Mill on Nationality

John Stuart Mill's thought has been central in works discussing the relationship between liberalism and nationality and in shaping liberal attitudes towards nationality. This book provides a thorough study of Mill's ideas, and aims to clarify the misconceptions surrounding his writings on nationalism.

To this end Varouxakis places Mill firmly within his socio-cultural context, examining his debates with his contemporaries as well as assessing his influence on other political thinkers. By analyzing the widely diverging interpretations of Mill's views from the early 1860s to the end of the twentieth century, this book presents a new understanding of his writings.

The book examines notions of "liberal nationalism," the importance of race, national character and politics, international relations, self-determination, foreign policy, cosmopolitanism and patriotism. Varouxakis' comprehensive work is an important contribution to scholarship in the history of political thought and intellectual history, as well as contributing to the current debates regarding nationhood, nationalism, patriotism, and the meaning of "Englishness."

This book provides a challenging new analysis of Mill's writings, and is therefore a valuable resource for students of philosophical or political thought at undergraduate and postgraduate level.

Georgios Varouxakis is a Lecturer in Politics in the School of Languages and European Studies, Aston University, Birmingham.

Routledge/PSA Political Studies Series
Edited by Michael Moran
University of Manchester

This series, published in conjunction with the Political Studies Association of the United Kingdom, aims to publish research monographs of
the highest quality in the field of political studies.

1. Postwar British Politics
From conflict to consensus
Peter Kerr

2. The Politics of Apolitical Culture
The congress for cultural freedom, the CIA and post-war American
hegemony
Giles Scott-Smith

3. Mill on Nationality
Georgios Varouxakis

Mill on Nationality

Georgios Varouxakis

London and New York

First published 2002 by Routledge
11 New Fetter Lane, London EC4P 4EE

Simultaneously published in the USA and Canada
by Routledge
29 West 35th Street, New York, NY 10001

Routledge is an imprint of the Taylor & Francis Group

Typeset in Times by Wearset Ltd, Boldon, Tyne and Wear
Printed and bound in Great Britain by Biddles Ltd, Guildford and
King's Lynn

British Library Cataloguing in Publication Data
A catalogue record for this book is available from the British Library

Library of Congress Cataloging in Publication Data
Varouxakis, Georgios, 1966–
  Mill on nationality / Georgios Varouxakis.
    p. cm.
  Includes bibliographical references and index.
  1. Mill, John Stuart, 1806–1873—Views on nationalism.
  2. Nationalism. I. Title.

JC311 .V295 2002
320.54–dc21

                                                    2001040816

ISBN 0-415-24968-6

To Fred Rosen
my generous *Doktorvater*

Much nonsense is talked as to the principle of nationalities, as about all approximate practical precepts which claim to be first philosophical principles.

(Walter Bagehot: Bagehot 1965–86, VIII: 157)

Sadly, while there are many books on the history of Marxist attempts to accommodate race and nationality..., there are few if any books which do the same for the liberal tradition.

(Will Kymlicka: Kymlicka 1995a: 208, n.7)

It is arguable that he [J.S. Mill] still retains a capacity to stir political passion, albeit in the curiously displaced form of conflicting scholarly interpretations. ... and it is presumably safe to predict that if he is to have a claim on the attention of any but scholarly specialists in the twenty-first century, it will be on account of the continued vitality of a political theory calling itself "liberal." How far he continues to be regarded as an embodiment of "Englishness" will depend in part on the needs which such refurbishings of national stereotypes have to meet in the future. ... The pressures likely to be felt in the future to explore and deal critically with somewhat different dimensions of Englishness may yet give a new and unexpected afterlife to Mill the relentless theorist, Mill the uncompromising partisan, and Mill the outspoken critic of English parochialism.

(Stefan Collini: Collini 1991: 340–1)

Contents

Acknowledgments

The first debt of anyone writing on J.S. Mill is to the late Professor John M. Robson and his collaborators in the Mill Project at the University of Toronto for having produced the superb edition of *The Collected Works of John Stuart Mill*. Mill scholarship has changed dramatically as a result of the publication as well as of the quality of this edition. My other great debt is to Professor Fred Rosen who supervised my PhD thesis on Mill at UCL in the early 1990s. There is no exaggerating his generosity with his time and advice nor the wisdom of the advice itself. His guidance was decisive in teaching me how to write comprehensibly in English and how to formulate an argument. Dedicating this book to him is the least I can do in an attempt to express my gratitude. I will always be grateful to my first teacher in political thought, Professor Paschalis M. Kitromilides, for having inspired me to continue my studies in this most fascinating of fields. Gregory Molivas has been a most valuable friend and a true mentor to me in many ways for the last eleven years. Both conversations with him and his inspiring example in perseverance and tenacity have proved vital in difficult times. My colleague Michael Sutton has been an extremely helpful and encouraging influence in more ways than he can imagine. I am also grateful to my former colleague David J. Howarth who has been a most valuable friend and, moreover, great fun to be with during the years which he spent at Aston University. In one way or another, I am most grateful for the help or advice which I have received from James H. Burns, Gregory Claeys, Janet Coleman, Jonathan Riley, Bernard Cottret, John W. Burrow, Geraint L. Williams, Cécile Laborde, Michael Drolet, Philip T. Schofield, Roger Crisp and Athena S. Leoussi. I was fortunate and privileged to have had my typescript looked at by Steve Turrington, cooperating with whom proved a most agreeable experience. For the remaining errors and problems I am, of course, solely responsible. Finally, my deepest gratitude goes to my family, who have supported me more generously than I could ever wish for: my mother, Chryssoula Varouxakis, my brother, Ioannis, and, far from least, my late hard-working father, Emmanouil, who died suddenly and prematurely some weeks before this book was completed. An earlier version of Chapter 3 has appeared in *Utilitas*, Vol. 10, No. 1 (1998), pp. 17–32. An earlier version of the latter parts of Chapter 4 has appeared in *History of European Ideas*, Vol. 24, No. 6 (1998), pp. 375–91. An earlier version of the greatest part of Chapter 5 has appeared in *Millennium: Journal of International Studies*, Vol. 26, No. 1 (1997), pp. 57–76. I am most grateful to the respective Editors of these journals and to Edinburgh University Press and Elsevier Science for permission to use the texts here.

1 Introduction

Interpretations of Mill's views on nationality

The Principle of nationalities is not a good in itself, a dogma of superstition to be pursued at all times blindly, but a means to an end, to be
applied rationally and discriminately towards that end.

(Walter Bagehot: Bagehot 1965–86, VIII: 152)

This theory assumes not so much that humanity ought to be divided into
national, sovereign states, as that people who are alike in many things
stand a better chance of making a success of representative government.

(Elie Kedourie: Kedourie 1985: 131–2)

John Stuart Mill is arguably the most influential major liberal theorist to
have engaged directly and thoroughly with the issues raised for liberalism and liberal politics by nationhood and nationalism.[1] It is hard to
overestimate the younger Mill's significance for – and influence on – the
British liberal tradition and liberalism more generally. From the time he
had Chapter V of L.T. Hobhouse's *Liberalism* (1911) dedicated to
himself and Gladstone (as the twin pillars of British liberalism in the
world of thought and in the world of action respectively) until today, he
has been considered a pivotal figure of liberalism, both as a political
philosophy and as an ideology.[2] As far as his native land was concerned,
Mill gradually became, "[f]rom dangerous partisan," extreme radical and
"un-English," a really "national possession," an epitome of liberal
Englishness.[3]

Now, developments in Anglophone normative political theory in the
1990s have brought Mill's attitude towards nationhood to the forefront of
theoretical debates on nationalism again. In a book published in the
mid-1990s, Professor Margaret Canovan complained about Anglophone
liberal political theorists' failure to address adequately issues of

nationhood. Canovan argued that they have traditionally tended to take the relatively stable nation-states in which they happened to live for granted, without further investigating the foundations of the solidarity that generates political power (Canovan 1996). And in works published also in the mid-1990s, Will Kymlicka commented on post-World War II liberal theorists' neglect of the issues of nationality and national minorities and suggested that any attempt to deal with these issues today from a liberal perspective will have to refer back to nineteenth-century liberal thought, which produced rich debates around the problems involved in the relationship between liberal principles and nationality (Kymlicka 1995a: 49–74; Kymlicka 1995b: 1–27). Around the same time, Stanley Hoffmann (in a Commentary he contributed to a French edition of John Rawls' lecture on "The Law of Peoples") observed of debates between communitarians (like Michael Walzer and Charles Taylor) on the one hand, and "mondialistes" (like Martha Nussbaum) on the other, that "la discussion de ce problème crucial a tout juste commencé"[4] (Hoffmann 1996: 132).

Commence it did, however, and, as a result, around the time these books were being written or published, political theorists were starting increasingly to discuss issues of nationhood, patriotism, the repercussions of national, ethnic or cultural belonging, and the feasibility of "multiculturalism." The tendency in question continues unabated.[5] Nor has it remained confined to the English-speaking world.[6] Among the most hotly debated issues are those regarding the relation of nationhood and national attachments to liberal political values, and of the compatibility between liberalism and certain versions of nationalism. The possibility of there being a version of particularistic attachment (called variously "patriotism," "nationality," or "liberal nationalism") which might be compatible with the political values and prerequisites of liberal democracy has proved most fertile ground for political theorists aspiring to contribute to debates relevant to contemporary concerns. A number of political theorists from both sides of the Atlantic have come up with various and divergent solutions to the challenges posed – or, according to some of them, the opportunities offered – to liberal democracy by the existence and apparent persistence of national or other particularistic attachments.

Most of these political theorists have also begun to heed to Kymlicka's injunction, and have paid ample lip-service to supposed nineteenth-century precedents or "traditions" for their respective positions (Tamir 1993: 62, 79, 92–3, 96–7, 124, 140–2; Miller 1995: 10, 97–8, 192–3; Miller 2000: 34, 36, 191 n.34; Viroli 1995: epigraph, 137–9,

144–55, 181–2; Viroli 2000: 272; Gray 1995: 99–100). Thus, one of the common characteristics among some of the major contributions to these debates has been a tendency to invoke a long pedigree for their respective prescriptions: they seem to feel a compulsion to endow their theories and recommendations concerning the appropriate attitude towards nationhood with "a liberal descent," as it were.[7] To an extent which should not surprise anyone familiar with the pre-existing literature on nationalism, most political theorists attempting to discuss questions of nationhood from a normative point of view feel obliged to turn to nineteenth-century debates on nationality.

John Stuart Mill is indisputably the central figure in the proposed pedigree that emerges from discussions of nationhood attempting to reconcile some kind of national attachment with liberal values. To name only the most discussed such contribution, David Miller straightforwardly borrowed the very notion and term "nationality" from Mill in order to propose an alternative, commendable version of particularistic attachment that can be, according to him, distinct from unpalatable versions of nationalism (Miller 1995: 10; also: 97–8, 192–3). As he puts it, his book "neither celebrates nationalism nor writes it off as some kind of irrational monstrosity. It sets out to explore and defend what I shall refer to as 'the principle of nationality'...." Rejecting earlier categorizations which attempted to identify a sanitized version of nationalism by distinguishing between two kinds of nationalism (i.e. distinctions such as those proposed by scholars like Hans Kohn or John Plamenatz between a "Western" and an "Eastern" form of nationalism),[8] Miller opts for a different term, less charged or tainted than "nationalism": "I prefer ... to use the term 'nationality' for the position I want to explore and finally defend, following here in the footsteps of (among others) John Stuart Mill, who employed the term in a sense similar to mine in chapter 16 of *Considerations on Representative Government*" (Miller 1995: 10; cf. Miller 2000: 36). Elsewhere Miller has written that

> Liberals ... very often disparage or dismiss national identities, not appreciating the role they have played (and continue to play) in supporting liberal institutions. Historically this was not so: contemporary liberals should be made to read, alongside the famous first chapter of Mill's *On Liberty*, the less famous sixteenth chapter of his *Considerations on Representative Government*, headed "Of Nationality, as Connected with Representative Government."
>
> (Miller 2000: 191 n.34)

Miller has also addressed the famous debate between Mill and Lord Acton, agreeing with Mill against Acton (Miller 2000: 34).[9] Miller's views have given rise to an extended debate since the publication of his *On Nationality*. Even his severest critics recognize his work as the most sophisticated of recent attempts by political theorists and philosophers to promote a sanitized version of national attachment purportedly compatible with liberal values (O'Leary 1996; Benner 1997). Besides David Miller, Mill's injunction that a liberal democracy, ideally, needs "citizens united by what Mill called 'common sympathies'" has recently received also John Rawls' approval (Rawls 1999: 23–5, and 23 n.17).

But Miller and Rawls have come to join a long tradition. Since 1861, rarely, if ever, has a liberal thinker addressed the issue of nationhood without feeling the need to reckon with the pronouncements of the author of *Considerations on Representative Government*. Mill's theorizing on these issues influenced decisively British and American liberal attitudes (including US President Woodrow Wilson's views on nationality) and is still taken as the starting point of relevant discussions today.[10] Thus, most subsequent scholars writing on nationality or nationalism, starting from Lord Acton a year after the publication of his *Considerations on Representative Government*, felt called upon to comment on Mill's contribution (Acton 1985–88, I: 409–33). Some major students of nationalism have criticized what they saw as Mill's naïveté or lack of perspicacity, especially in contradistinction to Lord Acton's purportedly prophetic warnings against nationalism (see, for instance, Kohn 1946: 35–8; Alter 1994: 61). Elie Kedourie considered Mill's position to have been the best formulation of what he called "the Whig theory of nationality" (Kedourie 1985: 131–3).[11] Others have seen Mill as the precursor and exponent *par excellence* of their more or less favoured position of "liberal nationalism" (Tamir 1993: 62, 140, 142; cf. Moore 2001), "nationality" (Miller 1995: 10, 97–8, 192–3; Miller 2000: 36, 191 n.34), or "patriotism" (Viroli 1995: epigraph; Viroli 2000: 272), or of what they see as the sober and balanced approach to nationalism characteristic of Isaiah Berlin's liberalism (Gray 1995: 99–100).

Existing accounts of Mill's views on nationality are based almost exclusively on the famous chapter on this issue in his 1861 book *Considerations on Representative Government* (Chapter XVI: "Of nationality, as connected with representative government").[12] For instance, received wisdom on the subject was exemplified recently by a political theorist as follows: "J.S. Mill's thoughts on it [nationalism] boil down to a chapter in which he views common nationality and language as necessary conditions for social unity and democracy" (Norman 1999: 57). Such a statement is problematic, both in its un-nuanced interpretation of what Mill's views were, and in its assertion that Mill's thoughts boil down to Chapter XVI of *Representative Government* only. Yet, this is the basis on which contemporary political theorists – and students of nationalism more generally – rest their discussions of what they consider to be the crown of classical liberal wisdom on the subject. In contrast to this state of affairs, this book offers a study of Mill's attitudes and pronouncements on nationality, patriotism, national character, national self-determination, and related issues, based on a great range of writings, from his major works through his innumerable journalistic articles to his voluminous correspondence. Writings that prove particularly useful and illuminating are those related to France and his constant Franco-British or Franco-English comparisons, as well as his writings on Ireland and the Irish question, the Celtic peoples more generally, India, and, last but far from least, his pronouncements on Englishness, the "English national character" and his recipes and subtle strategies aimed at its education and "improvement." The study of his views on what he called "national characters," their differences, and the factors affecting the formation of (and potentially changing, and "improving") national character proves a fruitful exercise, given the significance Mill attributed (or came to attribute, eventually) to national character and his compulsive interest in attempting to establish the social-scientific study of this category. These issues relating to Mill's treatment of national character have been neglected or underestimated as cursory in the extant literature.

The need for a book that should establish clearly where exactly Mill stood with regard to nationalism and nationhood becomes obvious from an examination of extant commentary on his utterances on these issues. This is because such an examination reveals that Mill's pronouncements on nationality have received all sorts of – sometimes strikingly – contradictory interpretations. To name but a few, Mill has been seen as:

- an English nationalist – a convert to "the system of mystical and nationalist enthusiasm enunciated by Wordsworth" (Newman 1987: 243–4) – but also, on the very contrary, as an example of what was – not groundlessly, the argument goes – perceived as the "*absence of* patriotism of any description among the forces of British radicalism" (Stapleton 2000: 247);

- a proponent of an "enthused nationalism" constituting a dishonourable exception to a "liberal continuum" of anti-nationalists (Vincent 1997: 279), and as "one of [nationalism's] staunchest defenders" (Lichtenberg 1999: 167), but also as completely insensitive and indifferent to the nationalist movements of Europe and thoroughly unappreciative of the significance of national consciousness (Harvie 1976: 154–5);
- as having offered a powerful argument in defence of what is today called multiculturalism (Poole 1999: 117–18), but also as the originator and exponent *par excellence* of liberalism's hostility to multiculturalism (Kymlicka 1991: 207–9, 212, 216 n.1; Parekh 1994; Kymlicka 1995a: 52–5, 72–3, 207 n.4; Kymlicka 1995b: 5–6, 22–3 n.8; Parekh 2000: 34–6, 40–7, 165–7);
- the quintessential "prophet" of commendable and enlightened English nationalism (Kohn 1946: 11–40);
- the classic exponent of the "Whig theory of nationality" (Kedourie 1985: 131–3);
- a precursor of Isaiah Berlin's supposedly nuanced and sober liberal attitude towards nationalism (Gray 1995: 99–100);
- a quintessential "liberal nationalist" (Tamir 1993; Moore 2001; and many others);
- an exemplary exponent of commendable "patriotism" as opposed to unpalatable "nationalism" (Viroli 1995; Viroli 2000);
- the precursor of a theory of "nationality" as distinct from nationalism (Miller 1995; Miller 2000);
- the direct ancestor of "[t]oday's cosmopolitan critic of particularism" (Judt 1994: 44–5);
- the major exponent of "the logically voluntarist version" of nationalism (Gilbert 1998: 64–8);
- an exponent of Anglo-Saxon ethnocentrism wishing to assimilate the Celtic nations, the French Canadians and other small groups (Kymlicka 1991: 207–9, 212, 216 n.1; Kymlicka 1995a: 52–5, 72–3, 207 n.4; Kymlicka 1995b: 5–6, 22–3 n.8);

and the list can go on. These widely divergent views are the result both of the subtlety and complexity of Mill's position (which means that people who did not have the whole picture could find isolated statements to support all sorts of arguments) and of the fact that all subsequent scholars who have commented on his views on nationality have based their judgments on their interpretation of one text only (*Representative Government*) or, very often, of certain oft-quoted sentences from that text.

But partial readings of Mill's own writings are not the only reason for the misrepresentations or half-truths that one usually reads on him. Another major problem is that Mill (as well as other thinkers) has fallen victim to all sorts of anachronistic misreadings of what some of his commentators did actually read, because it was not sufficiently contextualized. In the following chapters we will come across several examples of such anachronistic misreadings, but it is worth mentioning here the most striking. More often than not, when the issue of his attitude towards "race" is discussed, late-twentieth-century scholars have accused Mill of ambiguity at best, or of outright pandering to racial explanations (Steele 1970: 435; Mazlish 1975: 407; Mehta 1999: 15 n.22; Pecora 1997–8: 372). We will see in Chapter 3 that this is grossly unfair to the thinker who probably did more than anyone in Victorian Britain to discredit racial determinism. But this emerges through a close look at what he had to say on the matter in many different works, at his political activism, his correspondence, as well as through comparing his stance with that of his contemporaries, and, not least, through assessing how his contemporaries viewed him in respect to these matters. It is this kind of historical contextualization that is missing from most accounts of his thinking on such issues and which will be offered throughout this book.

Similar things can be said of the famous Mill–Acton debate on nationality. The two thinkers have been seen as representing two completely opposing attitudes towards nationality.[13] In fact, they were much closer to each other (and to some of their contemporaries such as Walter Bagehot or Matthew Arnold for example) than existing scholarship would have one believe. Mill abhorred nationalist sentiment as much as Acton did, and regarded nationalist tribalism as a "retrograde step in civilisation," as Acton put it. No less than Acton, Mill preferred the coexistence of various ethnic, racial and cultural groups in one state, enriching one another through the civilization-enhancing diversity that would result. He said as much in the very Chapter XVI on nationality which was criticized by Acton a year later. (*CW*, XVIII: 549)

Where they can rightly be said to have differed is in that Mill argued that, if a group had, regrettably, developed nationalist feelings so strong that they resented living in a state not their own, then there was trouble

and it should be addressed in the most realistic way. ("Where the sentiment of nationality exists in any force, there is a *prima facie* case for
uniting all the members of the nationality under the same government,
and a government to themselves apart" (Mill 1963–91 (hereafter referred
to as "*CW*"), XVIII: 547).) The other thing that is relevant here and
has escaped the attention of commentators on the Mill–Acton debate is
that Acton, who wrote "Nationality" at the age of twenty-eight, later
modified his view on the matter of dispute and came to adopt Mill's position, that it was probably necessary to allow nations to have their separate states wherever possible. No less interestingly, in a letter to
Gladstone, Acton stressed that "Nationality has to be dealt with discriminately. It is not always liberal or constructive" (Fasnacht 1952: 131). We
will see that this was the view of Mill. This was also the view of
Matthew Arnold, particularly explicit in his first foray into political
writing, his 1859 pamphlet *England and the Italian Question* (Arnold
1960–77, I: 65–96); and of Walter Bagehot, as the epigraph of this
chapter indicates.[14]

Another case of misinterpretation due to lack of adequate contextualization and to insufficient conversance with Mill's overall thought
is represented by the related charges of ethnocentrism and hostility
to diversity raised against the Victorian thinker during the last
decade, most notably by Will Kymlicka and Bhikhu Parekh respectively.

Kymlicka started by praising Mill for, as he saw it, "emphasiz[ing] the
importance of 'the feeling of nationality,'" and for being one of the
earlier liberal writers for whom "human freedom was tied to the existence, and consciousness, of a common cultural membership" (Kymlicka
1991: 207–9).

However, in a later work, Kymlicka came to address Mill's views
from the point of view of the question of minority groups and their
rights.

However, in the nineteenth century, the call for a common national
identity was often tied to an ethnocentric denigration of smaller
national groups. It was commonplace in nineteenth-century
thought to distinguish the "great nations," such as France, Italy,
Poland, Germany, Hungary, Spain, England, and Russia, from
smaller "nationalities," such as the Czechs, Slovaks, Croats,
Basques, Welsh, Scots, Serbians, Bulgarians, Romanians, and
Slovenes. The great nations were seen as civilized, and as the

carriers of historical development.[15] So some nineteenth-century liberals endorsed national independence for great nations, but coercive assimilation for smaller nationalities. Thus Mill insisted that it was undeniably better for a Scottish Highlander to be part of Great Britain, or for a Basque to be part of France, "than to sulk on his own rocks, the half-savage relic of past times, revolving in his own little mental orbit, without participation or interest in the general movement of the world...." Mill was hardly alone in this view.... nineteenth-century socialists shared this ethnocentric view, which was also invoked to justify the coerced assimilation of indigenous peoples throughout the British Empire.

(Kymlicka 1995a: 53)[16]

Similarly, in his Introduction to a collective volume he edited, Kymlicka tactfully takes issue with one of the contributors, Vernon Van Dyke, who accounted for liberals' and socialists' opposition to minority cultural rights in terms of liberal "individualism" or socialist "internationalism." For Kymlicka, in the cases of both liberalism and socialism, the refusal to accept the validity of claims for cultural minority rights "is exacerbated by an ethnocentric denigration of smaller cultures, and a belief that progress requires assimilating them into larger cultures." To prove this point Kymlicka offers two quotes, one from Mill and one from Engels, and goes on to assert:

For both liberals and Marxists in the nineteenth century, the great nations, with their highly centralized political and economic structures, were the carriers of historical development. The smaller nationalities were backward and stagnant, and could only participate in modernity by abandoning their national character and assimilating to a great nation.

For Kymlicka, it is "this conception of historical development, more than anything else, which has shaped traditional liberal and Marxist opposition to the rights of minority cultures." Therefore:

It seems misleading, then, to explain this opposition in terms of liberal "individualism" or socialist "internationalism." Instead, it reflects a rather blatant form of ethnocentric nationalism. Mill and Marx did not reject all group identities between the individual and the state. Rather, they privileged a particular sort of group – the "great nation" – and denigrated smaller cultures. They did not express an indifference to people's cultural identities or group loyalties. Rather, they insisted that progress and civilization required assimilating "backward" minorities to "energetic" majorities.

(Kymlicka 1995b: 5–6)[17]

Kymlicka misses the point, both by considering Mill's attitude to be ethnocentric,[18] and – especially – by emphasizing the factor of the size of a nation. Mill did not "[insist] that progress and civilization required assimilating 'backward' minorities to 'energetic' majorities" (Kymlicka 1995b: 6). Depending on the case, he often insisted, exactly on the contrary, that progress and civilization would be served by the absorption of backward majorities by energetic minorities. His hostility to Russian expansion and to Russia's absorbing any smaller, more "civilized" nationalities was a case in point. Kymlicka's theory would apply relatively more to Bagehot's attitude to the question of smaller versus larger nations. Bagehot did indeed stress why it was preferable in many respects for one to be a citizen of a "great" nation rather than a small nation, and did adduce arguments related to size. Although even Bagehot did concede that "The interest of the world is that it should be composed of *great nations*, not necessarily great in territory, but great in merit, great in their connecting spirit, great in their political qualities, vigorous while living, famous when dead" (Bagehot 1965–86, VIII: 149–50). But, in any case, Mill did not make size a criterion. Rather, his criterion when considering the advisability of one group absorbing another was, which one was more "advanced" and "civilized," and whether, therefore, the absorption would be to the benefit of the absorbed or to their detriment, in civilizational terms. There may be a lot of "political incorrectness" in Mill's pronouncements, from today's point of view, but his arguments were not referring to size in particular. Mill would have agreed with Bagehot that greater size offered opportunities for a broader and more interesting debate in many cases, but size was not the only criterion, and there were some nations great in size which he did not wish to see absorbing smaller nations, because the former were less "civilized" than the latter.

The other thing that should be borne in mind in addressing this issue is that Mill, as well as many of his contemporaries, when discussing the admixture of national or ethnic groups with one another, did not mean the absolute absorption and disappearance of the one group. Rather, what they had in mind was a kind of heterosis, whereby the best qualities of each group would be preserved and enhanced; it was a give and take, not the absolute disappearance of all the traits of one group and the adoption of those of the other.[19]

Even more has to be said in connection with some of Bhikhu Parekh's assertions regarding Mill's pronouncements. In a widely discussed and influential article entitled "Decolonizing Liberalism," as well as in his more recent significant book on multiculturalism Parekh has treated Mill as the epitome and most influential thinker in the liberal tradition with regard to the issues he discusses ("Since the liberal case was best represented by J.S. Mill..., I shall concentrate on him" (Parekh 1994: 86)). Parekh maintained in the former work that he sketched there "the outlines of a dominant strand of nineteenth-century liberalism of which Mill was the ablest and most influential spokesman." He therefore argued that "What I might call Millian liberalism had several distinctive features which it would be useful to identify and analyse" (Parekh 1994: 92). Parekh asserts that "some of the essential features of Millian liberalism" were that "it is Eurocentric, narrow, missionary and dogmatic," and further: "Although liberalism has mellowed over the decades and become less self-righteous, it has not yet fully liberated itself from its Millian legacy. This is as true of those who derive their inspiration from him as of those claiming to depart from him." In that context he takes Joseph Raz and Brian Barry to illustrate the point. According to Parekh, "Joseph Raz consciously departs from Mill in several respects, yet some of the implications of his thought are distinctly Millian" (Parekh 1994: 95). And "Barry's language, tone and basic message are distinctly Millian" (Parekh 1994: 99).

Parekh argues that "From time to time Mill ... came pretty close to sharing the crude racism of his time, but by and large he managed to avoid it."[20] He concedes that, unlike the racist writers, Mill "insisted that the non-Europeans once had their glorious periods and were not inherently inferior, that the Europeans too had their dark ages and were not naturally superior, and that the differences between them had a non-biological explanation." However, Parekh goes on to claim that:

Mill's own explanation was muddled.... For Mill the East had become stationary because it lacked individuality. That was so because it had fallen under the sway of despotic customs, and that in turn was due to bad forms of government and social structures. As to why and how the latter came into existence, he had no answer.

This is not true. Mill did have an answer. It may or may not be historically accurate or acceptable to Parekh or the rest of us today, but it is not true that Mill did not have an answer to the question. He had found that answer in a work of the French historian and statesman François Guizot. Having said this, I am not asserting that Guizot's explanation was historically impeccable or unproblematic. Nor is Parekh wrong in complaining that Mill "disposed of thousands of years of the arbitrarily homogenized East." I am simply saying that, following Guizot and recommending him and his explanation to the British public, Mill did have a politically functional argument concerning the causes of what he saw as Europe's "progressive" civilization and the reasons for its difference from what was the case in "the East." Without arguing that the explanation given by Guizot and Mill was as unproblematic as they thought, I am arguing that Mill's account of the difference between "Europe" and "the East" was more coherent than Parekh would have one believe. I would also argue that Mill was less of a "monist" than Parekh claims in his recent book on multiculturalism (Parekh 2000: 40–7), and that he had a much more complex and subtle attitude towards diversity than Parekh gives him credit for. It was exactly in the context of his explanation of the difference in the historical development of Europe from that of the East that Mill came up with his strongest argument in favour of diversity – by way of commenting on Guizot's historical works (see Varouxakis 1999: 296–305). Parekh goes on:

> Having disposed of thousands of years of the arbitrarily homogenized East, Mill went on to explain why Europe was able to come out of its backward past unaided. "What is it that has hitherto preserved Europe from this lot? What has made the European family of nations an improving, instead of a stationary portion of mankind? Not any superior excellence in them, which, when it exists, exists as the effect not as the cause; but their remarkable diversity of character and culture. Individuals, classes, nations, have been extremely unlike one another; they have struck out a great variety of paths, each leading to something valuable; and although at every period those who travelled in different paths have been intolerant of one another, and each would have thought it an excellent thing

if all the rest could have been [compelled] to travel his road, their attempts to thwart each other's development have rarely had any permanent success, and each has in time endured to receive the good which the others have offered. Europe is, in my judgement, wholly indebted to this plurality of paths for its progressive and many-sided development." For Mill the Europeans avoided the "Chinese" fate because of their "remarkable" diversity of character and culture.[21] In Europe individuals, classes and states[22] cherished their differences, struck out diverse paths of development, and resisted attempts at assimilation. As a result, they never entirely lost their vibrancy and creativity, so that a society passing through a bad period was able to draw inspiration and strength from the liveliness of the rest.

Parekh's comment follows:

Mill's explanation raised more questions than it answered. He did not explain ... why and when [Europe's] people began to develop the love of diversity. He did not explain either why the presence of different classes should by itself cultivate and sustain the love of diversity when similar social differences in India, China and elsewhere did not.

(Parekh 1994: 89–90)

However, Mill never wrote that Europeans developed a love of diversity. Nor did he speak of "the presence of different classes" as alone responsible for the outcome which he was describing. What Mill said on several occasions was that an astonishing array of different social, cultural, religious and political groups, values, ideas and centres of power kept up a struggle for predominance in Europe, all of them all the way wishing to preponderate exclusively and annihilate all the rest to extinction. A certain degree of diversity and struggle had existed also in Eastern societies (India, Egypt, China) as well as in ancient Greece, and the existence of different "elements of improvement" and the concomitant struggle between them had resulted in significant progress and achievements in civilization.[23] However, at some – relatively early – point in the history of these societies, one element, value, idea or class managed to win the struggle and preponderate exclusively, annihilating all the others and therefore ending the diversity and antagonism that had existed before. From that point onwards these societies, either perished once that one element of improvement (in this case, democracy) had exhausted the good it was able to offer, as happened to ancient Greece, or froze and became stationary for centuries (as India and Egypt, according to Guizot, and China as well, according to Mill and his British contemporaries for whom China was a cautionary tale against stationariness). In contrast to this plight, Europe was more fortunate, as a stormy struggle between all sorts of elements, values, centres of power, nations, and classes was kept up unabated, thanks to the fortunate fact that none of them was successful in the attempt to prevail completely (*CW*, XX: 268–70).[24]

Parekh then comes to an issue also discussed by Kymlicka: "Mill maintained that even as a civilized society had a right to rule over a primitive or semi-civilized society, a more civilized group or nationality within a civilized society had a right to 'absorb' and dominate inferior groups."[25] According to Parekh's interpretation of Mill's statement: "The Scottish Highlander and the Welsh would ... gain if absorbed into the British, by which Mill meant the English, way of life." However, Mill did not speak of absorbing them into the English "way of life" – many of whose most important traits he himself loathed and struggled strenuously to improve (see Varouxakis 2002: Chapter 2). Rather, as Mill put it in the passage quoted by Parekh immediately following the above statement:

> Nobody can suppose that it is not more beneficial to a Breton, or a Basque of French Navarre, to be brought into the current of the ideas and feelings of a highly civilised and cultivated people – to be a member of the French nationality, admitted on equal terms to all the privileges of French citizenship, sharing the advantages of French protection, and the dignity and *prestige* of French power – than to sulk on his own rocks, the half-savage relic of past times, revolving in his own little mental orbit, without participation or interest in the general movement of the world. The same remark applies to the Welshman or the Scottish Highlander, as members of the British nation.
>
> (*CW*, XIX: 549)

Mill spoke here of the benefit of being brought into the current of ideas and feelings of a highly civilized and cultivated people and of being "admitted on equal terms to all the privileges of French citizenship, sharing the advantages of French protection, and the dignity and *prestige* of French power," *not* about a way of life.

But Parekh (and Kymlicka, and many a Canadian theorist, following Parekh) become even more unfair to Mill when it comes to the latter's attitude towards Lord Durham and the Canadian issue. According to Parekh, the view stated earlier (that "The Scottish Highlander and the Welsh would ... gain if absorbed into the British, by which Mill meant the English, way of life") "lay at the basis of Mill's approval of Lord Durham's Report on Canada." As Parekh (1994: 91) puts it,

> Lord Durham was hostile to the "backward" French Canadians' "vain endeavour" to preserve their cultural identity, and insisted that their true interests lay in being subjected to the "vigorous rule of an English majority," that "great race which must ... be predominant over the whole" of North America.

According to Parekh, "Mill enthusiastically welcomed the Durham Report, calling it an 'imperishable memorial of that nobleman's courage, patriotism and enlightened liber[ali]ty.' "[26] Even less justice was done to Mill in Parekh's more recent work. According to Parekh:

> When Lord Durham's Report on Canada rejected the "backward" French Canadians' "vain endeavour" to preserve their cultural identity and insisted that their true interests lay in being subjected to the "vigorous rule of an English majority," Mill enthusiastically welcomed it, calling it an "imperishable memorial of that nobleman's courage, patriotism and enlightened liber[ali]ty" and urging "all legitimate means" to assimilate the French Canadians.
>
> (Parekh 2000: 46)

However, the reader will look in vain to find Mill's statement "urging 'all legitimate means' to assimilate the French Canadians," because Mill wrote no such thing. More importantly, Mill nowhere praised the Report's specific recommendations with regard to the assimilation of French Canadians. Rather, he praised the Report in Chapter XVIII of *Representative Government* ("Of the Government of Dependencies by a Free State"), for having introduced what had become "now a fixed principle of the policy of Great Britain ... that her colonies of European race, equally with the parent country, possess the fullest measure of internal self-government" (*CW*, XIX: 563). As Alexander Brady has aptly remarked:

Although Mill praised Durham's Report for advocating the general principle of colonial autonomy, he nowhere subjects it to a detailed and public analysis or meets the legitimate criticisms lodged against it at the time, especially those directed against the apparent impracticability of the formal terms for colonial autonomy.

(Brady 1977: xlvii)

However, to do justice to Parekh, Kymlicka and others who are critical of Mill for endorsing the Report, one could still retort that the fact that he did not discuss its details does not acquit Mill; that, in other words, since he praised the report as a whole, Mill can be blamed for accepting its concrete recommendations with regard to the French Canadians.

However, things are more complicated than that. It is well known that, at the time, in the late 1830s, Mill was strenuously trying to organize a distinct Radical Party in Parliament, and believed that Lord Durham, once back from Canada, would be the ideal person to be the leader of such a party, the ideal practical man of action (one could say, the British counterpart of the recently deceased Armand Carrel). Mill was absolutely explicit about this (see, for example, *CW*, VI: 433, 448–9). As a result, Mill was so keen to defend Lord Durham at the time against all sorts of attacks, some more justified than others, that he was bound to refrain from criticizing parts of Durham's comportment in Canada or his Report once he had returned, even if he did not fully agree with them. Now, this may or may not be a convincing argument with regard to the issue of the French Canadians, but there is no need to rely on this in order to make the case that Mill did not advocate the forceful absorption of the French Canadians nor, more generally, ignored their interests. There is, in fact, much more convincing evidence. As is usual with Mill and Mill scholarship, the misunderstanding is due to the fact that Parekh, Kymlicka and the others who criticize Mill on this count have read the one or two vague sentences he wrote on Durham's Report in *Representative Government*, but not his detailed commentary on the situation in Canada since the Canadian Rebellion, both before and once Durham had been sent to take charge of the situation. A perusal of those articles, all three of them written before the publication of Lord Durham's "Report,"[28] gives a completely different picture from that offered by Parekh and Kymlicka, and which is accepted wisdom on the subject today. What Mill did write on the issue of the two ethnic groups ("races") in Canada shows that he had a much subtler view than current scholarship gives him credit for.

The whole thrust of Mill's writings on the issue of Canada and Lord Durham's mission there was *in defense* of the French Canadians and their interests against what Mill presented as the unreasonableness, untenableness and greediness of the demands of the "English" party in Canada.[29] In his first article on the Canadian rebellion Mill blamed the "[j]ealousies between the two races" (quoting the Report of the Colonial Secretary) on the Executive Government, which "took part with one race, against the other – it took part with the English race, instead of being the umpire and arbitrator between both" (*CW*, VI: 428). Thus, "To this people, thus calumniated, it will now be for Lord Durham to do justice" (*CW*, VI: 429). In that article Mill raised directly the difficult question:

> If the English and the French inhabitants of Canada cannot live under each other's government, which ought to give way? The whole numbers of the British race in Lower Canada do not even, on their own computation amount to a third of the whole; . . . Here, then, is a body of men, positively not of American birth, strangers, mere new-comers, and a portion of them, particularly the trading classes, not even perhaps intending to remain permanently in the colony – who have actually the presumption (or somebody has it for them) to expect that the political constitution of a long-settled country is to be shaped to suit their convenience.

Mill's retort to the English Canadians and their supporters in Britain was, for as long as they were the minority, "let them be satisfied if they have a share of representation proportional to their numbers" (*CW*, VI: 431–2); and: "What *may* be done for the less numerous race [the English], if it is found impossible that both should live harmoniously under one government, is to give them separate Legislatures." If this system were adopted, "neither of the races would be legislated for by the other"; and a federal Legislature would be created, of delegates from the local Legislatures, which would discuss only "matters of common concernment to the three provinces" (*CW*, VI: 432). Mill went on:

> We entreat Lord Durham . . . so to act upon his declared resolution of knowing no distinctions of opinion, party, or race, as to provide, if provision be needful, for the interests of a minority, – not by putting them over the heads of the majority, or by any legerdemain contrivance to give them a power in the Legislature beyond what their

numbers entitle them to, – but either by the rigid exercise, for their protection against any meditated injustice, of the veto of the mother country...; or, if that will not content them, by separating the two races, and giving to each of them a legislature apart.

(*CW*, VI: 433–4)

In the second article on the matters involved ("Lord Durham and His Assailants"), Mill reiterated: "It is very well known what our opinion is of the conduct by which that insurrection was provoked; most unquestionably our own sympathies are not with the victors, but with the vanquished, in that melancholy struggle" (*CW*, VI: 441).

Now, before the famous "Report" was published, Mill had endorsed what had been known as Durham's plan, "the scheme, so far as yet matured, which he is understood to have had in view for the future constitution of the colony." The plan included a federal body, to be chosen by all the provinces, for decisions affecting the whole of Canada, while leaving the separate provinces to be self-governed by their own assemblies. According to Mill:

> This project ... had the further advantage, that it was the only legitimate means of destroying the so-much-talked-of nationality of the French Canadians. It would compel them to consider themselves, not as a separate family, but an integral portion of a larger body; *it would merge their nationality of race in a nationality of country*; instead of French Canadians it would make them British Americans; *and this without bringing into their house and home, into their social and domestic relations, the customs of another people (which, whether practised on all of them or on a part, would be one of the last excesses of despotism)*, or establishing, as hitherto, over not only their necks but those of the English population, a petty oligarchy of the latter.
>
> (Emphasis added: *CW*, VI: 458–9)

This does not sound like recommending "assimilation" of the French Canadians or "absorb[ing]" them "into the British, by which Mill meant the English, *way of life*" (Parekh 1994: 90);[30] or like agreeing with Lord Durham who purportedly "wanted the French Canadians to become English" (Parekh 1994: 91). Nor does it sound like Mill "urging 'all legitimate means' to assimilate the French Canadians" (Parekh 2000: 46), if by "assimilate" is meant to force them "to become English." Rather, Mill was adamant that he was recommending not absorption of the French by the English ethnic or racial group, but rather abandoning nationalist feeling and allegiance based on race and adopting "a nationality of country." This sounds more like what is proposed today as "constitutional patriotism" (cf. Sternberger 1982; Habermas 1995; Canovan 2000) than as English ethnocentric assimilationism. I am not pretending that there are no problems with what Mill proposed, or what Habermas and others are proposing today, problems fruitfully debated by political theorists these last few years. What I am saying is that we should see what Mill proposed for what it was, rather than through glasses tinted with "post-colonial" suspicion of everything an English liberal wrote or said.

Now, a great part of what Parekh discussed in relation to Mill referred to his attitude towards India, understandably given the younger Mill's (and his father's) role in the running of the East India Company. J.S. Mill's attitude towards India is a long story, in itself worth more than one book, and already the subject of important books, so I cannot enter it here in detail. However, to the extent that they affect overall judgments on his attitudes towards nationhood, culture and diversity, some scholarly pronouncements on Mill's attitude towards India and the Empire will need to be addressed here. Parekh again provides a case in point. After accusing Mill of having approved of Durham's assimilationist proposals, Parekh goes on to Mill's own Indian policy recommendations, doing him scarcely more justice:

> Just as Lord Durham wanted the French Canadians to become English, Macaulay wanted to make the Indians English in all respects save the colour of their skin. Liberals in other parts of the British empire felt the same way about the indigenous ways of life and thought. Drawing their inspiration from Mill they wondered why people should "blindly" adhere to their traditions and customs, and why the colonial rulers should not use a subtle mixture of education and coercion to get them to adopt the liberal ways of life and thought.
>
> (Parekh 1994: 91)

Now, reading this, one is almost bound to assume that Mill and Macaulay were at one in wishing to anglicize the Indians, even that Macaulay might have "[drawn] inspiration from Mill." This is grossly unfair, to the extent that the fundamental disagreements between J.S. Mill and Macaulay on exactly the latter's anglicization policies constitute one of the major *causes célèbres* of the administration of India. Lumping them together in the above statement does not help our understanding of the internal disagreements and nuances within liberal thought on imperialism.[31]

When all this has been said, what then, did Mill actually say and where did he stand on nationality?[32] Only the beginning of an answer can be given in this introductory chapter. As we have seen, Mill's oft-quoted statements on nationality, on which subsequent analyses have been based, are to be found primarily in Chapter XVI of *Representative Government* (1861) (*CW*, XIX: 546–52). Mill's definition of nationality was:

> A portion of mankind may be said to constitute a Nationality, if they are united among themselves by common sympathies, which do not exist between them and any others – which make them co-operate with each other more willingly than with other people, desire to be under the same government, and desire that it should be government by themselves or a portion of themselves, exclusively.

This feeling of nationality "may have been generated by various causes," none of which were "either indispensable, or necessarily sufficient by themselves" (*CW*, XIX: 546). He then stated his oft-quoted principle: "Where the sentiment of nationality exists in any force, there is a *prima facie* case for uniting all the members of the nationality under the same government, and a government to themselves apart." This is merely saying, he went on to assert, "that the question of government ought to be decided by the governed. One hardly knows what any division of the human race should be free to do, if not to determine, with which of the various collective bodies of human beings they choose to associate themselves."

In other words, as Alfred Cobban has commented on Mill's assertions at this point, national self-determination "is merely a statement, in different terms, of the principle of democratic, or at least representative, government" (Cobban 1969: 131). However, Mill's argumentation was not simply, or even mainly, based on the identification of the principle of national self-determination with the democratic principle of popular sovereignty. For he goes on to present more compelling reasons: "But, when a people are ripe for free institutions, there is a still more vital consideration. Free institutions are next to impossible in a country made up of different nationalities" (*CW*, XIX: 547). Among a people without "fellow-feeling," especially if they read and spoke different languages, the "united public opinion, necessary to the working of representative government," could not exist. Their mutual antipathies were generally much stronger than "jealousy of the government." And, above all, "the sympathy of the army with the people" was wanting in the case of such a state. Instead, soldiers of one nationality would regard members of the other nationalities which composed the state not just as strangers, but as enemies (cf. Horowitz 1994). And Mill went on to comment on the state of things he had just described:

> If it be said that so broadly marked a distinction between what is due to a fellow-countryman and what is due merely to a human creature, is more worthy of savages than of civilized beings, *and ought, with the utmost energy, to be contended against*, no one holds that opinion more strongly than myself. *But this object, one of the worthiest to which human endeavour can be directed*, can never, in the present state of civilization, be promoted by keeping different nationalities of anything like equivalent strength, under the same government.
>
> (Emphasis added: *CW*, XIX: 548)

For the preceding reasons, he opined, "it is in general a necessary condition of free institutions, that the boundaries of governments should coincide in the main with those of nationalities." This statement figures in every account of his views on nationality. Most of them, however, fail to refer to the sentence which immediately followed and qualified it: "But several considerations are liable to conflict in practice with this general principle." Then Mill spends more than half of the chapter to bring home this point, explaining the difficulties that precluded the application of the principle in a great variety of cases. "[G]eographical hindrances" were among such "considerations" which obliged people of different nationalities "to make a virtue of necessity, and reconcile themselves to living together under equal rights and laws" (*CW*, XIX: 548–9).

Other, more important, such "considerations," were moral and social. Experience proved, he asserted, that it was possible for one nationality to merge and be absorbed in another. And "when it was originally an inferior and more backward portion of the human race, the absorption is greatly to its advantage." The oft-quoted statement follows, where Mill asserted that it was "more beneficial to a Breton, or a Basque of French Navarre, to be brought into the current of the ideas and feelings of a highly civilized and cultivated people ... than to sulk on his own rocks, the half-savage relic of past times, revolving in his own little mental orbit, without participation or interest in the general movement of the world" (see above). This is followed by an emphatic declaration:

> Whatever really tends to the admixture of nationalities, and the blending of their attitudes and peculiarities in a common union, is a benefit to the human race. Not by extinguishing types, of which, in these cases, sufficient examples are sure to remain, but by softening their extreme forms, and filling up the intervals between them. The united people ... inherits the special aptitudes and excellences of all its progenitors, protected by the admixture from being exaggerated into the neighbouring vices.
>
> (*CW*, XIX: 549–50)

Such statements do not simply represent attempts by a British imperialist to legitimize his country's rule over other nations, as has sometimes been suggested. Mill had a genuine and earnest desire to see different national and ethnic groups merge their best qualities in the interests of the improvement of mankind. This son of a Scottish father (James Mill) and an English mother had spent much of his energy, during at least three decades (1820s–40s), trying to bring home to his fellow-countrymen what he saw as the advantages of combining different national and cultural traits – pertaining to different "national characters," in the vocabulary of his time – in order for a better national character to be attained to eventually. No other manifestation of this attitude is more striking than his almost life-long efforts to bring the British and the French closer to each other and to merge the best qualities of "Celt" and "Anglo-Saxon" in an improved hybrid national character. The same desire informed his views with regard to the continuation of the union between the Celtic peoples and the English in Great Britain. While he had ample praise for some qualities in the "character" of the "Anglo-Saxons," few British thinkers have ever been so critical of the English character, which he criticized at least as often as he praised it. His wish was to see it improve through contact and fusion with what he considered the character best designed to correct it, the Celtic – in which he included the French as well as the Celts of the British Isles.[33]

Despite scholars' obsessive focus on Chapter XVI, Mill had dealt with the issues he was to address there in a number of earlier writings, most explicitly in 1849, in his "Vindication of the French Revolution of February 1848" (*CW*, XX: 317–63). It was in the "Vindication" that Mill first enunciated the idea that the main justification for "nationality" was its potential conduciveness to free representative government. Although written at a time of revolutionary exuberance when his thought was most radicalized (see Chapter 5), this text shows beyond doubt that Mill was by no means blind to the contradictions and dangers involved in many nationalist movements. He was painfully aware of what Hans Morgenthau was to refer to later as the "A–B–C paradox" (Morgenthau 1957). And he condemned there as well, in the strongest terms, what is often called today "tribalism" (*CW*, XX: 347–8).

A major reason why Mill was favourably disposed towards several movements of national liberation was his belief that, in the conjuncture of mid-nineteenth-century Europe, the specific nation-states that would arise from the success of such movements were more likely to lead to the attainment of freedom than the multiethnic empires of Austria, Russia and Turkey (see, for example, *CW*, XXV: 1203). But he had a very clear idea of the difference and tension between national liberation (the attainment of "nationality," in the language of the time) and liberty within a state, and he endorsed the former only in so far as it seemed to be a necessary prerequisite for the latter. This is clearly stated in a letter to the Italian patriot, Pasquale Villari (28 March 1859): "I would understand that at a certain point in time one could put nationality before liberty, I could even forgive it, because liberty often needs nationality in order to exist" (my translation from French original: *CW*, XV: 610–11). Thus Mill accepted nationality only as a means to other ends. But he did not attach any intrinsic value to nationality *per se* or to the preservation of *national* cultures. Rather, Mill's attitude with regard to nationalism was informed by his paramount commitment to rationality.[34] It also has to be remembered that Mill, though much more appreciative of the importance of community than liberals are usually given credit for, did have a fundamentally individualist agenda. Politicians had to act in the "interest of the people": "Not that vague abstraction, the good of the country, but the actual, positive well-being of the living human creatures who compose the population" (*CW*, XXVIII: 67).[35]

Yet, while he condemned nationalist sentiment as it manifested itself in Eastern and Central Europe, as well as in France, at his time, and while he discarded excessive particularistic attachments as retrograde and impeding the advance of civilization, Mill was acutely aware of the need for cohesion in a society and of the imperative of replacing the more tangible attachments that held people together under older social and political arrangements (local feudal institutions, religious attachments, etc.) with a form of solidarity adapted to the revolutionary changes that had taken place in both society and politics during the late eighteenth and early nineteenth centuries. In his two reviews of Tocqueville's *Democracy in America* (1835 and 1840) Mill exhibits a sharp understanding of the changes entailed by the advent of modernity as far as people's allegiances were concerned (*CW*, XVIII: 61–3, 83, 87, 182, 195n).

If one takes into account Mill's various other references to the issue of patriotism and, not least, his political activism, where he put his theories to the test, a clear picture emerges. Mill should be seen as advocating a kind of "enlightened patriotism" (a term he used himself) in the sense of civic spirit. But – though it may sound a contradiction in terms – Mill's was a cosmopolitan patriotism. "Cosmopolitan patriotism" has many meanings, and the reader will have to wait until Chapter 7 for an exposition of what exactly I mean by the term in Mill's case. For one thing, like Bentham, Mill was cosmopolitan in outlook and ultimate moral allegiance. His ultimate goal being "the improvement of mankind," he clearly believed that the best practical way for an individual to serve this goal was through active and conscientious participation in the affairs and common concerns of one's own political community. A major part of this active involvement which Mill demanded from the individual was to be dedicated to an alertness over the behavior of one's political community *as* a community, in other words, its foreign policy. He wrote some extremely powerful texts calling on his compatriots to see to it that their government follow a moral and even-handed foreign policy. And he did not mince his words when it came to admonishing them each time he thought that they failed in the performance of that duty, or when the British government was behaving in a selfish manner dictated by narrowly conceived national interest – such as in the case of British policy towards the construction of the Suez Canal (*CW*, XXI: 109–24). But even more than conventional uses of the term "cosmopolitan," what will emerge from Chapter 7 is that Mill was promoting a patriotism that was cosmopolitan in the sense that it was outward-looking in its vocabulary and aspirations.

Thus, what this book aspires to show is that Mill has been grossly misrepresented in the extant literature, or rather, that the things that have been said of him with regard to nationality are partial truths (in his own vocabulary, "half-truths"). His thinking about nationality emerges here as having been much more subtle and nuanced than any of the existing accounts would have one believe.

2 "A liberal descent"?

Challenging the pedigree of "liberal nationalism"

"Liberal nationalism" is not a term or concept invented by political theorists or philosophers in the 1990s, although some of them seem to think so.[1] This being as it may, the "liberal nationalism" discussed in this chapter will be that debated by political theorists during the 1990s, independently of the existence of an earlier literature of studies on nationalism that had coined the term and discussed its meaning.

As we saw in Chapter 1, much has been written in recent years about the relationship between nationalism and liberalism, the main point at issue being the reconcilability of the two value systems with each other. A number of political theorists tend to assert that the two systems are not as antithetical or mutually exclusive as most twentieth-century liberal thinkers and scholars would have one believe. The theorists in question claim that liberalism and nationalism can be reconciled and so combined as to enhance each other, as they have, according to them, gone hand-in-hand at certain periods in the past. The discussion takes a philosophical-analytical turn, or tends to focus on the historical development of the relationship between the two movements, but in most cases the two approaches are combined and the historical approach is adduced in order to corroborate the philosophical assertions. A constantly recurring theme in the relevant literature is the invocation of nineteenth-century thinkers such as J.S. Mill, Mazzini, and others as examples of liberals whose work and public activity exhibited such a degree of sympathy for, or participation in, the nationalist movements of their time, that they can be taken to represent and exemplify the best expressions of a sound relationship between liberalism and nationalism. By the same token, there is a tendency to distinguish between "nationalism" – which, it is conceded, may have associations not wholly defensible in terms of liberal moral values – and the principle of "nationality," which is held to be not only defensible but also commendable. The very term is borrowed from the discourse of nineteenth-century thinkers, most notably J.S. Mill, and it is employed in an attempt to defend and promote a sanitized version of nationalism. Another line of argument adopted by some political theorists takes the form of a distinction between "nationalism" and "patriotism," with the latter being presented as a form of particularistic attachment that can be distinguished from nationalism and its unsavory implications.[2]

The tendencies described above have not met with universal enthusiasm. A number of political theorists, philosophers and social scientists have retorted that the argument that nationalism (or "nationality," or "patriotism") can, be not only reconciled with liberalism, but also reinforce and promote a liberal political order, has been overstretched and is fraught with both analytical flaws and politically dangerous implications. Thus, some powerful refutations of several of the arguments promoted by the champions of "liberal nationalism," "nationality," or of the neat distinction between "patriotism" and "nationalism" have been voiced.[3] Still, a lot more needs to be said in the direction of exposing the fallacies on which the theory of the compatibility between the two value-systems and movements rests, in respect both to its historical foundations and to their normative implications. The historical foundations being firmly focused on the nineteenth century, it will be argued here that the relationship between liberalism and nationalism was far from harmonious in the thought of the very theorists and activists that are supposed to exemplify best the happy synthesis of the two. The attitude towards nationalism of major liberal thinkers such as Benjamin Constant, Jeremy Bentham, John Stuart Mill and Alexis de Tocqueville – to name but the best known – was far from tension-free or unequivocal, and thinkers who are often lumped together were neither in agreement with one another nor unambiguous and always consistent with themselves in their respective approaches to some of the most important issues involved in this relationship.[4]

Thus, this chapter will attempt to give a sample of fundamental disagreements concerning the right attitude towards nationalism/patriotism between liberal thinkers who are supposed to be very close to each other on most important issues, namely Mill and Tocqueville. These are two thinkers, moreover, who have been explicitly presented as being at one in their endorsement of the "sentiment of nationality" from a liberal point of view (Gray 1995: 99–100; cf. Parekh 2000: 46, 347 n.9). Thus, in his book on Isaiah Berlin, John Gray has argued that:

One of the most significant aspects of Berlin's treatment of nationalism is its recurrence to an older, and in many ways a wiser, tradition of liberal thought. Nineteenth-century European liberal thinkers, by contrast with their Enlightenment predecessors and their twentieth-century successors, grasped the importance to human beings of collective identities other than, and more particularistic than, that of the species as a whole. It is a feature of the thought of Benjamin Constant, of Alexis de Tocqueville, of John Stuart Mill, for example, that they perceived in the sentiment of nationality an important source of social solidarity, and of the political stability of a liberal society. By contrast with twentieth-century liberals, such as Hayek and Popper, for whom nationalism is only tribalism revived and written large, these nineteenth-century liberals grasped the significance of membership in a common culture in sustaining allegiance to a liberal political order. Almost alone among twentieth-century liberal thinkers ... Berlin perceives that a liberal civil society cannot rest upon abstract principles or common rules alone, but needs a common national culture if it is to be stable and command allegiance. In this respect Berlin and Raz renew an unjustly neglected aspect of J.S. Mill's liberalism, that in which he emphasised the importance of the sentiment of nationality in a liberal culture.

(Gray 1995: 99–100)[5]

Gray's case is a characteristic example of the tendency alluded to earlier, of contemporary political theorists seeking to establish a pedigree for their respective prescriptions with regard to the compatibility between liberalism and nationalism. Gray (who has written extensively on J.S. Mill, and more recently wrote the book on Berlin from which the above quotation comes) makes no secret of his search for a "liberal descent,"[6] so to speak, for his own theorizing. Thus, in a newspaper interview, he spelt out his ambition as new Professor of European Thought at the LSE as follows:

I have been looking for a way of reformulating aspects of a British liberal tradition encompassing J.S. Mill and Isaiah Berlin in a way which is directly relevant to the needs of the present and the foreseeable future. I am interested in developing that tradition so it has something useful and illuminating to say about how human needs are to be met in a society such as we now are and will become in future decades.[7]

Whatever the similarities or affinities between Mill, Berlin and Gray might be in other respects, Mill was not a precursor of the kind of approach to nationalism Gray attributes to Isaiah Berlin. In his book on Berlin, Gray refers the reader to Mill's *System of Logic* as the work where, in his view, the British thinker "emphasised the importance of the sentiment of nationality in a liberal culture" (Gray 1995: 174 n.3). Though he does not give a reference to a specific page, it is obvious that Gray refers to Mill's oft-quoted passage where he outlined the three conditions of stability in political society. Mill included as one of these conditions "a strong and active principle of cohesion among the members of the same community or state." But he hastened to declare:

> We need scarcely say that we do not mean nationality in the vulgar sense of the term; a senseless antipathy to foreigners; an indifference to the general welfare of the human race, or an unjust preference of the supposed interests of our own country; a cherishing of bad peculiarities because they are national or a refusal to adopt what has been found good by other countries. . . . We mean a principle of sympathy, not of hostility; of union, not of separation. We mean a feeling of common interest among those who live under the same government, and are contained within the same natural or historical boundaries. We mean, that one part of the community shall not consider themselves as foreigners with regard to another part; that they shall cherish the tie which holds them together; shall feel that they are one people, that their lot is cast together . . . and that they cannot selfishly free themselves from their share of any common inconvenience by severing the connexion.
>
> (*CW*, VIII: 923)[8]

Yet, to what extent is this a text where Mill "emphasised the importance of the *sentiment* of nationality in a liberal culture"?[9] The very word "principle," which Mill uses (twice: "principle of cohesion," "principle of sympathy") goes a long way towards excluding the evocation of sentiments here. And his explanation of what he does *not* mean, in the first part of the passage quoted above, should leave one in little doubt as to the role of unreflecting sentiments in his appreciation of nationality. The above text from Mill's *System of Logic* is a call for reasoned public spirit, based on enlightened self-interest, rather than for particularistic, unreflective nationalist attachment resting on nationalist sentiment. But if further evidence is needed to prove that Mill was not so favorable to national attachments and sentimental particularistic preferences as Gray and many others would have one believe, a careful look at the very work usually invoked by those who present him as a quintessential "liberal nationalist" should suffice. In Chapter XVI of his *Representative Government* (1861) Mill said much more than the tediously reiterated statement: "Where the sentiment of nationality exists in any force, there is a prima facie case for uniting all the members of the nationality under the same government, and a government to themselves apart." However, as Alfred Cobban has poignantly commented, referring to this very passage:

> With his supreme capacity for digging deeper than his own principles, and sometimes, it is true, undermining them, Mill proceeds after this to introduce qualifications which completely alter the complexion of his views on nationality, but, as is usually the case, the general statement is remembered and the all-important modifications are forgotten.
>
> (Cobban 1969: 131)

A fuller analysis of Mill's position vis-à-vis nationalism/patriotism will be offered in the last chapter of this book, in the light of the insights gained by the preceding chapters. Yet, for the purposes of this chapter, one further statement from that very chapter on nationality should suffice. Let us remind ourselves that Mill wrote: "If it be said that so broadly marked a distinction between what is due to a fellow-countryman and what is due merely to a human creature, is more worthy of savages than of civilized beings, *and ought, with the utmost energy, to be contended against*, no one holds that opinion more strongly than myself." "*But this object*," he continued, "*one of the worthiest to which human endeavour can be directed*, can never, in the present state of civilization, be promoted by keeping different nationalities of anything like equivalent strength, under the same government" (Emphasis added: *CW*, XIX: 548). For the preceding reasons, he opined, "it is in general a necessary condition of free institutions, that the boundaries of governments should coincide in the main with those of nationalities." This phrase figures in every account of his views on nationality. Most of them, however, fail to quote the sentence immediately following it: "But several considerations are liable to conflict in practice with this general principle." Mill then gives a long list of reasons why this principle cannot apply to a great many cases (*CW*, XIX: 548–9). In other words, Mill accepted that nationalist sentiments were facts of life that had to be taken into account, but certainly not ones that should be encouraged, promoted, or cherished. In fact, he said in the above text, that unreasoned particularistic attachments "ought, with the utmost energy, to be contended against." Thus, one should take them into account when trying to promote other values – values which, for Mill, involve superseding such unreasoned and uncivilized attachments and sentiments. Even more explicitly, Mill had written in 1849 that it was far from his intention to "defend or apologise for the feelings which make men reckless of, or at least indifferent to, the rights and interests of any portion of the human species, save that which is called by the same name and speaks the same language as themselves." These feelings were "characteristic of barbarians." It was with the deepest "regret, not to say disgust," that he had witnessed the evidence which recent events (following the 1848 revolutions) had afforded, that, in some parts of Europe, as he put it, *"the sentiment of nationality* so far outweighs *the love of liberty,* that the people are willing to abet their rulers in crushing the liberty and independence of any people not of their own race and language" (emphasis added: *CW*, XX: 347). This sounds less as "emphasiz[ing] the importance of the sentiment of nationality," as Gray put it, and more like a repudiation of "tribalism . . . written large."[10]

Andrew Vincent's recent refutation of theories aimed at promoting some sanitized version of nationalism (such as Yael Tamir's "liberal nationalism" or David Miller's defence of "nationality" as having intrinsic ethical value) seems relevant here. Vincent's pragmatic verdict that: "[n]ationalism may be inevitable for the present, but is not a virtue to be promoted" (Vincent 1997: 275; cf. 294) could have been Mill's: it summarizes his position. In this context, it is ironical that all Vincent had to say on Mill was a rather dismissive parenthetic reference to him as an exception to a "liberal continuum" of thinkers opposed to nationalism: ". . .(if we leave aside J.S. Mill's enthused nationalism). . ." (Vincent 1997: 279).

But here we have to deal with another variety of theorizing on the relation between liberalism and particularistic attachments. It may be the case that "nationalism" cannot be reconciled with liberalism and liberal values, but what of "patriotism"? The most ambitious recent version of attempts to distinguish between bad, unacceptable, aggressive "nationalism," on the one hand, and a commendable "patriotism" on the other, has been Maurizio Viroli's *For Love of Country.* Interestingly, on opening the book, the reader is confronted with an epigraph which quotes parts of Mill's statement in the *System of Logic* to which Gray also referred (quoted above). The implication is, clearly, that statements such as Mill's constitute examples of a liberal endorsement of the "patriotism" Viroli goes on to defend in the book. But Erica Benner – among others – has shown convincingly why Viroli's distinction is not valid, either in its normative aspect or in its historical account, used to support the normative argument. Benner rightly asserts that there has been no clear-cut distinction between a language of patriotism and a language of nationalism in the historical periods Viroli addressed in order to establish his pet dichotomy. And she shows equally convincingly the implications of Viroli's failure to establish the distinction in his historical account for his normative proposal (Benner 1997: 191–8). It is worth quoting Benner's conclusion as a brief answer to the vexed question of the appropriate response to "nationalism," "patriotism," or "nationality" on the part of liberally minded people:

> It ... seems puzzling that [Miller and Viroli] want to give the contingent, disputed facts of nationality an independent ethical basis, or indeed to construct an ethical theory around them. If there is such a basis, I suspect that it is remarkably thin. We may choose to treat nationality as an intrinsic, unconditional value which can then be invoked to justify intolerance, repression and conflict. Or we can treat it as an undeniable social fact that sometimes supports "ethical" life and sometimes undermines it, depending on the way it ties in with other facts and values. Then we can try to limit the harm it can do while building on its strengths; but we will need a robust set of background constraints to guide the building. Both Miller and Viroli remind us that the sentiments of national belonging and patriotic partiality need not take irrational, undemocratic forms. We may now have to remind ourselves that national values still need anchoring in more fundamental principles of *freedom* and *political reason*.
>
> (Emphasis added: Benner 1997: 204)

It is such a reminder that will be attempted in the remainder of this chapter. It comes, not surprisingly, from the rich and far from unsophisticated debates on the relationship between nationality and liberal political values that took place in the nineteenth century – and to which Kymlicka enjoins we should turn. However, I do not intend to revisit here the well known debate between J.S. Mill and Lord Acton that is usually taken to be the crown of nineteenth-century liberal wisdom on the issue of nationality.[11] Rather, I hope to give here the gist of a serious disagreement between John Stuart Mill and Alexis de Tocqueville that emerges from their correspondence of the years 1840–3 (and which put an end to what seemed earlier a promising friendship and intellectual partnership).[12] Tocqueville has been time and again accused that he was "blind" to the significance of national differences and insensitive to the claims of the nationalities of Europe – both in his works and during his brief experience as Foreign Minister of the Second Republic. Yet, apparently he was more sensitive to the claims of nationality at home or, rather, he was aware, as a student of his thought put it, of "l'extraordinaire capacité mobilisatrice de la revendication nationale" (Mélonio 1991: 17).[13] He considered national feeling to be very precious because it was the only aspiration that transcended individual interests at a time when individualism and the "culte des intérêts matériels" seemed to him to threaten the social fabric of France and of atomized, democratic-egalitarian societies more generally. The great danger in the new commercial order was that individuals would be exclusively preoccupied with their own interests, and they would no longer aspire to any collective ideal in their capacity as citizens.[14]

When, in 1840, a serious diplomatic crisis broke out between France and the rest of the European Powers over the affairs of the Middle East, there was a general outcry for war in France on account of what was perceived as the dishonorable and humiliating treatment of France by the other Great Powers, most notably, of course, perfidious Albion. Tocqueville, who was then a Deputy, made some of the most belligerent speeches of his career, and sided squarely with those who advocated war.[15] For reasons that should not surprise anyone who has read his exaltation of the effects of war on the character of peoples under certain circumstances in his *Democracy in America*, Tocqueville was convinced that France should go to war against the rest of Europe, although he was equally convinced (as his private correspondence shows) that France was bound to be defeated in such a war.[16] In his correspondence of the time in question, and most notably in his exchanges with Mill, a serious dilemma is discussed, and the two liberal thinkers turn out to have very different views on how to deal with it.

Tocqueville argued that "the greatest malady that threatens a people organized as we are is the gradual softening of mores, the abasement of the mind, the mediocrity of tastes;... One cannot let a nation ... like ours ... take up easily the habit of sacrificing what it believes to be its grandeur to its repose, great matters to petty ones;..." And (as if he were addressing not just Mill, but, much more emphatically, Benjamin Constant's famous distinction between, on the one hand, "l'esprit de conquête et de l'usurpation," and, on the other, "l'esprit de commerce") Tocqueville went on:

> It is not healthy to allow such a nation to believe that its place in the world is smaller, that it is fallen from the level on which its ancestors had put it, but that it must console itself by making railroads and by making prosper in the bosom of its peace, under whatever condition this peace is obtained, the well-being of each private individual. It is necessary that those who march at the head of such a nation should always keep a proud attitude, if they do not wish to allow the level of national mores to fall very low.
>
> (Tocqueville 1985: 150–1)[17]

After a long interval, and only when Tocqueville apparently took the initiative and contacted him again (sending him his discourse to the *Académie Française*), Mill wrote back (on 9 August 1842) to thank him. After assuring Tocqueville of his own deep concern for "that country, to which by tastes and predilections I am more attached than to my own, and on which the civilization of Continental Europe in so great a degree depends," Mill returned to the subject of the Franco-British rift:

> I have often, of late, remembered the reason you gave in justification of the conduct of the liberal party in the late quarrel between England and France – that the feeling of orgueil national is the only feeling of a public-spirited and elevating kind which remains and that it ought not therefore to be permitted to go down. How true this is, every day makes painfully evident – one now sees that the love of liberty, of progress, even of material prosperity, are in France mere passing unsubstantial, superficial movements on the outside of the national mind and that the only appeal which really goes to the heart of France is one of defiance to l'étranger – and that whoever would offer to her satisfaction to that one want, would find the whole of her wealth, the blood of her citizens and every guarantee of liberty and social security flung down at his feet like worthless things. Most heartily do I agree with you that this one and only feeling of a public, and therefore, so far, of a disinterested character which remains in France must not be suffered to decay. The desire to shine in the eyes of foreigners and to be highly esteemed by them must be cultivated and encouraged in France, at all costs.

Notice how Mill transforms the "defiance to l'étranger" – which he deplores – into "the desire to shine in the eyes of foreigners and to be highly esteemed by them" – which he finds far more acceptable. However, having said this, he proceeded to lecture Tocqueville on more commendable ways of having his compatriots esteemed abroad:

> But, in the name of France and civilization, posterity have a right to expect from such men as you, from the nobler and more enlightened spirits of the time, that you should teach to your countrymen better ideas of what it is which constitutes national glory and national importance, than the low and grovelling ones which they seem to have at present. ... Here, for instance, the most stupid and ignorant person knows perfectly well that the real importance of a country in the eyes of foreigners does not depend upon the loud and boisterous *assertion* of importance, the effect of which is an impression of angry weakness, not strength. It really depends upon the industry, instruction, morality, and good government of a country:[18] by which alone it can make itself respected, or even feared, by its neighbours; and it is cruel to think and see as I do every day, to how sad an extent France has sunk in estimation on all these points (the three last at least) by the events of the last two or three years.
>
> (*CW*, XIII: 536–7)

Thus, the two great liberal luminaries of the nineteenth century were not exactly at one in their attitude towards nationalism. At first sight, Tocqueville could be taken as an exponent of French nationalism, which he would appear to endorse because he thought it was instrumental for the preservation of the mores of the French people, and of the public spirit that was bound to suffer in the emerging individualistic, commercial civilization. Mill shared Tocqueville's worries with a vengeance. But he abhorred his remedy. He reacted angrily (not only in this letter),[19] because he thought that Tocqueville's recipe was self-defeating and dangerous, especially on account of its irrationality. Though Mill was by no means less concerned than Tocqueville with the effect of policies (including foreign policy) on the mores and "character" of a people, he simply did not think that the promotion – or even the toleration – of jingoist policies and rhetoric would promote – or preserve – the right kind of mores and "character." But "nationalism" may mean many different things, and this debate brings us back to the question of whether there can be a distinction between "nationalism" and "patriotism." Liberals like Mill and Tocqueville argued strongly, on many occasions, in favour of bolstering a sense of solidarity and public spirit in the liberal-democratic society they aspired to. What are we supposed to call this component of their thought? Were they nationalists? (or, rather, "liberal nationalists," in Tamir's terms?) No, because I shall take nationalism to mean "putting the nation first."[20] If I may use the late George Armstrong Kelly's phrase in a slightly different context, Tocqueville, like Mill (and Constant), "put liberty first."[21] At the same time, both Mill and Tocqueville spoke often of the merits and the commendability of "patriotism." In fact, some of Mill's most interesting references to patriotism were made in his two celebrated reviews of Tocqueville's *Democracy in America*, by way of commending Tocqueville's (favorable) description of patriotism in America as enlightened self-interest.[22] Thus, at first sight, the two thinkers would appear to fit into a distinction such as Viroli's. But although it is tempting and convenient to categorize them as liberal patriots-as-opposed-to-nationalists, such a neat distinction between patriotism and nationalism is untenable in normative as well as historical terms, for the reasons adduced by Benner.

Moreover, the debate between Mill and Tocqueville seems to me to exemplify exactly why the distinction between a "good" patriotism and a "bad" nationalism is flawed and why we should rather always seek to subordinate nationalism/patriotism/nationality (however we choose to call it) to other, more commendable "liberal" values, rather than investing any "intrinsic" value in a principle or term that supposedly represents a better version of particularistic attachments (such as "patriotism" for Viroli and "nationality" for Miller).[23] This is so because, in the debate outlined above, Tocqueville and Mill were arguing about different approaches to building what they both would call "patriotism." The problem was, according to Mill, that Tocqueville's way was not that wholesome after all, because it was not based on reason, but rather was based on – and pandered to – lower feelings and unreflecting notions of national pride. Tocqueville's attitude and argumentation during the crisis of 1840 had not been consistent with his theoretical exaltation of the virtues of what he saw as the rational, enlightened patriotism of the Americans in *Democracy in America*. Mill had endorsed the latter, and his main grudge against Tocqueville in the aftermath of the crisis over the Near East was that the Frenchman's stance then promoted another kind of patriotism, unreflecting, unenlightened, irrational.

One may choose to call Mill's approach in this case "utilitarian," or even "English," besides "liberal." Or the approach could simply be taken

as a principled setting of priorities: rationality, morality, good government (and therefore, for Mill, free government) are set as principles or
values which should not be bypassed and sacrificed in the pursuit of the
goal of strengthening national solidarity and public spirit. National solidarity, public spirit, or "patriotism," were regarded by Mill as valuable,
even indispensable. That is why he was both candid and consistent with
himself when he conceded to Tocqueville that he "most heartily" agreed
with him that "this one and only feeling of a public, and therefore, so far,
of a disinterested character which remain[ed] in France must not be suf-
fered to decay." Yet, in the first place, it makes a world of difference
how he chose to phrase the feeling he approved, as opposed to the one
he had decried earlier. Instead of unreasoning, childish "defiance to
l'étranger," it was "[t]he desire to shine in the eyes of foreigners and to
be highly esteemed by them" that ought to be "cultivated and encouraged
in France." According to Mill, there were very different ways of cultivating this more properly termed "feeling." One was the "low and grovel-
ling" ideas of "what it is that constitutes national glory and national
importance" which the French seemed to entertain at that time – and
which he implicitly accused Tocqueville of condoning or encouraging,
by advocating that France should go to war in their name. In the second
place, Mill was juxtaposing his alternative vision of what a people should
be taught by its moral teachers and politicians to take pride in (and, consequently, to seek to excel in): namely "the industry, instruction, morality, and good government of a country."[24]

In conclusion, then, it has been seen in the above pages that thinkers
who would be taken to belong to the self-same camp or category according to most existing distinctions seeking to describe – while prescribing –
different attitudes towards nationalism or patriotism, could still be in fundamental disagreement about the ways in which it was permissible or
advisable to pursue the aims they are supposed to have shared. One
cannot help regarding this as a reflection on the limitations of the distinctions and categorizations in question.

3 Nations and nationhood I

Did race matter?

> Of all vulgar modes of escaping from the consideration of the effect of social and moral influences on the human mind, the most vulgar is that of attributing the diversities of conduct and character to inherent natural differences.
>
> (J.S. Mill, *Principles of Political Economy*: *CW*, II: 319)

> It is not in China only that a homogeneous community is naturally a stationary community.... It is profoundly remarked by M. Guizot, that the short duration or stunted growth of the earlier civilizations arose from this, that in each of them some one element of human improvement existed exclusively, or so preponderatingly as to overpower all the others; whereby the community, after accomplishing rapidly all which that one element could do, either perished for want of what it could not do, or came to a halt, and became immoveable. It would be an error to suppose that such could not possibly be our fate. In the generalization which pronounces the "law of progress" to be an inherent attribute of human nature, it is forgotten that, among the inhabitants of our earth, the European family of nations is the only one which has ever yet shown any capability of spontaneous improvement, beyond a certain low level. *Let us beware of supposing that we owe this peculiarity to any necessity of nature*, and not rather to combinations of circumstances, which have existed nowhere else, and may not exist for ever among ourselves.
>
> (Emphasis added: J.S. Mill, "De Tocqueville on Democracy in America [II]": *CW*, XVIII: 197)

After the misconstructions related to Mill's place in the pedigree of so-called "liberal nationalism" it is time now to address those related to his attitude towards "race," in order to be able to establish what he meant by nation and national character. Like his contemporaries, Mill paid a great deal of attention to the significance for politics of differences of what were called at his time "national characters." It will be argued further on that the category of national character was not as marginal in the younger Mill's thought as the cursory nature of references to it by subsequent students and the absence of its detailed consideration in existing scholarship would have one believe (to say nothing of statements implying that it amounted to little more than an argumentative weapon). Discussions about national and – what would be called today – cultural characteristics were, in Victorian Britain, inextricably associated with discussions about "race," and the term, "race," was often substituted for nation, nationhood, or national character.[1] A methodological difficulty that can complicate the examination of discussions on race during the nineteenth century arises from the fact that sometimes race was used in the sense that the term "culture" has today, without, that is, necessarily implying any belief in the doctrine of biological and hereditary transmission of mental and cultural traits.[2] Here race will be discussed inasmuch as it assumed a biological sense.

Even more importance was attached to the role of race in France at the same time (Seliger 1958: 273–82; Barzun 1965: 6, and *passim*).[3] It was certainly not accidental that Tocqueville came to examine seriously the possible significance of racial origin during his first stay in America (Drescher 1968: 274–6; Schleifer 1980: 62–72).

Mill was thus bound to address the question of the extent to which national character was formed or influenced by race or other physical factors such as climate.[4] His attitude towards the theories concerning these issues that were abroad at his time is illustrated in the following pages and the extent to which he followed the relevant scientific disciplines is assessed. For all his concessions to some of the stereotypes of the century Mill is shown to have been on the whole in the forefront of attempts to discredit the deterministic implications of racial theories and assert the ascendancy of "mind over matter," a view corroborated by the responses of his contemporaries. Criticisms by later scholars sometimes fail to place him in the context of his time and inevitably find his references to race unacceptable. For instance, E.D. Steele did less than justice to Mill when he wrote that "[h]is writings furnish examples of judgements on the basis of race or national character" (Steele 1970: 435). Though it is very much the case that he often made pronouncements on the basis of national character, Mill was far from equating or confusing the latter with race and denounced – and did a lot to discredit – the usual association of the two during the nineteenth century.[5]

In another instance of misconstruction of Mill's attitude to race, Vincent Pecora has argued, in reference to what Mill wrote on the causes of Chinese stationariness in *On Liberty* – as opposed to the diversity that had preserved Europe from the same fate (*CW*, XVIII: 273–4) – that: "it is hard not to understand this result as a product of innate racial disposition, for it is only an unexplained and seemingly natural 'diversity of character and culture' that, with proper nurturing, will save European nations and individuals from a similar fate" (Pecora 1997–8: 372). This is a gross mispresentation of what Mill wrote in that very text in *On Liberty*, as well as in *Representative Government* (*CW*, XIX: 458–9), his second review of Tocqueville's *Democracy in America* (1840) (*CW*, XVIII: 197),[6] or his two reviews of Guizot's works (see Varouxakis 1999). Mill does not talk of any "unexplained and seemingly natural 'diversity of character and culture.'" On the very contrary, his whole point in all the texts in question was that the diversity to which he (following Guizot) attributed Europe's "progressiveness" was *not* innate or natural in Europeans, but rather the result of historical accident, and that there would always be a serious danger of its disappearing if Europeans ever were to believe that it was natural to them and took it for granted. To blame the thinker who warned fellow-Europeans "Let us beware of supposing that we owe this peculiarity to any necessity of nature..." that he presented diversity "as a product of innate racial disposition" (Pecora 1997–8: 372) is to completely miss the point.[7]

Similarly, Bruce Mazlish wrote that "Mill even flirted with a kind of racial theory of character." Mazlish proceeded to substantiate this assertion by citing what Mill wrote to his French friend, Gustave d'Eichthal, on 14 September 1839, after having received the former Saint-Simonist's latest work which dealt with the relations between the black and the white races:

I have long been convinced that not only the East as compared with the West, but the black race as compared with the European, is distinguished by characteristics something like those which you assign to them; that the improvement which may be looked for, from a more intimate and sympathetic familiarity between the two, will not be solely on their side, but greatly also on ours; that if our intelligence is more developed and our activity more intense, *they* possess exactly what is most needful to us as a qualifying counterpoise, in their love of repose and in the superior capacity of animal enjoyment and consequently of sympathetic sensibility, which is characteristic of the negro race.

I have even long thought that the same distinction holds, though in a less *prononcé* manner, between the nations of the north and south of Europe; that the north is destined to be the workshop, material and intellectual, of Europe; the south, its "stately pleasure-house" – and that neither will fulfil its destination until it has made its peculiar function available for the benefit of both – until our *work* is done for their benefit, and until we, in the measure of our nature, are made susceptible of their luxury and sensuous enjoyment.

(Mazlish 1975: 407)[8]

The above text is not sufficient proof that Mill "flirted with a kind of racial theory of character." The term "race" was used quite loosely at the time this letter was written, and various characteristics were attributed to "races" as a matter of course, without reference as to whether they were biologically inherited or simply cultural traits occurring in these groups.[9] D'Eichthal's short work Mill was referring to was based on the assertion that the two races, the white and the black, were possessed of biologically inherited mental and social characteristics peculiar to each (Eichthal and Urbain 1839: 14–19). Of course, d'Eichthal's work drew implications very different from those characterizing the racial theories of the second half of the nineteenth century. Far from exalting racial purity, the whole point d'Eichthal was making was that the two races should associate with each other and produce the "race mulâtre." Yet, it remains the case that d'Eichthal's premises were based on theories asserting that the differences between whites and blacks were constitutional differences and that these physical differences resulted in the two races having different geniuses, habits, religious propensities, and so on.[10] What is not clear is how far Mill shared the premises behind d'Eichthal's benign theories.[11] But even if he did not object to them in 1839, his thought on the subject developed considerably during the following decades, and the Mill who wrote *The Subjection of Women* had moved a long way from any tacit acceptance of such premises and theories.

During the earlier years, Mill's most direct and explicit public reference to the subject of race – to which he himself drew attention in later instances (*CW*, XV: 691) – was made in his review of the five first volumes of Michelet's *Histoire de France*, written in 1844. After praising Michelet for having endeavoured to assign to the several races that were mixed on French soil "the share of influence which belongs to them over the subsequent destinies of his country," Mill observed:

> It was natural that a subjective historian, one who looks, above all, to the internal moving forces of human affairs, should attach great historical importance to the consideration of Races. This subject, on British soil, has usually fallen into hands little competent to treat it soberly, or on true principles of induction; but of the great influence of Race in the production of national character, no reasonable inquirer can now doubt. As far as history, and social circumstances generally, are concerned, how little resemblance can be traced between the French and the Irish – in national character, how much! The same ready excitability; the same impetuosity when excited, yet the same readiness under excitement to submit to the severest discipline – a quality which at first might seem to contradict impetuosity, but which arises from that very vehemence of character with which it appears to conflict, and is equally conspicuous in Revolutions of Three Days, temperance movements, and meetings on the Hill of Tara. The same sociability and demonstrativeness – the same natural refinement of manners, down to the lowest rank – in both, the characteristic weakness an inordinate vanity, their more serious moral deficiency the absence of a sensitive regard for truth. Their ready susceptibility to influences, while it makes them less steady in right, makes them also less pertinacious in wrong, and renders them, under favourable circumstances of culture, reclaimable and improvable (especially through their more generous feelings) in a degree to which the more obstinate races are strangers. To what, except their Gaelic blood, can we ascribe all this similarity between populations, the whole course of whose national history has been so different?
>
> (*CW*, XX: 235)

A little further on Mill disagreed with a specific instance of Michelet's application of the racial model of explanation. The French historian had attributed to race (the Germanic race in this case) what he called "that voluntary loyalty of man to man, that free adherence, founded on confiding attachment, which was characteristic of the German tribes, and of which, in his opinion, the feudal relation was the natural result." Michelet had asserted that this "personal devotedness and faith in one another" of the Germans was missing in the case of the Gauls, who were already possessed by "that passion for equality which distinguishes modern France."[12] Mill's comment follows: "We think that M. Michelet has here carried the influence of Race too far, and that the difference is better explained by diversity of position, than by diversity of character in the Races." Mill accounted for the difference by the circumstance of the conquerors being a small body scattered over a large territory, which prevented them from relaxing the bonds which held them together.[13] "Similar circumstances would have produced similar results among the Gauls themselves" was his retort to Michelet (*CW*, XX: 237).

The above qualification notwithstanding, Mill's adherence to some of the views that were abroad at his time, concerning the significance of race in the formation of national character, was part of his approach to the subject. And when, sixteen years later, he was criticized by Charles Dupon-White that he had denied the influence of races, Mill replied (in a letter of 6 April 1860) that he had "pleinement" admitted this influence in his article on Michelet. This having been said, however, and as far as theoretical discussion is concerned, it is the limit of his adherence to the commonplace views on the significance of race that is more remarkable than the fact of the adherence itself. In that same letter Mill proceeded to explain to Dupon-White that, though he did not deny the significance of the racial factor, what he disagreed with was the tendency, which was most conspicuous in the nineteenth century (as a result of that century's reaction against the eighteenth century), "celle d'attribuer toutes les variétés dans le caractère des peuples et des individus à des différences indélébiles de la nature, sans se demander si les influences de l'éducation et du milieu social et politique n'en donnent pas une explication suffisante."[14] It was, he said, like the habit of primitive peoples to attribute whatever they were doing to direct inspiration from a god. Thus, in the case Dupon-White had referred to, that of the differences of character between "les peuples celtiques" and "les peuples anglo-saxons," Mill's comment was that he agreed with his French correspondent that "la race y entre beaucoup." Yet, he hastened to add: "mais quant à leur goût pour ou contre la centralisation, je vous demanderai si la diversité dans le développement historique de la France et de l'Angleterre dont vous avez fait une esquisse si vraie et si instructive, ne suffisait pas à elle seule comme explication"[15] (*CW*, XV: 691).

Thus, while accepting vaguely that racial origin is one of the factors influencing the formation of national character, Mill went further to establish that racial predisposition in itself could prove nothing and was liable to be modified out of any recognition through the agency of circumstances such as institutions, historical accidents and human effort.

An instance of Mill's careful depreciation of the role of both race and, more generally, physical causes occurs in the very article on Michelet, closely following the theoretical discussion of the significance of race. There, after having admitted the importance of the influence of "geographical peculiarities" in the formation of national character (*CW*, XX: 237), he proceeded to praise Michelet for not being unaware of the tendency of provincial and local peculiarities to disappear:

> A strenuous asserter of the power of mind over matter, of will over spontaneous propensities, culture over nature, he holds that local characteristics lose their importance as history advances. In a rude age the "fatalities" of race and geographical position are absolute. In the progress of society, human forethought and purpose, acting by means of uniform institutions and modes of culture, tend more and more to efface the pristine differences. And he attributes, in no small degree, the greatness of France to the absence of any marked local peculiarities in the predominant part of the population.
>
> (*CW*, XX: 238)

Many other instances occur – in Mill's correspondence in particular – where he protested against the inordinate importance that he thought most of his contemporaries accorded to race.[16]

In 1850 he attacked his erstwhile friend Carlyle for having asserted that negroes were born servants to the whites who were "born *wiser*."[17] Mill reprobated Carlyle for his disrespect of "the analytical examination of human nature"; failure to apply the mode of analytical examination "to the laws of the formation of character" had led Carlyle to "the vulgar error of imputing every difference which he finds among human beings to an original difference of nature" (*CW*, XXI: 93). Some lines further on Mill spoke his mind with regard to the theoretical issues involved:

> What the original differences are among human beings, I know no more than your contributor, and no less; it is one of the questions not yet satisfactorily answered in the natural history of the species. This, however, is well known – that spontaneous improvement, beyond a very low grade, – improvement by internal development, without aid from other individuals or peoples – is one of the rarest phenomena in history; and whenever known to have occurred, was the result of an extraordinary combination of advantages;[18] in addition doubtless to many accidents of which all trace is now lost. No argument against

the capacity of negroes for improvement, could be drawn from their not being one of these rare exceptions.[19]

Mill concluded: "It is curious withal, that the earliest known civilization was . . . a negro civilization. The original Egyptians are inferred, from the evidence of their sculptures, to have been a negro race: it was from negroes, therefore, that the Greeks learnt their first lessons in civilization" (*CW*, XXI: 93). And it is well known which side Mill took during the Governor Eyre controversy (see Semmel 1962).

In his writings on Ireland, it was one of Mill's main aims to show that the alleged failings of the Irish were not "natural" to them, but were due to English misgovernment. In his *Principles of Political Economy*, he wrote, concerning the Irish, that it was a "bitter satire on the mode in which opinions are formed on the most important problems of human nature and life," to find people "imputing the backwardness of Irish industry, and the want of energy of the Irish people in improving their condition, to a peculiar indolence and *insouciance* in the Celtic race." He commented that: "*Of all vulgar modes of escaping from the consideration of the effect of social and moral influences on the human mind, the most vulgar is that of attributing the diversities of conduct and character to inherent natural differences*" (Emphasis added). Any race would be indolent and idle, he stressed, if the arrangements under which they lived and worked resulted in their deriving no advantage from forethought or exertion. The certain degree to which Mill did indulge in stereotypes concerning primordial racial (or geographical) characteristics, is no less apparent in this very passage, as is his way of drawing from these premises he shared with his contemporaries different conclusions than the conclusions most of them did:

It is very natural that a pleasure-loving and sensitively organized people like the Irish, should be less addicted to steady routine labour than the English, because life has more excitements for them independent of it; but they are not less fitted for it than their Celtic brethren the French, nor less so than the Tuscans, or the ancient Greeks. *An excitable organization is precisely that in which, by adequate inducements, it is easier to kindle a spirit of animated exertion.* It speaks nothing against the capacities of industry in human beings, that they will not exert themselves without motive. No labourers work harder, in England or America, than the Irish; but not under a cottier system.

(Emphasis added: *CW*, II: 319)

Another important instance of Mill's pronouncing on race occurs in *The Subjection of Women*. In his attempt to discard theories of women's inferiority founded on alleged physical differences between men and women and inferences thereof, he enlisted the example of national characters and their alleged racial determination. His mode of arguing in this respect was by admitting the existence of some primordial physical differences between different human groups (races, sexes), and subsequently trying to prove that social circumstances, human will-power and self-discipline ("mind over matter" as he had said *à propos* of Michelet) could lead such physical predispositions to directions opposite to those they were supposed to be destined to take. Among his examples were, of course, the omni-present French, as well as other groups such as the Irish, the Greeks, the Romans, and the English. Mill protested against "the unspeakable ignorance and inattention of mankind in respect to the influences which form human character," which was, he asserted, the greatest of the difficulties which impeded "the progress of thought, and the formation of well-grounded opinions on life and social arrangements." He developed this subject as follows:

> Whatever any portion of the human species now are, or seem to be, such, it is supposed, they have a natural tendency to be: even when the most elementary knowledge of the circumstances in which they have been placed, clearly points out the causes that made them what they are. Because a cottier deeply in arrears to his landlord is not industrious, there are people who think that the Irish are naturally idle. Because constitutions can be overthrown when the authorities appointed to execute them turn their arms against them, there are people who think the French incapable of free government. Because the Greeks cheated the Turks, and the Turks only plundered the Greeks, there are persons who think that the Turks are naturally more sincere;...[20]

But History taught another lesson, by showing "the extraordinary susceptibility of human nature to external influences, and the extreme variableness of those of its manifestations which are supposed to be most universal and uniform" (*CW*, XXI: 277). And in an attempt to refute arguments to the effect that the alleged "greater nervous susceptibility of women is a disqualification for practice" (*CW*, XXI: 307), Mill employed the example of races to assert that experience of races did not show those of excitable temperament "to be less fit, on the average, either for speculation or practice, than the more unexcitable." His examples were the French and the Italians, compared with the Teutonic races, especially with the English, the Greeks and Romans compared with the northern races, and so on.[21] Statements such as these made in *The Subjection*, written in Mill's maturity, offer not only a theoretical rejection of biological determinism, but also would suggest an unequivocal belief in the malleability of human nature and therefore in the improvability of the character of the various nations.[22] But, while declaring his rejection of physical determinism, Mill spoke in a way that betrays his use of many of the stereotypes of his contemporaries based on race, climate or geography. Where he differed is in that he asserted that the alleged natural predispositions in question could lead to results very different than those they seemed to lead to at present, if they were appropriately guided by institutions and human will.[23]

If one compares Mill's letters to d'Eichthal (1839, 1840) and his review of Michelet (1844) with all his later pronouncements on race, there seems to be a shift of emphasis in his statements around the middle of the nineteenth century. In the early 1840s he asserted that race was one of the factors that influenced national character and should therefore be studied and taken into account. From the end of that decade onwards, and with increasing intensity, he went out of his way to stress how little importance race had. This shift was probably due to his growing realization of the uses to which racial theories were being put. Historians of anthropological or racial theories have stressed the increasing occurrence during the second half of the century of overtly racist theories which – unlike d'Eichthal's orientalist ethnological ventures of Saint-Simonist inspiration – led to conclusions disturbing to Mill with regard to issues such as slavery, international relations, the government of dependencies, as well as women's rights.[24] The worst consequence of the growing popularity of racial theories was the determinism (or, as Mill would put it, the fatalism) that followed as the main implication of the acceptance of such theories. Another factor that, during the 1840s, must have brought home to Mill the full implications of the attribution of mental and moral characteristics to physiological differences was Comte's insistence on the inferiority of women, on the grounds afforded by Gall's phrenological studies.[25]

Apparently it was not accidental that Mill was singled out as the target of more than one article written by one of the major exponents of racial determinism in Britain. James Hunt was the founder (1863) and President of the Anthropological Society of London. He was "an ardent racialist" and strongly in favour of slavery (Burrow 1968: 118–36).[26] He was a follower of the Edinburgh anatomist Robert Knox. Knox has been called Gobineau's British counterpart (Sternhell 1987: 414), "an almost hysterical racialist," who had asserted, in *The Races of Man* (1850), that "race is everything; literature, science, art – in a word, civilization, depends on it" (Burrow 1968: 130). Hunt dedicated an entire article to an attack on Mill's explicit rejection of racial explanations in the *Principles of Political Economy* and his failure to take any account of the racial factor in his other major works, *Considerations on Representative Government* and *On Liberty* (Hunt 1866: 113–35).[27] Hunt did not fail to pay ample lip-service to Mill's qualities as a thinker and logician, and maintained that he wrote the article on "Race in Legislation and Political Economy" in order to induce Mill and his followers to cease neglecting what Hunt regarded as the scientifically proven all-importance of the racial factor. Hunt had earlier written an article entitled "Race in History," in which he had attacked directly the historian H.T. Buckle (who professed to be influenced by Mill's *Logic*) and also extended his criticisms to J.S. Mill and Bentham (Rainger 1978: 63–4).[28] Hunt's 1867 presidential address to the Anthropological Society was "another attack on Mill" (Rainger 1978: 64). There is no evidence of Mill's having read Hunt's articles referring to himself or the rest of the anthropologist's writings.[29] But, if he did, they do not seem to have convinced him at all, if one is to judge from Mill's even more outspoken denunciation of racial determinism in *The Subjection of Women*.[30]

For all his exhortations for the scientific study of differences among societies Mill does not seem to have followed closely developments in the new disciplines of ethnology and anthropology. Besides his failure to refer to most of the main figures in the field and their work, there is also his own admission to the same effect. When, in 1863, the Anthropological Society was founded by Hunt and his followers who had broken away from the Ethnological Society (Rainger 1978: 51–70), Mill wrote to Max Kyllmann (who had apparently referred to that Society in his previous letter to Mill):

> The Anthropological Society I hear of for the first time from your letter. I should suppose from the publications it announces that its objects must be very much the same as those of the Ethnological Society which already existed. The names mentioned are all new to me except two: Capt. Burton ... and Mr Luke Burke. ... It is possible that some of the others may be distinguished names, *for I am very little acquainted with the present state of this class of studies*.
>
> (Emphasis added: *CW*, XV: 840–1)

Though Mill was acquainted and even corresponded with a number of scientists whose work was related to the issues involved in the study of races, he did not regard studies in the field of natural sciences as relevant to his interest in character. He found more congenial the approach of scientists such as his acquaintance, Thomas Henry Huxley, who "considered a subject such as human heredity to be a scientific matter from which he personally would draw no political or nonscientific conclusions" (Rainger 1978: 65).[31] Referring to an article written by Huxley in 1865 Mill wrote to J.E. Cairnes that it was particularly good, "notwithstanding what I venture to think heretical physiology, which, however, he clearly sees, and as clearly shews, not to affect in the smallest degree the moral, political, or educational questions, either as regards negroes or women" (*CW*, XVI: 1057–8).[32]

What has been argued so far is not meant to obscure the fact that Mill's failure to develop his projected science of "ethology," in combination with his pre-Darwinian approach to the natural sciences[33] must be held to account for the fact that he did find himself obliged to accord race a certain – unclear – role (simply because he had not gone as far as he had hoped in developing the science that would demonstrate beyond doubt the way in which character was formed by circumstances). Though he made strenuous efforts during the last three decades of his life to depreciate the importance of physical factors in the formation of national character, it has already been seen that he stopped short of denying them any significance whatsoever. This was less obvious in his theoretical statements on these subjects than in his tacit assumptions and his use of language.

The extent to which these tacit assumptions concerning the relation of physical factors to national character could compromise some of his theoretical arguments can be tested in a reference to French national characteristics, which appears in Chapter III of his *Considerations on Representative Government* ("*That the Ideally Best Form of Government is Representative Government*"). Mill asserted that, when it came to "the influence of the form of government upon character," the superiority of popular government over every other would be found to be "still more decided and indisputable." This question depended upon "a still more fundamental one – viz. which of two common types of character, for the general good of humanity, is it most desirable should predominate – the active, or the passive type" (*CW*, XIX: 406). In this context Mill came to the subject of the passive character's envy:

In proportion as success in life is seen or believed to be the fruit of fatality or accident and not of exertion, in that same ratio does envy develop itself as a point of national character. The most envious of all mankind are the Orientals. In Oriental moralists, in Oriental tales, the envious man is markedly prominent. . . . Next to Orientals in envy . . . are some of the Southern Europeans. The Spaniards pursued all their great men with it. . . . *With the French, who are essentially a southern people*, the double education of despotism and Catholicism has, in spite of their impulsive temperament, made submission and endurance the common character of the people, and their most received notion of wisdom and excellence . . .

(Emphasis added: *CW*, XIX: 408)

It is not entirely clear what Mill held to account for the character traits attributed to the French. Is it the fact that they are "essentially a southern people"? Or is it "the double education of despotism and Catholicism" that "in spite of their impulsive temperament, made submission and endurance the common character of the people . . ."? It would indeed make sense, given Mill's aim to convince his readers that "the passive type of character is favoured by the government of one or a few, and the active self-helping type by that of the Many" (*CW*, XIX: 410), to assert that it was despotism that made the French passive and envious. But then, what does their being "essentially a southern people" have to do with this argument?[34]

Of course, the confounding of sets of causes of different nature is no contradiction in Mill's own terms, given his assertion that race and other physical factors do have some small part in the formation of national character. What generates considerable difficulty is that, by allowing race the part he did, Mill was unable ever to define clearly and unequivocally the exact nature of the concept of national character and its legitimate unit. In other words, for all his talk of national character, he did not define what groups had a "character," what exactly constituted a nation. Most times he spoke of it as a political unit, referring to the inhabitants of what is called today a nation-state, but he also often spoke of ethnic, cultural or "racial" groups as possessing a national character. Thus, while he spoke sometimes of the Scottish and the Welsh characters as fairly distinct from the English, it seems that he often included the Scotch and Welsh in what he called the English character.

Thus, some of Mill's arguments concerning national character are rendered ambiguous due to his having indulged in discussions involving assumptions related to race or climate and geography more often than he would consciously – or theoretically – have admitted and condoned. At the same time, in order to do him justice it should not be lost sight of that, in doing so, he was in good company. Compared with most of his well known contemporaries[35] Mill can be said to have indulged in the temptation of racial explanation remarkably less than them (except probably Tocqueville, whose position was similar to Mill's). Though he lacked the scientific buttressing he needed, he made strenuous efforts to use what materials he had (mainly consisting of carefully selected historical examples) in order to substantiate his claims concerning man's progressive nature.

The study of Mill's views with regard to race leads to a broader conclusion concerning his political thought and activity, namely to a corroboration of recent interpretations of Mill stressing the overwhelming significance of his commitment to rationality as a unifying and fundamental constituent of his conception of virtue and the good life (Skorupski 1989; Jones 1992). As part and parcel with this view comes the recognition of the extent to which "Mill was always a child of the enlightenment" (Skorupski 1989: 5; cf. Mandelbaum 1971: 198–9) in his overall outlook and the underlying purposes of his intellectual and political activity. The analysis of Mill's pronouncements on race attempted in the preceding pages comes to support the view that sees Mill as in essence attempting to adapt and translate to the intellectual climate of the nineteenth century a world-view and aspirations rooted in the Enlightenment of the eighteenth century while purging the latter of what he saw as its historical immaturity and naiveté.[36] Mill often presented himself as somehow standing above the dispute between the two centuries and effecting a mature synthesis of what was good in each. Yet, all the concessions he was prepared to make to opposite viewpoints notwithstanding, when it came to a test he opted for what he would call the eighteenth-century position. This attachment to an eighteenth-century viewpoint is exemplified in Mill's treatment of differences of national character between various "portions of mankind." For all his assertions of originality and distance from what he called "the eminent thinkers of fifty years ago" (Collini *et al.* 1983: 133), in dealing with differences of national character he consciously declined to follow the directions contemporary discussions were taking, especially from the moment he came to realize the decidedly non-enlightenment implications these directions were bound to have. (He explicitly referred to the emphasis placed on race and physical factors in the formation of national character as a result of the reaction of the nineteenth century to the philosophy of the eighteenth (*CW*, XV: 691).[37]) Thus, although his discussions of national character strike one as incomparably more sophisticated than those of thinkers such as Hume or Montesquieu, it remains the case that the framework within which he conducted such discussions was far closer to Hume and Montesquieu than it was to Gobineau, Robert Knox, Matthew Arnold, Lord Acton, Marx, Carlyle, Comte, or the spokesmen of the London Anthropological Society in the 1860s. His deliberate effort to concede as little importance as possible to race and other physical factors, even at the risk of being – as he actually was – exposed to the criticism that he was not sufficiently scientific, was the result of a strong determination to stand by certain assumptions about rationality and capacity for improvement that were dear to him.

4　Nations and nationhood II

National character and politics, or the discrete charm of Englishness

We have now established that Mill, contrary to claims based on anachronistic misreadings of parts of his work, was in the forefront of attempts to discredit the deterministic implications of racial theories and assert the ascendancy of "mind over matter"; that he went out of his way to insist that the racial factor was far from being the most important factor in the formation of "national character." We now need to come to the meaning, development, and significance in Mill's thought of the category of national character itself. Thus, in the following pages it will be shown, first, that the category of national character came to be, eventually, considerably more significant in Mill's thought than the cursory nature of references to it by subsequent students would suggest. Second, it will be shown that it was Mill's life-long study of France and the French, and the conclusions to which this study led him regarding both the French and what he called the "English national character," that informed decisively his views on this concept and its significance.[1]

Discussions of "national characters" have a long history. Political thinkers have indulged in them much more than the relative scarcity of commentary on this aspect of their concerns would suggest. Talk of national characters has been understandably discredited since World War II in particular, and thus embarrassment about the political implications of the concept came to compound the difficulties inherent in its very nature – inextricably related to the perplexities characterizing the notions "character" and "nation" themselves.[2] Earlier political thinkers, however, were more casual about these matters, and collective characteristics and their significance for politics have been among the concerns of political thought at least since Aristotle. Besides cursory references in the works of most thinkers, some proceeded to theoretical discussions of the very category. Thus, David Hume wrote an essay entitled "Of national characters," and certainly Montesquieu and Voltaire were far from alone in making much of the differences of character between nations (Hume 1994).[3] In the nineteenth century such references, if anything, intensified.[4] Thus, it is hardly surprising that the younger Mill should be interested in such matters.

National character, and the "science of national character"

But what exactly did Mill mean by the term, "national character"? It can hardly be overstressed that "national character" is a concept more often employed than defined,[5] and Mill is no exception to this tendency – nor are subsequent commentators of his thought. The closest he came to defining national character was when he spoke in the *Logic*, of "the character, that is, the opinions, feelings, and habits of the people" (*CW*, VIII: 905). As this does not go very far, what he meant will have to be traced through a great number of writings. It has to be clarified that Mill talked of national character in two different – though interconnected – senses. In the first place, he spoke of the importance of national character as an end of legislation and social reform. Institutions could not be considered advisable if they did not provide for the improvement of the collective character of the people who were to live under them. In the second place, he spoke of differences of national character between different "portions of mankind" as an existing fact, and of the need for legislators or social reformers to take them into account in the calculation of the means they were to employ in order to achieve their goals (attaining to a better collective or "national" character being one of the main goals, as far as Mill was concerned).[6] It will be mainly in this latter sense that national character will be discussed here.

More important than the fact that Mill discussed national character itself, was his genuine desire to proceed to its "scientific" study. It is well known that he had envisaged in his *Logic* (Book VI, Chapter v) the creation of a new branch of science. The title of that chapter was "*Of Ethology, or the Science of the Formation of Character.*" Further on in the same Book (VI) he spoke of the appropriate methods of the overall "social science" and of the different branches of sociological speculation that could with advantage be studied separately (*CW*, VIII: 900–7). Among the "hypothetical or abstract sciences" which could profitably be "carved out of the general body of the social science" there was one, which could not be passed over in silence, "being of a more comprehensive and commanding character than any of the other branches into which the social science may admit of being divided." He referred to "what may be termed Political Ethology, or the theory of the causes which determine the type of character belonging to a people or to an age." Of all the subordinate branches of the social science, this was "the most completely in its infancy." The causes of national character were "scarcely at all understood, and the effect of institutions or social arrangements upon the character of the people is generally that portion of their effects which is least attended to, and least comprehended." Yet, he asserted, "the laws of national (or collective) character" were "by far the most important class of sociological laws" (*CW*, VIII: 904–5). In the first place, "the character which is formed by any state of social circumstances is in itself the most interesting phenomenon which that state of society can possibly present." In the second place, "it is also a fact which enters largely into the production of all the other phenomena." And, "above all, the character, that is, the opinions, feelings, and habits, of the people, though greatly the results of the state of society which precedes them, are also greatly the causes of the state of society which follows them; and are the power by which all those of the circumstances of society which are artificial, laws and customs for instance, are altogether moulded" (*CW*, VIII: 905). Here Mill spoke in a vein reminiscent of his criticisms of Bentham (in the 1830s) on account of what he saw as the latter's neglect of the educative function of institutions (*CW*, X: 9, 105).

Further on he observed that those branches of social science, such as Political Economy for instance, which had been cultivated as separate sciences, were hopelessly deficient with regard to what he called "the theory of the manner in which their conclusions are affected by ethological considerations." He offered a telling example: "In political economy for instance, empirical laws of human nature are tacitly assumed by English thinkers, which are calculated only for Great Britain and the United States." For example, "an intensity of competition is constantly supposed, which, as a general mercantile fact, exists in no country in the world except those two." English political economists, and English people in general, had "seldom learned that it is possible that men, in conducting the business of selling their goods over a counter, should care more about their ease or their vanity than about their pecuniary gain." Yet, those who knew "the habits of the Continent of Europe" were "aware how apparently small a motive often outweighs the desire of money-getting, even in the operations which have money-getting for their direct object." That was why, "[t]he more highly the science of ethology is cultivated, and the better the diversities of ... national character are understood, the smaller, probably, will the number of propositions become, which it will be considered safe to build on as universal principles of human nature" (*CW*, VIII: 905–6). Here Mill talked more in terms of differences of national character, that had to be taken into account in any calculation and arrangement – which is the sense in which Whewell had blamed Bentham of neglecting national character and in which Mill had asserted that Bentham had not in fact neglected it (*CW*, X: 104–5).

It is well known that Mill did not go very far beyond stating the project of founding the science of ethology, stipulating its aims and general principles, and asserting its urgency and importance (cf. Leary 1982). Subsequent commentators have never tired of criticizing Mill on this account, and sometimes he has been presented as more sanguine or more inconsistent than his words show him to have been. In a study of his thought focusing on the concept of "character," Janice Carlisle, among some fair criticisms of Mill's failure to formulate cogently his proposed science of ethology, raises also some criticisms which are not justified. The difficulty arises when the account comes to the discussion of the study of the character of groups, such as nations:

> [I]n this context ... Mill raises the problem ... of describing any given character in ways that will win general acceptance. Here Mill seems to involve himself in contradictions and confusions from which there is no escape. The first sections of the chapter refer to "familiar maxims," the "common wisdom of common life," as the knowledge of human nature that needs to be tested against the "really scientific truths" constituted by causal laws,[7] but in his footnote on groups, "current popular maxims" become the evidence of "the character of a nation [as it] is shown in its acts as a nation":[8] popular wisdom serves as both the raw data and the analytical conclusions of the science of ethology.... Such common maxims are, as well, the fallacies that Mill has worked so hard to debunk.
>
> (Carlisle 1991: 141)

The "footnote on groups" Carlisle refers to is in Book VI, Chapter v of the *Logic*. There Mill wrote:

> The most favourable cases for making such approximate generalizations are what may be termed collective instances;... Thus the character of a nation is shown in its acts as a nation; not so much in the

acts of its government, for those are much influenced by other causes; but in the current popular maxims, and other marks of the general direction of public opinion; in the character of the persons or writings that are held in permanent esteem or admiration; in laws and institutions, so far as they are the work of the nation itself, or are acknowledged and supported by it; and so forth.

(*CW*, VIII: 867n)[9]

It is difficult to see any "contradictions and confusions" as far as the above statements are concerned. It is not accurate that, in this footnote, "popular wisdom" serves as "the analytical conclusions of the science of ethology." What Mill says is that popular maxims are part of the raw data that the scientific observer, the "ethologist," has to take into consideration and to study. To say that popular wisdom serves as the analytical conclusions of the science of ethology is to say that Mill takes the various popular maxims, sayings, national and local stereotypes for incontestable truths of the science of ethology. Carlisle's criticism would be well-founded, for instance, if Mill had said or implied that what the English populace think of the French should be part of "the analytical conclusions of the science of ethology" on the subject of *the French* character. But this is not what Mill said in the footnote in question. What he did say about popular sayings, maxims, or stereotypes of this kind is that they should be part of the material that the ethologist should study in order to reach conclusions about the national character of those who hold these maxims and stereotypes – rather than about the objects of these maxims and stereotypes.[10] Thus such "popular wisdom" is as far from being part of "the analytical conclusions of the science of ethology" as the popular customs, sayings, or proverbs of a given tribe or region are from being part of the "analytical conclusions" of the contemporary discipline of social anthropology for instance.[11]

In discussing the overall role of the projected science of ethology and of Mill's focus on national characters in his *œuvre* Carlisle asserts that "[a]lthough Mill never wrote a theoretical treatise on ethology, during the mid-1840s and into the 1850s and the 1860s, he worked to put into practice the claims he made for it in his *System of Logic*." She singles out the *Political Economy*, the long series of articles on Ireland in the *Morning Chronicle*, and *The Subjection of Women*. According to Carlisle "[a] consistent definition of ethology emerges from these essays as well as consistent proof that the science became, for Mill, less a powerful tool of inquiry than a powerful mode of persuasion." She proceeds to assert:

Whenever Mill chose a subject for sustained ethological analysis during the last three decades of his career, he invariably chose groups remarkable for their common status as marginal, dispossessed, or disenfranchised: the geographically and politically marginal Irish, the socially and economically disadvantaged working classes, and the politically and professionally dispossessed group constituted by all women, in England and Ireland, in all classes. Such choices again reveal the political nature of the inquiry. These were the groups whose circumstances were most in need of change.

Carlisle goes on to write that Mill's comments "on middle-class, male-dominated, English commercial society emerge, by contrast, only apropos of some other topic." And:

Mill's analysis of the English is fairly specific; he remarks on the provincialism that allows ignorance of French thought and French politics and French history, the toadying of the English classes to their betters, the stultifying narrowness of English manners and morals, and the rampant commercialism that saps energy for all pursuits and values other than the monetary and the material. Such comments, however, and the consistent portrait of English national shortcomings that they draw are usually elicited by more sustained discussions of topics not English, not middle-class, and not male. . . . Ethology, the science whose laws will guide the reformer's methods, is to be practised on the dispossessed.

(Carlisle 1991: 144–5)

But it is debatable whether "Mill's analysis of the English is fairly specific" and whether he remarked only on the issues mentioned above with regard to the English character. Mill also discussed manifestations of the English character with regard to virtue, veracity, the passion not to have arbitrary power exercised over oneself, the "struggling, go-ahead" and self-helping character of "the Anglo-Saxons," the English nation's tenderness of conscience, their aversion to war, and all sorts of other topics. Most of these were part of the stock in trade of Victorian discourse and English self-perception (cf. Varouxakis 2002: Chapter 4). These comments on the English character were made in key points of key texts as diverse as the *Political Economy*, the *Logic*, *Representative Government*, the *Inaugural Address*, *The Subjection of Women*, and an impressive number of newspaper articles, to say nothing of his exchanges on the differences of national characters with d'Eichthal, Comte, and many others in his correspondence with them. What Mill called "ethological" considerations and concerns are amply present in all these writings, and the English character is far from appearing parasitically.

Recently Peter Mandler has also argued that "Mill never developed his theory of national character, or applied it specifically to the English" (Mandler 2000: 238). Yet, there are statements which go some way towards indicating that it was the study of the peculiarities of the English character that was in the centre of these concerns. Besides his general theoretical assertion that one can never get to know a foreign country as well as one's own,[12] there is also his emphatic statement in a letter to Comte that since his early youth he had been occupied in the study of the English character, accompanied by the complaint that Continental observers were falling into gross misunderstandings of the character of their insular neighbour (*CW*, XIII: 696–7 – letter of 26 March 1846. Cf. *CW*, XV: 656).

Thus, in the first place, besides the character of the "dispossessed," that of the English was at least of equal interest to Mill, and was extensively discussed by him, in what he would call ethological terms. In the second place, any discussion of Mill's ethological ventures should not fail to take into account his innumerable comments on the character of one more group. His comments on this group, throughout his life, abound with remarks of an "ethological" nature, by no means less than his comments on the Irish, the labouring classes, and women. The group alluded to are the French. Besides, through a study of Mill's ethological observations on the French, a better estimation of the status of his comments on *the English* national character can also be achieved, as the observations on the character of the French were most often given in the form of comparisons between them and the English. It is characteristic that, whenever Mill spoke of differences of national character in the abstract, theoretically, in his various attempts to demonstrate the significance of ethological inquiry, in works such as the *Logic*, *The Subjection of Women*, or the *Political Economy*, all the examples he used either were exclusively, or included – in a central position, along with other examples – that of the differences between the English and French characters with regard to the issue in question.[13]

The importance that Ethology had for Mill has been captured by Alexander Bain. With reference to Mill's review article of 1844 on Michelet, Bain noted that while writing that article, he was "projecting in his mind his next book, which was to be on the new science, first sketched in the *Logic*, and there called 'Ethology.'" Mill's first biographer added that "[w]ith parental fondness, he cherished this subject for a considerable time; regarding it as the foundation and cornerstone of Sociology." After describing Mill's failure with this project Bain concluded that:

> He was all his life possessed of the idea that differences of character, individual and national, were due to accidents and circumstances that might possibly be, in part, controlled; on this doctrine rested his chief hope in the future. He would not allow that human beings at birth are so very different as they afterwards turn out.
>
> (Bain 1882: 78–9)

National characters, states of society, and stages of civilization

Though Mill's interest in differences of national characters has not gone entirely unnoticed, it is still the case that his increased relativism – in comparison to his father and Bentham – has been acknowledged and discussed mainly in terms of his insistence that different stages of civilization (or states of society) required different institutional arrangements.[14] Yet, Mill himself stressed the importance of another kind of relativism in his thought. An instance where this is obvious is in the oft-quoted text winding up his assessment of the significance of his boyhood stay in France in his *Autobiography* (*CW*, I: 63). The emphasis in that statement is on J.S. Mill's superiority to other "English" thinkers (including his father) not on account of his historical relativism and comprehension of the differences between different stages of civilization, but rather, on account of the alertness he believed he acquired, thanks to his interest in France and French thought, to differences between nations and national viewpoints – with no reference to their being nations belonging to different stages of civilization. In other words, his acquaintance with France alerted Mill to the importance of one more dimension where relativity had to be applied, that of differences of national character.[15]

In Mill's argumentation in the *Logic* on the significance of the study of national character, the notion of "state of society" or "state of civilization" appears in connection with "national character" (*CW*, VIII: 905 – Book VI, Chapter ix, section 4). There are references or allusions to the different meanings of the two concepts long before the *Logic* was written. In an early letter to Gustave d'Eichthal Mill censured the Saint-Simonians for thinking "that the mind of man, by a sort of fatality or necessity, grows and unfolds its different faculties always in one particular order, like the body; and that therefore we must be always either standing still, or advancing, or retrograding." To this Mill retorted that he believed "that different nations ... may and do advance to improvement by different roads; *that nations ... nearly in an equally advanced stage of civilization, may yet be very different in character.*"[16]

It is obvious that the problem of the reformer-legislator is quite complicated, since he has to ascertain both the stage of civilization and the character of a nation if he is to heed Mill's injunction that he should adapt his means – institutions – to these two elements in order to carry both forward. In "Bentham" (1838), Mill uses examples which can leave no doubt that he recommends that there should be different institutional provisions between nations which he regarded as being "nearly in an equally advanced stage of civilization" and yet "very different in character": obviously he regarded England and France as cases in point, and apparently the same applied to the case of the Germans and "the people of Northern and Central Italy." In such cases it was not so much the difference in the degree (or "stage") of civilization already attained that rendered differences in legislation advisable, but rather differences of "character" (*CW*, X: 104–5). In that text, both stage of civilization and national character (though none of them is mentioned by name) seem to be factors that may necessitate modifications in the legislation appropriate for each particular people. But there are many instances in Mill's writings where "state of civilization"[17] and "national character" are mentioned together as factors to be taken into consideration with little or no comment as to the degree of attention due to each and the concrete significance of each. At times they seem hardly separable and yet in other instances Mill spoke of them in terms that indicate that he considered them to be distinct. Thus in 1836, in "State of Society in America" he remarked that there were in his time four great nations, England, France, Germany and the United States, and that each of these possessed, "either in its *social condition*, in its *national character*, or in *both*, some points of indisputable and pre-eminent superiority over all the others." At the same time each of them had "some deep-seated and grievous defects from which the others are comparatively exempt." Hence, the "state of society" in each, and "the type of human nature which it exhibits," were "subjects of most instructive study to the others" (emphasis added: *CW*, XVIII: 94).

It was in the *Logic* that Mill attempted to give a definition of what he meant by "state of society" or "state of civilization": "the simultaneous state of all the greater social facts or phenomena."[18] In arguing for the importance of his projected "Political Ethology" in the same work, Mill had spoken of "the character which is formed by any state of social circumstances" as being "in itself the most interesting phenomenon which that state of society can possibly present." And "above all, the character, that is, the opinions, feelings, and habits, of the people, though greatly the result of the state of society which precedes them, are also greatly the causes of the state of society which follows them" (*CW*, VIII: 905). If the relative status of state of society and national character can be inferred from the relative status of the sciences that were designed by Mill to study each of them – "the general Science of Society" (or Social Science, or Sociology) and "Political Ethology" respectively – it is the "state of society" that emerges as the most important consideration. Political Ethology was supposed to be but a branch of the broader Social Science. This having been said, however, Mill is adamant that "ethological considerations" (arising from the findings of the study of national characters, the causes of their formation and their differences) were to be the most indispensable considerations. His remarks concerning the importance of Political Ethology for Social Science, and the statement that national character is at the same time the result of the preceding state of society *and* to a very great extent the cause of the following state of society, go some way towards pointing to the complexity of the considerations involved and the difficulty of always attributing the phenomena under examination to either exclusively or principally. A close examination of Mill's comments on the affairs and character of the foreign people he was most interested in (and conversant with) may shed some more light on the relevant concepts.

The French in Mill's early writings: *La Jeune France* and the generation factor

As early as in April 1832, in introducing what was intended to be a regular co-operation with the Saint-Simonian journal *Le Globe*, Mill declared his earnest commitment to help the editors of *Le Globe* towards enabling "two nations, each of which possesses so many of the elements of greatness and goodness, but developed in an unequal degree, to understand each other" and "to make them do justice mutually to each other's merits, and acquiesce in the necessary results of those laws of human and of external nature which have made the characters of the two nations different."[19] Mill went on to inform his French friends that he had this object "deeply at heart." That this was actually the case is shown by the impressive volume of his writings on France and the French, which were aimed at imparting to his compatriots what he saw as his peculiarly close conversance with the "character" of the French. No less eager was he to discover – for himself, as well as for his readers – "the laws of human and of external nature which [had] made the characters of the two nations different." It was this search that constituted his principal "ethological" inquiry throughout his life.[20] The first exercises of this search were given scope in Mill's newspaper writings of the early 1830s, the greatest number of which (in the early years of the decade especially) dealt with France, its politics and its prospects after the revolution of July 1830.[21] His last public comments on the French character were made in the major works of the 1860s, among which *Representative Government* will receive attention here.

The term "national character" itself does not appear in these newspaper articles before December 1830 (*CW*, XXII: 215), but what could be considered to be its ingredients (on the basis of Mill's own use of the term later) were commented on from July onwards. In these writings it is the term "state of society" which is frequently used with regard to France (see, for example, *CW*, XXII: 130, 136). Mill was sanguine about the prospects of France in the months immediately following the July Revolution, and believed that the fact of the Revolution itself would help carry the state of society of France forward.[22]

What deserves particular attention here is his extraordinary reliance on the generation factor during the 1830s. In May 1831, Mill asserted that the French had undergone "some rather remarkable metamorphoses since the days of their grandfathers." The French "of the present day" were "a far more serious people than the English" and their national character was "grave, earnest, and enthusiastic."[23] He went on to present to his readers some of the characteristics of the generation of young men, "*la jeune France*," which distinguished them from their predecessors and justified the high hopes he had set on them in the aftermath of the July Revolution (*CW*, XXII: 308–9).[24] Earlier, in the letters he sent his father from Paris, after he had rushed there shortly following the July Revolution, one cannot fail to notice the extraordinary extent to which he dwelt upon the hopes he harbored on account of the age and acquirements of the people he met (see, for instance, *CW*, XII: 63–5). He was to pursue the subject of the "young men" some weeks later, in his fourth article of the "Prospects of France" series in the *Examiner* (10 October 1830). There he dealt at length with what he called "the entire question between the gerontocracy and the young men" and explained the superiority of the young men to the older generations in terms of their respective experiences, related to the circumstances of France and the institutions under which the two groups had received their early impressions (*CW*, XXII: 154–6). Such an explanation of differences between human groups was consistent with Mill's belief in the influence of circumstances upon the formation of character. It was a sort of "ethological" analysis *avant la lettre* that he applied here.[25] Mill was by no means alone in attributing importance to the generation factor in France at the period in question (see Spitzer 1987: 3, 4, 270 n.3). What is remarkable about Mill's portrayal of this generation is his total failure to refer to one of its main characteristics, namely its intensely nationalistic attitude.[26] Many, in fact some of the most important, of Mill's frustrations with regard to France were to arise from his having underestimated the degree to which national grandeur was valued by the generation which he expected to renew France's and Europe's politics. He was to come, before the end of the year, to admit that he was no less than "shocked and disgusted" by the eagerness for war in which the French belonging to that generation were all but unanimous (*CW*, XXII, 214–15).[27] Aside from the young men's unpalatable nationalism, the frustration of his hopes for rapid progress in the early 1830s was to be an important factor that led Mill to attribute more and more importance to durable elements in the national character and rely comparatively less on what a change of generation could effect.

What could be ascribed to the "state of society"?

It has been seen already that Mill considered France and Britain to be at the same stage of civilization, as well as that he used the terms "stage of civilization," "state of civilization" and "state of society" interchangeably. In consequence, if one were to take Mill's word literally one would have to proceed reluctantly to any reference to differences in the states of society of France and Britain. But Mill was not always strictly consistent in his use of these terms. He spoke of "the state of society or the state of civilization" as being one and the same thing in the definition he gave in the *Logic* (*CW*, VIII: 911–12), and he also used "state of civilization" and "stage of civilization" interchangeably in *Representative Government* (see, for instance, *CW*, XIX: 379, 393, 394, 396–7, 404), where the countries of western Europe and north America were treated as having reached more or less the same – most advanced – stage of civilization. However, there are other statements in his works which can justify introducing a partial distinction between stages of civilization and states of society. While Britain and France were both at the same stage in terms of Mill's – and his father's – implied evolutionary scale of civilizations, they might not necessarily have identical states of society. This last remark should follow logically from Mill's definition of a state of society as being "the simultaneous state of all the greater social facts or phenomena." The long list of such social facts or phenomena which follows this statement in the *Logic* (*CW*, VIII: 911–12) renders it legitimate for one to assume that, as some of these facts did differ between countries such as Britain and France, their states of society could not be exactly identical. What confuses things and, to an extent, appears to contradict this assumption, is the fact that Mill proceeded, in the same text, to insist on the existence of what he called "Uniformities of Coexistence between the states of the various social phenomena" and the "*consensus* of the various parts of the social body" (*CW*, VIII: 912. Cf. *CW*, VIII: 899).[28]

Yet it has been seen that Mill had himself, earlier (in 1836), spoken of England, France, Germany, and the United States as countries exhibiting differences in both their national character and their "social condition" or "state of society" (*CW*, XVIII: 94). It is therefore obvious that in that case (1836) Mill spoke of countries which he considered to be at the same level or stage of civilization as exhibiting differences in their states of society. Besides, he again spoke of the states of society of various western European countries and the United States as being different in a letter of 1844, after he had published the *Logic*.[29] Clearly, two countries could be equally advanced in civilization (in terms of an implied linear trajectory of civilization) and yet exhibit a great number of differences. The question to be asked is what part of these differences could be ascribed to what Mill called the national characters of the two nations, and what part of them could be better accounted for by reference to the rest of "the greater social facts or phenomena" which constituted their respective states of society. Such were, for example, according to Mill's definition, "the degree of knowledge ... existing in the community, and in every class of it; the state of industry, of wealth and its distribution; the habitual occupations of the community; their division into classes, and the relations of those classes to one another; ... their form of government, and the more important of their laws and customs" (*CW*, VIII: 911–12). One can assume that some of these social facts could be expected to change faster than others. The last one mentioned could be significantly altered with a simple change of regime or constitution. The question is to what extent changes in such components of the state of society of, say, France were expected by Mill to alter the overall situation in the country. Only thus is it possible to establish the importance he accorded to what he called the national character of the French at different stages.

There are instances in Mill's writings of the 1830s, where various characteristics of French society and the French people were presented as the results of what Tocqueville came later to mean by a "state of society."[30] Thus, in 1833, the interest of the French populace in the arts and their respect for art-works and monuments were accounted for in terms of France's being "an unaristocratic country" (*CW*, XXIII: 655 – 15 December 1833; cf. *CW*, XXII: 308–9). But Mill used "state of society" in a much more casual manner than Tocqueville did, and in most cases it had very little to do with Tocqueville's ideal-typical use of the concept.[31]

In an article Mill wrote following the Paris insurrection of June 1832, the failure of the French to show the "habitual reverence for law which is so deeply rooted in the minds of all classes of Englishmen" was described as an historical accident. England was more fortunate in that it had a long history of rule of law, which engendered this salutary habit in the English nation. Though Mill's words were hardly complimentary to the French, he did not present them as a people inherently deficient in terms of "national character" or "race," but only as a people placed in less favorable circumstances, suffering from bad laws and precedents (*CW*, XXIII: 485–6 – 24 June, 1832). And in 1837, in "Armand Carrel," he wrote of a habit he was later (*Representative Government, CW*, XIX: 420–1) to present as a serious defect of the French national character, in terms that would suggest that he hoped, then (1837), that it was only a question of time when the French would be able to form better "constitutional *mœurs*." Thus he wrote that it was "the grievous misfortune of France, that being still new to constitutional ideas and institutions," she had not yet known what it was to have a fair government. A chance had occurred before the July Revolution, under the moderate Martignac ministry. The July Revolution had "intervened." But there was still hope for France, though probably not in the immediate future (*CW*, XX: 190–2).[32]

From 1848 to *Representative Government*

A development that could be expected to raise Mill's hopes for France was the Revolution of February 1848. As he wrote to a correspondent on 29 February 1848, he was "hardly yet out of breath from reading and thinking about it. Nothing can possibly exceed the importance of it to the world or the immensity of the interests which are at stake on its success" (*CW*, XIII: 731).[33] In the part of her book dealing with Mill's comments on the February Revolution and the acts of the Provisional Government that had been formed following that event, Iris Wessel Mueller wrote that "Mill maintained that a [constitutional] monarchy would be uncongenial to the character and habits of the French just as it was suited to the thought and feelings of the English" (Mueller 1968: 179). The text she refers to is from Mill's "Vindication of the French Revolution of February 1848,"[34] published in April 1849. He had argued there that

> constitutional royalty is in itself a thing as uncongenial to the charac-
> ter and habits of the French ... as it is suited to the tone of thought
> and feeling characteristic of England. From causes which might be
> traced in the history and development of English society and govern-
> ment, the general habit and practice of the English mind is compro-
> mise. No idea is carried out to more than a small portion of its
> legitimate consequences.

Constitutional royalty was congenial to the English relish for "discordance between principle and practice." On the contrary, the French were impatient of "discrepancy between theory and practice." Since the constitutional King was not supposed to govern, the French could see no reason why they should pretend to have a sovereign King. "A constitutional monarchy, therefore, was likely in France ... to be but a brief halt on the road from a despotism to a republic" (*CW*, XX: 331–2).[35]

Mueller accompanied the statement quoted above with a footnote which seems to imply that there was some discrepancy or shift between Mill's stance here, in 1849, and his earlier remark in the article on Armand Carrel, written in 1837: "In 1837, however, Mill had stated in reference to Armand Carrel's reasons for wanting a republic that 'they are, no doubt, refuted by the fact, that the public mind was not ripe for a republic, and would not have it. ...' Later, the fact of the revolution seemed to demonstrate for Mill the popular readiness for a republic" (Mueller 1968: 179, fn.35).[36] However, it is far from clear whether Mill believed that the French had become ready for a republic in 1848. He stressed in the "Vindication..." (April 1849) that "though a republic, for France, was the most natural and congenial of all the forms of government, it had two great hindrances to contend with." One was "the political indifference of the majority – the result of want of education, and of absence of habits of discussion and participation in public business." The other was "the dread inspired by the remembrance of 1793 and 1794." These two causes "prevented the French nation in general from demanding or wishing for a republican government; and as long as those causes continue, they will render its existence, even now that it is established, more or less precarious" (*CW*, XX: 332). Thus, the assertion that the republic was congenial to the French character did not necessarily mean that the French were ready for it. In that same work Mill stipulated his conditions of the advisability of a constitution in any given case. In the first place, codes and Constitutions "should not violently shock the pre-existing habits and sentiments of the people"; and, in the second place, "they should not demand and presuppose qualities in the popular mind, and a degree of interest in, and attachment to, the institutions themselves, which *the character of the people*, and *their state of civilization*, render unlikely to be really found in them" (emphasis added). He went on:

> These two are the rocks on which those usually split, who by means of a temporary ascendancy establish institutions *alien from*, or *too much in advance of*, the condition of the public mind. The founders of the English Commonwealth failed for the first reason.... Charlemagne's attempt to construct a centralized monarchy amidst the distraction and anarchy of the eighth century, failed for the other of the two reasons specified. Its success would have required, both in the governors and the governed, a more cultivated intelligence, a greater comprehension of large views and extended interests, than existed or was attainable in that age, save by eminently exceptional individuals like Charlemagne himself.
>
> (Emphasis added: "Vindication," *CW*, XX: 356–7)[37]

His appraisal of the situation in France in 1849 with regard to these matters followed, and it did not betray excessive optimism: "If the establishment of republicanism in France should turn out to be premature, it will be for the latter reason." Although "no popular sentiment is shocked by it, the event may prove that there is no sufficient attachment to it, or desire to promote its success; but a readiness to sacrifice it to any trivial convenience, personal *engouement*, or dream of increased security" (*CW*, XX: 357). Thus, it would seem that the French national character was averse to (or not fitted for) constitutional monarchy, and rather more prone to a republic or a despotism. However, the French people were not sufficiently advanced on the road most suited to their character as to be "willing" and "able" to do what was required to sustain a republic.

As Mill was to put it later in *Representative Government*, there were "three fundamental conditions" of the adaptation of a form of government to the people who were to be governed by it. First, "[t]he people . . . must be willing to accept it; or at least not so unwilling, as to oppose an insurmountable obstacle to its establishment" (*CW*, XIX: 376). It seems that this first condition corresponds to some extent to the first condition of the viability or advisability of a Constitution in the 1849 article ("Vindication"), namely that the Constitution "should not violently shock the pre-existing habits and sentiments of the people." If that were to be the case, presumably the people would be unwilling to accept it. The case for drawing a parallel between the 1849 text and *Representative Government* is reinforced when Mill comes to enlarging upon the second condition stipulated in the latter essay. With regard to that condition (that the people must be "willing and able to do what is necessary to keep [the political machinery] standing")[38] Mill says:

> But there are also cases in which, *though not averse to a form of government – possibly even desiring it – a people may be unwilling or unable to fulfil its conditions.* . . . Thus a people may prefer a free government, but if, from indolence, or carelessness, or cowardice, or want of public spirit, they are unequal to the exertions necessary for preserving it; if they will not fight for it when it is directly attacked; if they can be deluded by the artifices used to cheat them out of it; *if by momentary discouragement, or temporary panic, or a fit of enthusiasm for an individual, they can be induced to lay their liberties at the feet even of a great man, or trust him with powers which enable him to subvert their institutions*; in all these cases they are more or less *unfit for liberty*: and though it may be for their good to have had it even for a short time, they are unlikely long to enjoy it.
>
> (Emphases added: *CW*, XIX: 377)[39]

It would be tempting then, to draw a distinction between a form of government which offends (and is incompatible with) the deeply rooted traits of the national character of a people (therefore being inappropriate for them either permanently, or at least for a very long time), and a form of government which could be compatible with the national character of the people in question, but required in addition to be on a level with their current state of society. A form of government could be "the most natural and congenial of all forms of government" for a people, and yet they may not be prepared for it. They might be deficient in political education, or prevented from supporting a form of government due to an unfortunate association of that form with an event in their recent history. It can be presumed that such impediments could count only in the short run, that they applied to what Mill called the "state of society" of that people, which could be expected to change and progress. Therefore, the people in question could be expected *to become* ready and fit for the particular form of government sooner or later, if the right course were taken.[40] But, no matter how convenient such a distinction might be for analysis, Mill complicated the matter by making "national character" part of the considerations applying to the latter condition. Codes and constitutions "should not demand and presuppose qualities in the popular mind ... which *the character of the people*, and *their state of civilization*, render unlikely to be really found in them" (emphasis added: *CW*, XX: 356). The example of the failure of Charlemagne's venture, which Mill gave, seems to apply more to what he called the "stage of civilization." As to the reasons why he thought the experiment of republicanism could fail in France, they belonged, Mill said, to the second category specified by him (presupposing qualities that are not to be found in the *character* and the *state of civilization* of the people). But, in this particular case, no clear distinction can be drawn between reasons attaching to national character and those attaching to the state of civilization or state of society. It may turn out that there is "no sufficient attachment" to the republic, or desire to promote its success, but "a readiness to sacrifice it to any trivial convenience, personal *engouement*, or dream of increased security."

Now, some of the difficulties involved in reconciling Mill's assertion that the republic was better suited to the French character than constitutional monarchy with his admission that "the event may prove that there is no sufficient attachment to [the republic], or desire to promote its success..." can be lifted by bearing in mind the protean character of the concept of the republic. In Mill's former assertion the emphasis seems to have been more on the republican form of government in the strict sense of a constitutional government without a hereditary head of state. Mill maintained that, rather than a constitutional monarch who reigned but did not govern, the French character was apt to prefer either an absolute monarch who did actually govern, or an elected head of state. Now, as far as the latter assertion is concerned, it has to be remembered that Mill was referring to the specific republic that had recently been established in France. The way he voiced his worries about the French people's preparedness for that government suggests that he was referring not so much to the question of the head of state but rather to what he was to call later (in *Representative Government*) the French people's "attempt at representative government by the whole male population" (*CW*, XIX: 421). Mill was doubtful whether the French were prepared, not for a non-hereditary head of state, but rather for free representative government under universal manhood suffrage. The proximity of the conditions he laid down for the success of the republic in 1849 and those he stipulated for the success of free representative government in 1861 point to the same assumption.[41]

Mill was not clear whether it was the state the French were in at the moment he was writing, or something deeper and more ineradicable in their national character, that was most likely to impair the success of the republican experiment. The whole thing becomes less difficult to grasp if we bear in mind that still, in 1849, Mill must have meant "national character" to be as malleable as he had presented it in the *Logic*, being at the same time the result of the preceding state of society and the main cause of the state of society that was to follow. In any case, he was not clear as to exactly how durable, or how malleable this character was.

If Mill was vague and possibly undecided in 1849, he seems to have grown more conclusive and to have come to regard the French character as more rigid by 1861, as some references to the French in *Representative Government* indicate. The statement discussed below refers explicitly to the French national character rather than to the state of society the French were in at the time, and is, more or less explicitly, to the effect that this national character of theirs had incapacitated the French from establishing or enjoying the full benefit of a free representative government. In *Representative Government*, Chapter IV (*"Under What Conditions Representative Government is Inapplicable"*), Mill spoke of "positive defects of national character" as being one of the "infirmities or short-comings in a people ... which *pro tanto* disqualify them from making the best use of representative government" (*CW*, XIX: 418).[42] In that context he wrote a little further on of two very different "states of the inclinations" which affected decisively the efforts of individuals and nations: one was "the desire to exercise power over others"; the other was "the disinclination to have power exercised over themselves." He asserted that: "*The difference between different portions of mankind in the relative strength of these two dispositions, is one of the most important elements in their history*" (emphasis added: *CW*, XIX: 420). It is worth noting that here, instead of pointing to the history of the "different portions of mankind" as accounting for "the relative strength of these two dispositions," Mill focuses on the extent to which it is the latter which has affected the former.[43] He continues:

> There are nations in whom the passion for governing others is so much stronger than the desire of personal independence, that for the mere shadow of the one they are found ready to sacrifice the whole of the other.[44] Each one of their number is willing, like the private soldier in an army, to abdicate his personal freedom of action into the hands of his general, provided the army is triumphant and victorious, and he is able to flatter himself that he is one of a conquering host. . . .[45] A government strictly limited in its powers and attributions, required to hold its hands from overmeddling, and to let most things go on without its assuming the part of guardian or director, is not to the taste of such a people. In their eyes the possessors of authority can hardly take too much upon themselves, provided the authority itself is open to general competition. An average individual among them prefers the chance, however distant or improbable, of wielding some share of power over his fellow-citizens, above the certainty, to himself and others, of having no unnecessary power exercised over them.

These, he went on, were "the elements of a people of place-hunters."[46] By such a people "equality alone is cared for, but not liberty."[47] And the contests of political parties "are but struggles to decide whether the power of meddling in everything shall belong to one class or another, perhaps merely to one knot of public men or another." The idea such a people entertained of democracy was "merely that of opening offices to the competition of all instead of a few." With them, "the more popular the institutions ... the more monstrous [is] the over-government exercised by all over each, and by the executive over all." The remark that follows leaves very little doubt as to which national character Mill had in mind throughout this presentation of the tendency in question:

> It would be as unjust as it would be ungenerous to offer this, or anything approaching to it, as an unexaggerated picture of the French

people; yet the degree in which they do participate in this type of character, has caused representative government by a limited class to break down by excess of corruption, and the attempt at representative government by the whole male population to end in giving one man the power of consigning any number of the rest, without trial, to Lambessa or Cayenne, provided he allows all of them to think themselves not excluded from the possibility of sharing his favours.

(*CW*, XIX: 420–1)

On the other hand, "[t]he point of character which, beyond any other, fits the people of this country for representative government, is, that they have almost universally the contrary characteristic" (*CW*, XIX: 421).[48]

A hardening of Mill's position is discernible. In the early writings, France was faring badly because it had not known better things, because of bad institutions and misgovernment, historical accidents, etc., but Mill was eager to see changes that would enable France to "speedily outstrip all the rest of the world in the career of civilization" (*CW*, XXII: 134). In *Representative Government*, on the other hand, one is left with the impression that the character of the French made them more or less unfit for free government. Earlier he relied heavily on the generation factor and the *jeune France*. When he was disappointed he came to attribute more importance to "national character," or rather, what comes to the same thing, he came to consider "national character" more durable and obstinate, less easily and less rapidly changeable than he thought in the 1830s. Characteristically, in one of his last comments on France, Mill pointed again to the French character as being primarily responsible for the problems of France. When, after the Franco-Prussian war, Dupont-White asked him whether he thought that France was in decadence,[49] Mill replied by commenting that it was certain that the French character had very serious flaws, most clearly demonstrated during the unhappy year that had just passed. But he asserted that he believed these flaws to have existed in no smaller degree during what were called "les plus beaux jours de la France" (*CW*, XVII, 1864).[50]

To the extent that a turning point should be sought, it seems to have been the aftermath of 1848, the fact that the establishment of a representative government with universal manhood suffrage ended up in Louis Napoleon's becoming an emperor almost unopposed. Though Mill would have found some of Walter Bagehot's views on national character crude, it seems that Bagehot's appraisal of the impact of 1848 and its aftermath on explanatory models applies, to a certain extent, to Mill as well. According to Bagehot, the events of 1848 "had ... taught thinking persons ... that of all ... circumstances ... affecting political problems, by far and out of all question the most important is *national character*" (Bagehot 1965–86, IV: 49).[51]

By the time he wrote his *Representative Government* Mill had abandoned the ambition he had spelt out in earlier writings of establishing a scientific study of differences of national character with the express purpose of thereby identifying the institutions most appropriate to carry each particular society to the next stage of progress of which it was susceptible. What he did, instead, in *Representative Government*, was to focus on representative democratic government as the best government only for the most advanced stage of civilization. What is implicit, however – as can be seen from the remarks quoted above – is that he had come to believe that the free representative government he was proposing was the most appropriate form of government only for a particular national character, that of the English and the Americans. For the rest he despaired of solutions. All he had to offer were hints.

Finally, there is a parallel that cannot fail to suggest itself here. In his remarks in *Representative Government* presented above Mill articulated a distinction which can be said to be, to an extent, reminiscent of other distinctions between different perceptions of liberty. In terms of such distinctions, proposed by thinkers as diverse as De Lolme, Priestley, Constant, and Berlin, it can be argued that Mill suggested (more or less implicitly) that the English "national character" was fitter for what others have called "liberty of the moderns" or "negative liberty" than the French character was. This should go some way towards indicating, first, how important differences of what he called national characters came to be for J.S. Mill, and second, the extent to which he did theorize on "Englishness."

5 International relations, intervention/non-intervention and national self-determination

Few questions are more topical or urgent in international ethics, particularly since the end of the Cold War, than those related to the ethics of third-party intervention in intrastate or secessionist conflicts. While current debates may focus on specific issues important to our era, discussions about the ethics of third-party intervention in sovereign states are not new, and actually owe much to arguments developed over 150 years ago. John Stuart Mill is a key figure when it comes to understanding debates on the ethics of intervention. Therefore, we need to establish what his exact views were, as well as how and in what context they emerged and subsequently developed, if we are fully to appreciate and make use of them in contemporary debates. And, as we will see in the last part of this chapter, Mill's pronouncements on intervention were inextricably related to his overall attitude towards "nationality." Although students of Mill's thought have paid little attention to his views on international relations and the foreign affairs of Britain, specialists in international relations have, to a greater extent, taken notice of his contributions. Thus there are some short accounts of his views on international politics, or references to them in more general works.[1] As the author of one of the most ambitious such accounts put it: "Although his principal writings were not in the field of international relations, an examination of [Mill's] works indicates that he had a more than cursory interest in foreign affairs and a rather consistent set of beliefs that can, without stretching the meaning of the term, be considered a theory of international relations" (Miller (Kenneth) 1961: 495).

Mill's place in debates on non-intervention

In recent decades, students of international theory have tended to regard the younger Mill as the originator and exponent *par excellence* of one of the main versions of the theory of non-intervention. He is held to have made one of the most significant contributions to discussions on this subject, and his arguments are considered to be relevant to contemporary debates (cf. Mayall 1991).

R.J. Vincent treats most subsequent debates on intervention – most notably during the Cold War – as so much repetition of the arguments put forward by Richard Cobden and J.S. Mill. The former espoused "a near-absolute doctrine of nonintervention" (Vincent 1974: 45), while the latter asserted the right to counter-intervention in cases where a foreign power had already intervened.[2] Carsten Holbraad considers Mill's position to be central to the development of what he calls the "humanitarian" branch of "progressive theory" in the context of British discussions about the Concert of Europe (Holbraad 1970: 162–3). Holbraad also speaks of Mill's views on the subject of intervention as having "influenced Gladstone's theory of the Concert of Europe" (Holbraad 1970: 165). He further asserts that Mill's was the dominant influence "during the great crisis in the Eastern question and in the following years" until the time of the crisis over Armenia and Crete (Holbraad 1970: 175–6). Some commentators have noted that Michael Walzer's attempt to deal with the problems of intervention and non-intervention owes a lot to Mill (Smith (Michael Joseph) 1992: 213–14; Johnson (Peter) 1993: 81–2; McCarthy 1993: 81–2). A closer examination of Walzer's views bears this assertion out (see especially Walzer 1992: 86–101). Even accounts of the "right of counter-intervention" in purely legal terms recognize Mill's pronouncements as the starting point of discussion on the matter (Perkins 1987: 172).

Yet, despite the fact that scholars often acknowledge Mill's contribution to our contemporary theorizing about intervention, the broader sweep of his views is not as widely known. Thus, Mill's debt to French debates on intervention has been entirely ignored, although, as will be shown in the following pages, French debates were decisive in forming Mill's views, notably the argument in favour of counter-intervention. Consequently, the aim of this chapter is to elucidate the full scope of Mill's contribution to debates on intervention and to disentangle the different nuances and shifts of emphasis that characterize his views on the matter. These have been lost to subsequent commentators who usually quote only from Mill's later works.

Mill's later – and best known – position

Just as contemporary students of international relations acknowledge the significance of his pronouncements for current debates, Mill himself was no less convinced of the novelty of his ideas on non-intervention in British debates during the last century. The closest he came to formulating a general theory on this question was in his article "A Few Words on Non-Intervention," written in 1859.[3] He started the theoretical part of the essay by stating emphatically that "[t]here seems to be no little need that the whole doctrine of non-interference with foreign nations should be reconsidered, if it can be said to have as yet been considered as a really moral question at all" (*CW*, XXI: 118). It is what he asserted in this text that is generally known today as Mill's theory on intervention and non-intervention.

In "A Few Words..." Mill addressed the issue of the appropriateness of third-party intervention. He stated that when we ask whether one country is justified in "helping the people of another in a struggle against their government for free institutions," our answer is bound to be different, "according as the yoke which the people are attempting to throw off is that of a purely native government, or of foreigners." Mill clarified at this point that he regarded as "foreigners," "every government which maintains itself by foreign support." Thus, he went on, when the contest was only with native rulers, "and with such native strength as those rulers can enlist in their defence," intervention was not justified. The reason was that it was almost certain that intervention, even if successful, would not be "for the good of the people themselves."[4] He elaborated as follows:

> The only test possessing any real value, of a people's having become fit for popular institutions, is that they, or a sufficient portion of them to prevail in the contest, are willing to brave labour and danger for their liberation.... No people ever was and remained free, but because it was determined to be so; because neither its rulers nor any other party in the nation could compel it to be otherwise.[5]

Mill was adamant that things had to be different, however, when the struggle in question was against a foreign yoke, or against "a native tyranny upheld by foreign arms." No matter how attached to freedom a people were, and even if they were "the most capable of defending and making a good use of free institutions," they might be unable to contend successfully for free institutions "against the military strength of another nation much more powerful." For him, it followed that "[t]o assist a people thus kept down, is not to disturb the balance of forces on which the permanent maintenance of freedom in a country depends, but to redress that balance when it is already unfairly and violently disturbed." In order, therefore, for the doctrine of non-intervention to be "a legitimate principle of morality," all governments must accept this principle, and it must bind the "despots" as much as the free states.[6] If the despots did not consent to be equally bound by it, its profession by free states could only produce the result "that the wrong side may help the wrong, but the right must not help the right." Thus, Mill concluded:

> Intervention to enforce non-intervention is always rightful, always moral, if not always prudent. Though it be a mistake to give freedom to a people who do not value the boon, it cannot but be right to insist that if they do value it, they shall not be hindered from the pursuit of it by foreign coercion.
>
> (*CW*, XXI: 123–4)[7]

The origins of the argument for counter-intervention

It is with regard to the debate on the limits of the principle of non-intervention that Mill's conversance with France came to bear most on his thinking on international relations.[8] Martin Wight has noted[9] that, when Talleyrand was asked in 1832 to explain the real meaning of the word non-intervention, he replied: "C'est un mot métaphysique, et politique, qui signifie à peu près l[a] même chose qu'intervention."[10] Wight's comment was that, "[t]his was the practical judgment of a diplomatist in *a generation which had explored the problems of intervention and non-intervention with more conscious thoroughness than any before or since*."[11] Perhaps Mill's ideas on intervention and counter-intervention were as complex and influential as they have turned out to be partly because they were formed most decisively by the debates in question – debates that took place in Talleyrand's country in the early 1830s.

No scholarly attempt has been made to follow the development of the idea of counter-intervention in Mill's thought, nor to identify any possible influences on his views on this subject. Holbraad asserts that the idea of what he calls "intervention for humanitarian ends ... originated in the writings of John Stuart Mill." He adds that "[i]t was the struggle of the Italian subjects of the Austrian Emperor ... which inspired Mill to formulate his doctrine of intervention," referring to the debates on intervention that followed the February Revolution of 1848 in Paris (Holbraad 1970: 163–4).

Vincent seems to imply that Mill's advocacy of counter-intervention in "A Few Words..." (1859) had been anticipated by the Italian nationalist Giuseppe Mazzini in 1851.[12] In fact, the views associated with Mill's name were anticipated by some French politicians and publicists two decades before Mazzini adopted them in the work Vincent refers to. Mill's argumentation is strikingly reminiscent of that used by Lafayette, Armand Carrel, and other representatives of the French Left, the so-called "party of movement" (*parti du mouvement*). In the early months of the Orléans monarchy (1830–48), these opposition leaders used the arguments in question to urge the French government that had come to power after the July revolution of 1830 to intervene in favour of suppressed nationalities that had revolted in the aftermath of the "Three Glorious Days" in France. Opponents of King Louis Philippe's "peace at any price" policies regarded the revolts in Belgium and Poland, as well as in Italy, as sister revolutions that France should support.[13] These views were put forward in the Chamber of Deputies most vocally by Lafayette, and in the press by Armand Carrel, chief editor of *Le National*, which, according to Jeremy Jennings, "was, in a sense, *the* paper of the July Revolution" (Jennings 1991: 498).

These arguments are to be found in many articles written by Carrel, in particular during the first months of 1831.[14] However, there is no need to quote Lafayette or Carrel here, nor to resort to speculation, as Mill put forward to the British public the gist of the argument of the French opposition in an article he wrote in the *Examiner* for 10 April 1831 (*CW*, XXII: 299–301).

It has to be stressed that Mill was not happy at all with the war fervour of the French opposition. He considered it a dangerous distraction from what was more important than any national liberation movement: the progress of political reform in France. His first references to the intervention issue betray a deep-seated fear that a war in which France would be involved would halt the march of civilization, corrupt the French "national character," and result in a repetition of the Napoleonic experience, imperiling France's own liberty, and reawakening painful and destructive national antipathies.

On 19 December 1830, Mill condemned forcefully the war-like spirit that was abroad in France, and censured the French for what he saw as their abandonment of the principle of non-intervention. He remarked that discussions in the French Chambers were almost monopolized by the questions of the organization of the National Guard[15] and the arrangements for putting the army on a war footing. Mill further observed that the French seemed to "desire nothing so much as an opportunity for showing their neighbours" how well "prepared for war" they were. A month earlier the French had been "as quiet, as could reasonably be required," on the affairs of Belgium. However, now, "the insurrection in Poland has kindled them into a perfect flame." And he went on to comment: "*We have been shocked and disgusted by the language of the leading French papers on the subject of the Polish revolution. The principle of non-intervention, on which they insisted so strongly a few weeks ago, is now scattered to the winds*" (emphasis added: *CW*, XXII, 214–15). Mill seemed then, in December 1830, to subscribe to a traditional and absolute version of the doctrine of non-intervention and, at any rate, to have no understanding of, or sympathy for, the stance of the French opposition.

Again, on 23 January 1831, Mill wrote disapprovingly that "General Lamarque made another of his vehement exhortations to war" in the French Chamber of Deputies (*CW*, XXII: 247–8).[16] He went on to complain of the warlike tone of Mauguin's speech on the same occasion.[17] In his next reference to French reactions to the affairs of Belgium and Poland, on 6 February 1831, Mill again implied regret that their agitation over these events abroad was distracting the French from more relevant concerns, but this time in a less critical tone, enumerating the negative impact a war in Europe would bring in its wake (*CW*, XXII: 258–9).

On 13 March 1831 he wrote that, unlike most other commentators, he believed that the probabilities of a major war that would involve France were diminishing. He went on to account for his optimism:

> The French may be assured, that the English people will approve of their *enforcing* the principle of non-intervention against the despotic powers, but will disapprove of their *violating* that principle, in order to crusade in support of the subjects of other states against their governments, however just the resistance of such subjects may be, or however certain their destruction, if not aided from abroad.
>
> (*CW*, XXII: 284 – emphases in original)

On 10 April 1831, he wrote in the same vein as he had done in December and February, that it was "unfortunate in a thousand ways for all Europe," that the question of peace and war should have come to complicate the difficulties of France's internal political situation at that moment. This development had come "to place the popular party, in the estimation of many who would otherwise have sympathized with them, manifestly in the wrong," exposing everything that had been gained to new hazards. He believed that the defeat of France, in case war did come, would "stop the march of civilization for another half century" (*CW*, XXII: 299).

However, having said as much, he then proceeded to present the case of the French opposition, and this time he seemed to have both digested and accepted the validity of their main arguments. The similarity of his argumentation in this article with what he was to write on the subject of intervention in 1859 (in "A Few Words...") is indicative of the impact that his reading of French newspapers and debates during the preceding months (between December 1830 and April 1831) had on his thought with regard to this question.[18] Thus, he accompanied his expression of grief at the fact that the question of war had perplexed the situation of France with the following comments: "We must be just, however, to what is called (incorrectly) the war party in France. They do *not* advocate a crusade for liberty, or a war of propagandism. They know well that the improvement of a nation is not advanced, but retarded, by popular institutions imposed upon it by foreign force." It was not for foreigners to judge, Mill wrote, whether a nation would benefit by a constitutional government, before it had put forth its strength and seized such a government. Because, no matter the form of a government, unless it was "vigorously upheld by a preponderance of the physical and intellectual strength of the nation itself, sufficient to overmatch all domestic attempts at its overthrow," it would have to be carried on "in the spirit and with the machinery of a despotism" (*CW*, XXII: 299). For this reason,

> The so-called war party have not the folly to think of quixotizing through all Europe, giving liberty to nations by the sword.[19] But they say that when a nation *has* put itself in motion – when it *has* shown itself eager for liberal institutions, and ripe for them, by subverting all domestic opposition, vanquishing the strength of an established Government, and giving itself, by its own strength, without foreign aid, a constitution more favourable to the progress of civilization, – that then no one ought to be permitted to rush down upon it with the overpowering strength of another nation not equally advanced, not equally prepared for an improvement in its government, and overwhelm a united people by superiority of brute force. They say that

non-intervention by one nation in the affairs of another should be laid down by France as an inflexible rule, which she should herself observe, and of which she should enforce the observance on all other Governments.

(*CW*, XXII: 299–300)

Mill went on to say that the French opposition asserted that this policy was also in the best interests of France itself. They believed that the existence in France of a government founded on popular will, and "established on the ruins of legitimacy and divine right," was bound to give an impulse to "the democratic spirit" throughout Europe, which, if not restrained, would undermine and eventually overthrow the thrones of all absolute monarchs. The opposition were therefore convinced that the monarchs would regard it as "the sole chance of saving their existence as despots," to "extinguish the spirit of liberalism in France" (*CW*, XXII: 300).

Those French liberals who comprised the so-called "war-party" believed that such a struggle against despotic powers was as inevitable as had been the French revolutionary struggle against the European powers in 1792.[20] In that forthcoming contest, the "war party" expected and wished to have for their "natural allies" the people of all countries in Europe aspiring to free institutions. This was why they were wary of allowing all, to whom they might appeal in their hour of need, "to be crushed, one after another, not by their own governments, but by the armies of foreign despots." If their potential allies were thus crushed, the despots would then have no enemy but the French, and would seize the first favorable moment for pouring their troops into France, making it necessary for her people to fight for their very existence on their own soil. It was on these grounds, Mill stressed, that Lafayette, "and the numerous body whose opinions he represents," contended "for the enforcement, by arms, if necessary, of the principle of non-intervention" (*CW*, XXII: 300).[21]

Then Mill judged the argument, asserting that, if France had been a united nation, "headed by a government which could trust the people, which the people trusted, and which was able and dared to call forth the national enthusiasm," the policy proposed by the opposition would have been "the true policy of France," and "its almost infallible result would have been not war but peace." He gave as evidence the stance of the French government in the case of Belgium a few months earlier as an example of what could be achieved by a simple declaration by a power, provided it could convince other powers that it was able to command the unanimous support of its people.[22] It was Louis Philippe and his Chambers, that had "marred this glorious position." They did so by "placing themselves in a state of hostility against the spirit of the nation," and thus destroying "the *prestiges* of its power." The result was that they gave the despotic governments the impression that they were too busy fighting internal squabbles for them to be credible and formidable abroad (*CW*, XXII: 301).[23]

It follows from the above that some qualifications to the principle of non-intervention, which Mill presented as a re-interpretation, or rather, as a stricter interpretation of the principle (in 1859, but also earlier, in 1837),[24] were very much in line with the arguments of the French opposition in the early 1830s.

What may require further comment is the apparent shift in Mill's attitude *vis-à-vis* the advocacy by the French opposition of an energetic counter-interventionist foreign policy. While he started off by declaring that he was "disgusted" by the warlike tone of the French papers, he came very close indeed to vindicating their cause. The period from December 1830 (when he wrote, expressing his disgust) until April 1831 (when he came to the defence of "what is called (incorrectly) the war party") is crucial. Unfortunately, Mill's extant letters from these months reveal no clues concerning this issue. However, there is an indication of another kind. It was precisely during the months in question that Carrel and other members of the opposition elaborated their interpretation of the "principe de la non-intervention." A look at the contents of Carrel's articles in *Le National* is revealing. One needs only to read the headings of the articles to see that non-intervention had come under scrutiny. On 8 January 1831, Carrel wrote: "Qu'est-ce que la non-intervention?" (Carrel 1857–9, II: 5–12); on 29 January, he reported extensively on the "Discussion à la Chambre sur la Pologne," with particular references to different interpretations of the principle of non-intervention, and to the speeches of Bignon, Lafayette, and others (Carrel 1857–59, II: 52–7 – especially p. 56). Mill most probably read Lafayette's entire speech in the governmental organ, the *Moniteur Universel*, of 29 January,[25] judging by the resemblance of the arguments put forward by the veteran French politician on that occasion and Mill's presentation of the cause of the opposition – including his particular reference to Lafayette – in the text quoted above (*CW*, XXII: 299–301). Additionally, just a couple of weeks before Mill wrote his defence of the views of the opposition, Carrel had written (20 March) "De l'interprétation que donne le nouveau ministère au principe de la non-intervention" (*Œuvres*, II: 176–83; see also *ibid.:* 184–90). It should be stressed, however, that Carrel and his paper had gone further than just advocating the principle in the way Mill presented it. Although he made use of the same counter-intervention argument as Lafayette, Carrel, the former soldier, did not conceal that his aim was, in fact, a crusade for liberty. Thus, Mill did not follow Carrel entirely on this issue. Instead, in the *Examiner*, he presented the considerably milder arguments that had been put forward by Lafayette. This could explain why Mill mentioned only Lafayette by name.

Continuity in Mill's advocacy of the theory

In his later writings about international affairs, besides adducing the theoretical and moral justification of counter-intervention in cases where the despotic powers had already "interfered" with a people, Mill employed another argument propounded by the French opposition. It was grounded on expediency and national security. Accordingly, it was considered not only fair but also necessary for constitutionally governed France in the 1830s to aid nationalities which revolted against the despots in order to have the former as allies against the latter.

Similarly, Mill argued that it would be equally necessary and wise for Britain to do exactly the same in the 1840s and 1850s. In his 1859 article, "A Few Words...," Mill accompanied the moral argument about the legitimacy of counter-intervention (already quoted) with an illustration of the advisability for Britain to follow the principle proposed:

> It might not have been right for England (even apart from the question of prudence) to have taken part with Hungary in its noble struggle against Austria [in 1849]; although the Austrian Government in Hungary was in some sense a foreign yoke. But when, the Hungarians having shown themselves likely to prevail in this struggle, the Russian despot interposed ... it would have been an honourable and virtuous act on the part of England to have declared that this should not be, and that if Russia gave assistance to the wrong side, England would aid the right.
>
> (*CW*, XXI: 124)

He conceded that considerations of prudence ("the regard which every nation is bound to pay to its own safety") might have prevented England from taking this position single-handed, but added that "England and

France together could have done it." Had they done so, the Russian armed intervention that followed the 1849 Hungarian revolt against Austria "would never have taken place, or would have been disastrous to Russia alone." Instead, Mill argued, all that England and France gained by not intervening on the side of the Hungarians was "that they had to fight Russia five years afterwards, under more difficult circumstances, and without Hungary for an ally" (*CW*, XXI: 124).[26] Mill's recommendation for future British policy followed:

> The first nation which, being powerful enough to make its voice effectual, has the spirit and courage to say that not a gun shall be fired in Europe by the soldiers of one Power against the revolted subjects of another, will be the idol of the friends of freedom throughout Europe.

Such a declaration alone, he asserted, would ensure "the almost immediate emancipation of every people which [desired] liberty sufficiently to be capable of maintaining it." As for the nation which would make that declaration, it would soon find itself at the head of "an alliance of free peoples, so strong as to defy the efforts of any number of confederated despots to bring it down." Mill thought that "the time may not be distant when England, if she does not take this heroic part because of its heroism, will be compelled to take it from consideration for her own safety" (*CW*, XXI: 124). In other words, Mill allocated to England after 1851 the international role that he, along with the French radicals themselves, earlier believed France was rightfully aspiring to, before France itself had become – in his eyes at any rate – a despotic power.[27]

Mill repeated the version of the principle of non-intervention discussed above during what could be called his equivalent to an electoral campaign before the Westminster election in 1865. Having been asked by his constituents to state his basic principles on some key questions, he asserted, when it came to discussing foreign policy:

> Every civilized country is entitled to settle its internal affairs in its own [way] and no other country ought to interfere with its discretion, because one country, even with the best intentions, has no chance of properly understanding the internal affairs of another: but when this indefeasible liberty of an independent country has already been interfered with; when it is kept in subjection by a foreign power, either directly, or by assistance given to its native tyrants, I hold that any

nation whatever may rightfully interfere to protect the country against this wrongful interference. I therefore approve the interposition of France in 1859 to free Italy from the Austrian yoke, but disapprove the intervention of the same country in 1849 to compel the Pope's subjects to take back the bad government they had cast off.

(*CW*, XVI: 1033)

However, it was not a necessary consequence "that because a thing might rightfully be done, it is always expedient to do it." Thus, Mill wrote that he would not have voted for a war on behalf of Poland (in 1863) or Denmark (in 1864), because "on any probable view of consequences I should have expected more evil than good from our doing what, nevertheless, if done would not have been, in my opinion, any violation of international duty" (*CW*, XVI: 1033).[28]

One could be tempted to argue that Mill's attempt to defend the stance of the French opposition should be interpreted in terms of strategy. One could assert that, wishing to see reform succeed at home, Mill was bound to vindicate everything the French *parti du mouvement* stood for, including an interventionist foreign policy that was hardly destined to commend them to the British public. However, viewing Mill's comments on intervention as mere attempts of a British radical to justify his French counterparts at a moment when radical reform was at stake in both countries would fail to account for the fact that Mill continued, on different occasions throughout his life, to advocate the principles and arguments he first put forward in his early newspaper articles on France.

In particular, we could note that, during his 1865 election campaign of sorts, Mill declared that he approved of France's 1859 intervention in Italy on the grounds that it was undertaken in order to help a people struggling against a foreign yoke. His statement that he approved of Louis-Napoleon Bonaparte's intervention in Italy is one of the occasions that prove that he stuck to the interpretation of non-intervention he first adopted in 1831. Mill approved of the French intervention despite the fact that it was carried out by a government he sympathized least with, that of Louis-Napoleon (Napoleon III). This particular example serves to support the argument that Mill did not advocate the principle of counter-intervention earlier (i.e., from the early 1830s) merely to vindicate the policies of the French Left.[29]

In the wake of 1848: continuity or radicalization?

Nonetheless, we can discern a shift of emphasis in Mill's statement of 1865. This can best be understood through a discussion of his pronouncements in the aftermath of the revolutions of 1848. His statements following 1848 constitute the one occasion on which Mill might be taken to have modified the principle he set forth. That is, he seems to have asserted then, in 1849, that liberal powers had a right "to assist struggling liberalism," without making this conditional upon an already ongoing "interference" by a power in the affairs of the struggling country. Though there is a certain ambiguity about what exactly Mill asserted in the 1830s and in "A Few Words..." (1859), his statements on these occasions were circumspect enough for him to be understood as advocating counter-intervention only as a response to prior intervention. At first sight, Mill's statement in 1859, justifying intervention in cases where a foreign yoke is holding down a people, could be taken to imply that liberal powers had a right to aid indiscriminately struggles for national liberation from multiethnic empires. However, his exposition of what he meant, in the concrete example of the Austrian Empire, shows that this interpretation cannot be taken for granted. The statement that "[i]t might not have been right for England (even apart from the question of prudence) to have taken part with Hungary in its noble struggle against Austria; although the Austrian Government in Hungary was in some sense a foreign yoke" (*CW*, XXI: 124), leaves one baffled and confused. Was Mill advocating intervention in all cases where an ethnic group claimed national status and statehood against a "foreign" power that was keeping it down, as was the case with the Hungarians and other subject ethnic groups of the Austrian and Ottoman Empires? Or was he asserting that such intervention was warranted only in cases where a third foreign power had already intervened to aid the oppressors in keeping their hold over the nation in revolt?[30]

Mill had been more explicit a decade earlier. In April 1849, he had published in the *Westminster Review* an article intended to be a "Vindication of the French Revolution of February 1848."[31] In particular, the article was a reply to Lord Brougham's attack on almost everything the Provisional Government of France had done (Brougham 1848).[32] One of Brougham's targets had been the declaration of intent by the new French government with regard to foreign policy, in the shape of Alphonse de Lamartine's *Manifeste aux Puissances*.[33] The two main issues Mill addressed in his reply were the French repudiation of the treaties of 1815 which had been imposed on France by the victorious powers after the Napoleonic Wars, and the assertion of France's right, in Mill's own words, "to afford military aid to nations attempting to free themselves from a foreign yoke" (*CW*, XX: 343). When it came to discussing the latter issue, "the doctrine, that one government may make war upon another to assist an oppressed nationality in delivering itself from the yoke," Mill admitted that Brougham was by no means alone in his indignation against "such a breach of received principles, such defiance of the law of nations," but was, rather, backed by a large body of English opinion (*CW*, XX: 344).[34]

Mill's reply to Brougham was outspoken, and with radical overtones: "May we venture, once for all, to deny the whole basis of this edifying moral argumentation?" It was true, he conceded, that "[t]o assist a people struggling for liberty is contrary to the law of nations," and Pufendorf, Burlamaqui, or Vattel would not have approved of such action. And yet: "So be it. But what is the law of nations? Something, which to call a law at all, is a misapplication of terms. The law of nations is simply the custom of nations." For Mill international law was no more than "a set of international usages" which "in an age of progress" were as subject to improvement and as changeable as any other human institution (*CW*, XX: 345).[35] Further, since there was no legislature, or Congress of nations, to alter any part of "that falsely-called law, the law of nations," the improvement of international morality could only take place "by a series of violations of existing rules" (*CW*, XX: 345). Accordingly, Mill maintained that new principles and practices were being introduced into the conduct of nations towards one another. Thus, one "entirely new principle was for the first time established in Europe, amidst general approbation, within the last thirty years." This new principle was that other countries had a right to step in and settle among themselves what they considered reasonable terms of accommodation whenever two countries, or two parts of the same country, were engaged in war, and "the war either continu[ed] long undecided, or threaten[ed] to be decided in a way involving consequences repugnant to humanity or to the general interest."[36] If these terms of accommodation were not accepted, third countries should interfere by force, and "compel the recusant party to submit to the mandate." This new doctrine of intervention had already been acted on by a combination of the great powers of Europe "in three celebrated instances."[37] The cases he had adduced appeared to Mill to establish sufficient precedents to justify the practice of such intervention as part of what he termed as the new "international morality" (*CW*, XX:

346). It can be argued that it is the case for what could be called "humanitarian intervention" that Mill was defending in the above text.[38]

Having established the "new principle" that nations were allowed to "forcibly interfere with one another for the sole purpose of stopping mischief and benefiting humanity," Mill proceeded to present a specific case where such interference was most justified. This was the case where what was at stake was "preventing the liberty of a nation, which [cared] sufficiently for liberty to have risen in arms for its assertion, from being crushed and trampled out by tyrannical oppressors, and these not even of its own name and blood, but foreign conquerors" (*CW*, XX: 346).

There are two distinct, if interconnected, ideas being advanced here. In the first place, he asserted that arguments based on "the law of nations" and which advocated complete and strict non-intervention were untenable, if for no other reason than because the European powers themselves had established a precedent, "within the last thirty years" of interfering for "stopping mischief and benefiting humanity."[39] Having established this principle, he claimed, secondly, that no grounds for such intervention could be stronger than in the case of a revolted nation which had demonstrated the strength of its desire for liberty through an armed uprising for its assertion, and whose liberty was in danger of being crushed and trampled out by tyrannical oppressors who also happened to be foreign conquerors.

Holbraad focuses his discussion of Mill's views on the "Vindication." After quoting Mill's declaration that every liberal government or people "has a right to assist struggling liberalism, by mediation, by money, or by arms, wherever it can prudently do so; as every despotic government, when its aid is needed or asked for, never scruples to aid despotic governments," Holbraad observes in a footnote that,

> [i]n 1859, when the fate of Italy was being decided, he again took up the subject of intervention. Repeating the argument set forth in 1849, *he added a new rule*: "Intervention to enforce non-intervention is always rightful, always moral, if not always prudent."
>
> (Emphasis added: Holbraad 1970: 164–5n)

However, the rule was not new. Mill had advocated it in 1831 (in the *Examiner* articles: *CW*, XXII: 284, 299–301) and in 1837 ("The Spanish Question": *CW*, XXXI: 359–88). But Holbraad's remark is important because it draws our attention to the fact that Mill did not actually refer, explicitly at any rate, in 1849, to the principle of counter-intervention aimed at enforcing non-intervention.

One may suggest that Mill implied the principle of counter-intervention at various points in the 1849 work, as for example in the proviso: "as every despotic government ... never scruples to aid despotic governments." Yet, it remains true that there was no clear assertion of the right to intervene in order to enforce non-intervention; the justification Mill offered in 1849 was not grounded on the right to enforce non-intervention in cases where "the despots" had already intervened. Rather, Mill asserted that at times "when ... the most important interests of nations ... were interests of opinion," no one paid the least regard to "the pretended principle of non-interference."[40] Thus, in 1849, there was a certain departure from his earlier (1831, 1837) position, as well as his later (1859) position. He seems to have adopted a more radical position in 1849. Whether this was due to an eagerness to vindicate Lamartine, or whether it reflected a genuine radicalization of his attitude at a moment of revolutionary exuberance may have to remain a matter of speculation.[41] Scholars have not noticed this divergence between the 1849 text and that written in 1859 and Mill's views are taken to be consistent and identical throughout his writings.[42] Usually, only one of the two texts (1849 or 1859) forms the basis of scholarly discussion.

All that can be said in an attempt to fit the stance Mill adopted in the 1849 "Vindication" with the rest of his writings on the subject of intervention is to suggest that he took for granted that the despots would and did intervene against national struggles. Therefore, he went out of his way to vindicate the French Provisional Government's *Manifeste* with its pro-nationalities overtones, justifying this position in terms of duty by a liberal power to assist struggles for national liberation.

What is perhaps more important in accounting for the apparent difference of emphasis between Mill's writings is that his focus in 1849 was not the question of intervention or non-intervention itself and *in abstracto*, but rather the merits of the principle of *nationality*. In his onslaught on Lamartine's *Manifeste*, Brougham had particularly directed his venom against nationality, which he described as "[t]hat new-fangled principle, that new speculation in the rights of independent states, the security of neighbouring governments, and indeed the happiness of all nations, which is termed *Nationality*, adopted as a kind of rule for the distribution of dominion" that was advocated "by the Paris school of the Law of Nations and their foreign disciples."[43] In his reply, Mill felt obliged to counter Brougham's argument by concentrating on showing why the claims of nationalities deserved satisfaction, rather than on discussing the merits of intervention or non-intervention in the abstract.

By doing so, Mill somehow also answered the complicated question of whether a country was allowed to interfere to help a minority ethnic group that had revolted in a foreign country against their own government. Mill did this by giving (implicitly) the national – or ethnic – group in revolt the status of a nation that was fighting with foreigners. The extent to which he was bolder in the "Vindication" becomes apparent if one compares his statements there with his more qualified and reluctant statement in 1859 concerning Hungary and "its noble struggle against Austria" (*CW*, XXI: 124). It is obvious that in 1859 Mill was not that clear and outspoken about what to recommend in a case such as that of Hungary, which is indicated by the qualified and uncertain expressions ("might," "although," "in some sense") that he used in the 1859 text (*CW*, XXI: 124). The main difference between the 1849 "Vindication" and the other texts in which the subject of intervention was discussed is that, in 1849, Mill took the radical step of maintaining openly and unequivocally that liberal countries had a right, and perhaps a duty, to intervene and assist struggles of national liberation, whether or not a "despotic" power had already intervened to assist the state whose integrity was threatened by the national revolt. In 1849, Mill seemed to imply that the very fact that a nation was under a "foreign" occupation (the fact that the liberty of a nation was "trampled out by tyrannical oppressors ... not ... of its own name and blood, but foreign conquerors") constituted a form of intervention with the political development of that nation. In line with this notion, Mill (as well as Lamartine[44]) considered the Italians' attempts at unification to be their own affair, while the attempts by Austria to obstruct Italian unification for the sake of retaining its own Italian territories were to be considered interference by foreigners. In 1849, Mill implied, to all intents and purposes, that the legitimate unit in international politics was the nation, not the state. Or, to put it differently, that national allegiances might be more important than existing territorial arrangements. The difference is one of criteria of legitimacy, and is revolutionary in its implications.

The reference to these questions in the "Vindication" is important for our understanding of Mill's later, and much better known, statements about nationality in *Representative Government* (1861). In the latter work he had come to state more carefully many of the bold statements he formulated in 1849. However, there is at least one major idea in the 1849 essay to which Mill held with little, if any, qualification in Chapter XVI of *Representative Government*, but rather elaborated on it: the idea that the main justification for "nationality" and its aims was its potential conduciveness to free representative government.

For all his concessions to the nationalists, Mill was not blind to the contradictions and dangers involved in many nationalist movements. He condemned categorically and in the strongest terms what is often called today "tribalism." It was far from his intention, he hastened to declare, to "defend or apologise for the feelings which make men reckless of, or at least indifferent to, the rights and interests of any portion of the human species, save that which is called by the same name and speaks the same language as themselves." These feelings, he wrote, "are characteristic of barbarians" (*CW*, XX: 347).

But it was exactly because of these deplorable characteristics of nationalist sentiment that the latter should be humored, wherever possible, if the damage it could do to the cause of free government was to be prevented: "But grievous as are these things, yet so long as they exist, the question of nationality is practically of the very first importance." When portions of mankind which live under the same government "cherish these barbarous feelings," they are "scarcely capable of merging into one and the same free people." This is because "[t]hey have not the fellow-feeling which would enable them to unite in maintaining their liberties, or in forming a paramount public opinion." As a result, the government would be able, "by playing off one race and people against another, to suppress the liberties of all."[45] The example of the Austrian Empire was adduced (*CW*, XX: 347–8). Therefore: "Nationality is desirable, as a means to the attainment of liberty; and this is reason enough for sympathizing in the attempts of Italians to re-constitute an Italy, and in those of the people of Posen to become a Poland."

So long, indeed, as a people are incapable of[46] self-government, it is often better for them to be under the despotism of foreigners than of natives, when these foreigners are more advanced in civilization and cultivation than themselves. But when their hour of freedom, to use M. de Lamartine's metaphor, has struck, without their having become merged and blended in the nationality of their conquerors, the re-conquest of their own is often an indispensable condition either to obtaining free institutions, or to the possibility, were they even obtained, of working them in the spirit of freedom.

(*CW*, XX: 348)

Epilogue

In an article surveying the prevailing trends in the study of the issues related to intervention and non-intervention in recent decades, Richard Little delineates the distinction between empirical and normative analysis (Little 1993). As he puts it, it is a conventional distinction "which derives from the epistemological position often referred to as positivism" (Little 1993: 26). Little goes on to challenge the line drawn by positivists between "facts" and "values" and the concomitant "division of labour . . . between social scientists and moral philosophers." In opposition to the assertions by positivists to the effect that there is a "logical gulf between the demands of morality and the dictates of self-interest" (Little 1993: 27), Little maintains that we need to supersede the juxtaposition between self-interest and morality, and seems to endorse recent attempts to develop this new approach in the context of intervention and non-intervention. It is arguable that such an approach was advocated by Mill. What Mill did was to try to convince his compatriots that, in many – though not all – cases, the course of action required by the demands of morality was at the same time dictated by their enlightened self-interest. Exactly as the spokesmen of the French Left had done in the early 1830s, he asserted in the 1840s and 1850s that liberal powers such as France (in the 1840s, before the second Bonaparte's coup in 1851 rendered France a "despotic" power) and Britain had not only a moral right, but also a clearly discernible interest in assisting liberal movements aimed against the despotic powers. Thus, his ultimate appeal was to a combination of morality and prudent self-protection. He did not bother to abide by any positivist orthodoxy. What he endeavored was epistemologically less ambitious, though it was, perhaps, morally and politically ambitious. To use his own words, he tried in each case "either as theorist or as practical man, to effect the greatest amount of good compatible with his opportunities" (Mill, *Autobiography*: *CW*, I: 87).

6 Foreign policy and the public moralist
Fighting ethnocentric "half-truths"

Je voudrais qu'on crucifiât le premier homme qui osât dire à la tribune d'un peuple des injures contre un autre peuple. Il faut des générations entières pour guérir le mal que cela peut faire dans un jour. Cela est bien méprisable dans un siècle qui a tant besoin du concours des hommes énergiques et éclairés de tous les pays avancés pour l'œuvre difficile de réorganiser la société européenne.[1]

(J.S. Mill, letter to Alexis de Tocqueville, 20 February 1843: *CW*, XIII: 570–1)

I do not know how a public writer can be more usefully employed than by telling his countrymen their faults, and if that is considered anti-national I am not at all desirous to avoid the charge.

(J.S. Mill, letter to Macvey Napier, 20 October 1845: *CW*, XIII: 683)

The great instrument of improvement in men, is to supply them with the other half of the truth, one side of which only they have ever seen: to turn round to them the white side of the shield, of which they seeing only the black side, have cut other men's throats and risked their own to prove that the shield is black.

(J.S. Mill, letter to Gustave d'Eichthal, 7 November 1829: *CW*, XII: 42)[2]

An essential part of Mill's conception of his role as a "public moralist" (the Victorian equivalent to what later epochs would call a public intellectual),[3] was his self-appointed task to educate, shame or cajole his compatriots out of their narrow, smug, and ethnocentric ways of thinking and feeling into a more enlarged and – it is not too much to say – more cosmopolitan way of perceiving the world. This "least parochial of writers" (Collini 1999: 143) seems to have considered it no less than immoral to stick to one's ethnocentric point of view with no interest in, and understanding of, the viewpoints of other nations and cultures. Not the least of the reasons for this attitude was his boyhood stay in France for a year, at the age of fourteen, with the family of Samuel Bentham, Jeremy's brother.[4] By no means less than the other celebrated "Francophile" of Victorian cultural and social criticism, Matthew Arnold, Mill tended to deprecate ruthlessly what was narrow and parochial in English culture and thought and to celebrate what was broader, shared, enlarged, pan-European, cosmopolitan, the result of the admixture and interaction of different cultures and a contribution to the general fund of a shared universal – or, at any rate, European – civilization.[5] It was for this reason that Mill spent an extraordinary amount of time and energy trying to acquaint the British public with French politics, philosophy, political and social thought, literature, and, far from least, historiography. In review article after review article he castigated what he saw as the lamentable inattention of his compatriots to the remarkable and exciting movement of thought and ideas taking place on the other side of the English Channel. He saw France as a laboratory of mankind in the realm of new ideas and movements in the same way as his compatriots (and most Continental observers) saw Britain as a laboratory in terms of industrial and economic development. Throughout the 1830s and 1840s Mill almost tediously reiterated his exhortations to his fellow-countrymen to enlarge their horizons by a better acquaintance with what was taking place or being contemplated in France, for even the experiments that were bound to fail were worth studying and drawing conclusions from. Thus, there is nothing surprising in the fact that the editors of the *Collected Works of John Stuart Mill* have calculated that the one word which appears more times than any other in his *œuvre* is "France" – to say nothing of French names and French books (O'Grady 1991: xxix).[6]

Mill was not alone in his almost compulsive interest in France. I have enumerated elsewhere various reasons that led a number of Victorian thinkers to observe France and to write about things French, particularly French politics (Varouxakis 2002: Chapter 1). It has to be emphasized, however, that, among thinkers that can be called "political," it is only Matthew Arnold that may be taken as having exhibited a comparable degree of interest in studying and pointing to France. And though Arnold's attacks on the English "philistines" and their "narrow civilisation" and his evocation of the excellencies of France have been amply celebrated, it is usually forgotten that Mill had done the same things at least as vociferously as Arnold, starting more than three decades before Arnold.[7] Now, in Mill's own case, this evocation of a foreign country – moreover, the foreign country *par excellence*, the anti-England, to paraphrase Michelet (Michelet 1974: 224) – performed several functions. In the context of what is discussed in this book, we need to look at two of them here. One dimension of Mill's enterprise with regard to France is the educative dimension, his attempts to teach and "improve" the "national mind" and "national character" of his compatriots through a better acquaintance with the country he (as well as many of his contemporaries) considered the best suited to serve as a mirror to Britain, France. A second dimension of Mill's involvement with France worth examining here was related to his strenuous efforts to contribute to the improvement of both the relations between the two countries, and, most crucially, between the two peoples – in terms of mutual perceptions, understanding and feelings.

The battle against ethnocentrism

To start with the first dimension, Mill – as well as some of his contemporaries – had developed no less than a full theory concerning the importance of studying a foreign country and its culture for one's intellectual development, as well as for one's better acquaintance with one's own country and culture (cf. Varouxakis 2002: Chapter 1). The study of a foreign country, like the study of history, conduced to the expansion of one's intellectual horizon, and it went some way towards making amends for the "accident of birth" of one's being born in a particular country and epoch. Thus, he wrote in 1836 that nations, no less than individuals, until they had compared themselves with others, were "apt to mistake their own idiosyncrasies for laws of our common being, and the accidents of their position, for a part of the destiny of our race." As a result, "[t]he type of human nature and of human life with which they are familiar, is the only one which presents itself to their imagination." Thus, it was "[t]he correction of narrowness" that was "the main benefit derived from the study of various ages and nations: of narrowness, not only in our conceptions of what is, but in our standard of what ought to be." The individualities of nations were as useful to the general improvement, as the individualities of persons: "since none is perfect, it is a beneficial arrangement that all are not imperfect in the same way."

> Each nation, and the same nation in every different age, exhibits a portion of mankind, under a set of influences, different from what have been in operation anywhere else: each, consequently, exempli-

fies a distinct phasis of humanity; in which the elements which meet and temper one another in a perfect human character are combined in a proportion more or less peculiar. ... when each nation beholds in some other a model of the excellencies corresponding to its own deficiencies; when all are admonished of what they want, by what others have (as well as made to feel the value of what they have by what others want), they no longer go on confirming themselves in their defects by the consciousness of their excellencies, but betake themselves, however tardily, to profiting by each other's example.

Whoever made up his system of opinions from the contemplation of only one nation, was "in imminent danger of falling into narrow and one-sided views" (*CW*, XVIII: 94). Or, as he put it in 1867, "unless we ... possess [the] knowledge, of some other people than ourselves, we remain, to the hour of our death, with our intellects only half expanded." Given that "[i]mprovement consists in bringing our opinions into nearer agreement with facts"; and given at the same time that this could not be achieved "while we look at facts only through glasses coloured by those very opinions," his solution was: "But since we cannot divest ourselves of preconceived notions, there is no known means of eliminating their influence but by frequently using the differently coloured glasses of other people: and those of other nations, as the most different, are the best" (*CW*, XXI: 226).[8]

From his first biographer a few years after his death to Stefan Collini very recently, commentators on his thought have said of Mill that "[h]e always dealt gently with [the] faults [of France], and liberally with her virtues" (Bain 1882: 78) and that "his habitual way of speaking of England, the English people, English society, as compared with other nations, was positively unjust, and served no good end."[9] Though understandable – in view of the harshness of some of Mill's comments on the English – Bain's criticism misses the point, especially as far as its latter part is concerned: it was Mill's conviction that he *did* serve a very good end by being over-critical of England and the English while extolling liberally the virtues of other countries such as France. He was far from being a starry-eyed Francophile. But he did not see what purpose it would serve to confirm the English in their anti-Gallican prejudices by adding to the commonplace expositions of the faults of the French. What was needed was "to place by [the] side" of these faults "those excellencies which are often the bright side of the same qualities." This attitude constituted a deliberate strategy of a man who considered himself one of "the moral teachers of England, those who are labouring for the regeneration of England's national character."[10] In the article where the above phrases occur ("The English National Character," June 1834: *CW*, XXIII: 717–27), Mill attacked vehemently one of the most Anglophile Frenchmen of the nineteenth century, Philarète Chasles. Chasles attracted Mill's attack because he had criticized in a review of Edward Bulwer-Lytton's *England and the English* (1833) the British author's harsh criticisms of some faults in the English national character. The worst of these so-called vices of the English character was, according to Bulwer-Lytton and Mill, "the universal and all-absorbing struggle to be or to appear rich." The Anglophile French reviewer had taken issue with Bulwer-Lytton's strictures. On the contrary, in his review he extolled the beneficial consequences of the English spirit of commerce. However, according to Mill, Bulwer-Lytton's "harshness" was "deserved." He opined that such commendation of England as that attempted by Chasles was "worse than the ancient antipathy" between England and France. Mill's retort to the French reviewer was: "We want you to sympathize in our virtues, not in our faults," adding that "*[t]he disposition to hold fast by a favourite vice does not stand in need of any foreign support*" (emphasis added). It was his belief that the reverse of this statement was true as well, that prompted Mill to write publicly in the way he did: it seemed to him that *the eradication* of favourite vices *did* stand in need of "foreign support" – in the shape of his use of France as a mirror to England. To use his own terms from a text already quoted concerning "the benefit derived from the study of various ... nations," the English nation had to "[behold] in some other [nation] a model of the excellencies corresponding to its own deficiencies."

Besides Mill's indirect exposition, in the passages just referred to, of the spirit guiding him in his writings on France, there is an indication of another kind to corroborate the view that there was a deliberate strategy in his commenting on France: there is a certain difference between the public as opposed to the private Mill. While in his correspondence he emerges fairly critical, from very early on, of what he considered to be faults in the French character, he raised his criticisms less often in his public writings, where he chose to set the emphasis on extolling what he regarded as qualities in the French character and exhorting – directly or indirectly – the English to emulate them. It also appears that Mill was too sensitive to other people in Britain criticizing the French, even when he had himself raised the same or similar criticisms earlier. He seems to have believed that his own criticisms were constructive, because he censured France *"en ami,"* which was not always the case with others.

As a French reviewer of a work written by Mill put it: "Comme tous les esprits élevés, qui veulent accroître la civilisation de leur patrie en la comparant à des civilisations différentes, il dédaigne de flatter son pays, et ne craint point de lui signaler les qualités de ses rivaux, qu'il voudrait lui voir acquérir. S'il a encouru un reproche parmi ses compatriotes, c'est d'être le censeur un peu morose de l'Angleterre et le panégyriste un peu complaisant de la France" (Forcade 1859: 988–9).[11]

The public moralist as bridge-maker

Like some other Victorian thinkers, Mill saw himself as conducting a life-long struggle against what he called half-truths. There is at least one area of his thought and activity where his near-obsession with combating half-truths and attempting to make people see "the other side of the shield" is free from objections and has a lot to recommend it today no less than during Mill's life-time. I am alluding to international relations – in the extended sense of relations between peoples rather than in the strict sense of diplomatic relations. Mill's handling of the sensitive issues connected with the relations between Britain and France, as well as between the two peoples, amounts to no less than a theory of the appropriate role of intellectuals in bringing about a better understanding between different nations, averting mutual misunderstandings, irrational wars, combating chauvinism and national smugness, and working towards meeting the need of the "concours des hommes enérgiques et éclairés de tous les pays avancés pour l'œuvre difficile de réorganiser la société européenne"[12] (Letter to Tocqueville, 20 February 1843: *CW*, XIII: 571). No matter what the case might be with regard to other issues (such as the reconcilability of the world-views of Bentham and Coleridge for instance), there is nothing philosophically or politically untenable about applying to international disputes the theory that:

> The great instrument of improvement in men, is to supply them with the other half of the truth, one side of which only they have ever seen: to turn round to them the white side of the shield, of which they seeing only the black side, have cut other men's throats and risked their own to prove that the shield is black.
>
> (*CW*, XII: 42)[13]

Mill was not a starry-eyed cosmopolitan. He was acutely and painfully aware of the obstacles to be overcome before his Saint-Simonian friends' plans for European unity could even be discussed (see, for example, *CW*, XV: 702–3; *CW*, XVII: 1800–1). But the alertness to the difficulties only affected his means and strategies, not his ultimate goals. His strategy, as it emerges from an examination of his handling of Franco-British disputes, was remarkable for its consistency and perseverance. Appreciating that in the increasingly democratized societies that were emerging in the world scene international relations were bound to be affected by the feelings and wishes of peoples more than they ever had been in the past, and being aware of the "new style" of international politics that the French Revolution had introduced (cf. Kedourie 1985: 9–19), Mill believed that a better understanding and the cultivation of friendly dispositions between the peoples themselves was a necessary condition for the preservation of peace.[14] His perception of his role as a public moralist included his adoption of a subtle attitude in this domain.

Throughout the 1830s, Mill made strenuous efforts to contribute to the amelioration of the dispositions and feelings of the British and the French towards each other. That the preservation of peace in Western Europe and of a good atmosphere in the relations between "the two greatest nations in the world" (*CW*, XXII: 303; cf. *CW*, XXIII: 644; *CW*, XX: 125), Britain and France, was of paramount importance to Mill from very early on is clear from his writings in the *Examiner* on French affairs in the early 1830s. We have already seen (Chapter 5) that, though it could be said that his aim there was to vindicate the policies of the French left (the so-called "parti du mouvement") rather than to criticize them, he did show himself impatient with what he saw as their excessive concern with the affairs of Belgium and Poland and the danger that this attitude posed for the cause of reform in Europe – in Britain no less than in France.

But besides the earnest desire to see peace preserved, Mill also made concerted efforts during the early 1830s – as he did throughout his life – to contribute to the easing of tensions between British and French public opinion. In 1843 he said that he would like to see crucified the first man who would dare use in the tribunal of a people abusive language against another people (*CW*, XIII: 571).[15] He showed himself no less solicitous of the preservation as well as cultivation of friendly dispositions between the two peoples in his early newspaper writings. His first aim was to commend the French opposition, the *parti du mouvement*, to the British.

It has been seen that he defended the so-called war party in April 1831.[16] And he went out of his way to stress in his newspaper writings that *The Times* and the rest of the English press were wrong in attributing anti-English feelings to the French liberals (see *CW*, XXII: 182–4; cf. *CW*, XII: 115). In this spirit, writing in the *Examiner* on 3 June 1832 Mill censured *The Times* for having asserted, some days earlier, that the internal affairs of France were of no concern of the British public, because they were not connected with "English interests" (*The Times*, 1 June 1832, p. 2). He deplored the implications of such an assertion for the morality of the nation, and then commented that this was "but a poor sample of English feeling from the 'leading journal,' on the very day which brings us the news of a patriotic banquet at Paris," during which

> Armand Carrel, the Editor of the only influential Paris newspaper in which there lingered some remains of anti-English feeling, was selected, perhaps for that very reason, to give, as a toast, "The People of England," with expression of the warmest sympathy and congratulation upon our late glorious though pacific Three Days.
>
> (*CW*, XXIII: 466–7)[17]

In the context of his attempts to bring like-minded Frenchmen and Englishmen closer many of Mill's articles seem to have been written in order for them to be read on both sides of the Channel.[18] One such article was that for the *Examiner* of 2 December 1832 ("French and English Journals"). It was addressed at least as much to Carrel and the French "popular party" as to the British readers of the *Examiner*. Mill was commenting on an article written by Carrel in *Le National* on 31 October 1832 entitled "Des correspondances des journaux anglais." In that article the French liberal journalist had complained about what he saw as the unfair treatment of his own paper – and of French news more generally – by some British newspapers and their Paris correspondents. Carrel's first target had been the London *Globe and Traveller*, which had apparently misrepresented what Carrel had written in an earlier article, and accompanied its version with an anti-Gallican gibe. Carrel's comment was: "This is but one example among a thousand of the dishonesty and levity with which all French affairs are treated in the *juste-milieu* Papers of London, while their brethren here are preaching about the possibility of an alliance with England."[19] A similar complaint followed about an anti-French comment in the *Courier*.

This was a serious situation, requiring Mill's intervention. An influential French liberal was criticizing the anti-French tone of British papers, which were ostensibly liberal, in order to prove that some French politicians'[20] advocacy of an alliance with England was chimerical. Mill's answer was that "the above strictures on the English Journalists" were just, but that the journalists "must not be confounded with the English people." The truth was, "(and our friends of the *National* must not allow themselves to forget it)," that while the French journals represented "the most generous and high-minded portion of the French public," their English counterparts represented "the baser and more sordid part of ours." Mill explained why the French should not be misled into regarding the two journals Carrel had referred to as in any way representative of or influential on the English people. He proceeded to offer a complex sociological explanation of the reasons why the English press should not be taken to represent the feelings of the English public at large (*CW*, XXIII: 529). And he concluded:

> M. Carrel compliments *The Times* on its occasional relaxations of anti-French spirit:[21] we can assure him that the "touches of generosity" which he speaks of, find a responding chord in every English bosom which Toryism has not petrified; while the spirit to which those touches are exceptions is very generally regarded as an instance of the antiquated John-Bullism, which, in many other things besides this, distinguishes that Journal. We can assure him [M. Carrel], moreover, that the close union between France and England, which he seems to think chimerical, is earnestly desired by all parties in this country except the Tories; for our *juste-milieu* feels its cause bound up with the French *juste-milieu*, and our *mouvement* with the French *mouvement*.
>
> (*CW*, XXIII: 529–30)

And Mill went on to assure the Frenchman of the sympathy and identification of the "popular party" in England with their counterpart in France. The declarations of solidarity with his "friends and brothers the French patriots" that follow border on the melodramatic (*CW*, XXIII: 530).[22]

Not long before Mill had this article published in the *Examiner* he had written to W.J. Fox (18 October 1832), that his friend André Marchais,[23] "who pays me the compliment of making me the depository and instrument of all the plans he forms for bringing about a good understanding between the patriotic party in France and the best of the English radicals," had suggested something which appeared to Mill "highly important" and for which he was asking for Fox's support. He explained to him that an association had been formed at Paris, of which his "excellent friend" Marchais was the secretary, aiming at promoting the liberty of the press, and especially raising subscriptions to pay the fines imposed on newspapers as a result of Louis-Philippe's persecution against the liberal press. He went on to inform Fox that those among the French patriots who knew enough of the English radicals "to desire their co-operation and sympathy" were anxious to obtain subscribers in England for their association, "and above all they wish that the Political Unions should bear *some public testimony of sympathy and fraternity*" (emphasis added) on that important occasion. Mill asked Fox to do all he could in order to bring both these things about. He commented further:

> The more you see and converse with French people, the more importance you will attach to things of this kind. Every such mark of sympathy produces a great momentary effect; but they require to be, again and again, repeated: for so few Frenchmen ever come here, that they do not learn, except from such public occurrences, that the English people, all but the Tories, esteem, and wish well to, the French.
>
> (*CW*, XII: 121–2)[24]

In November 1833 Mill took the failure of the Reform Ministry to respond positively to what he saw as a French friendly overture deeply to heart. The French government had proposed to the British a measure that would allow the newspapers of each country to be distributed by the mails of the other on the same terms with its own, free of postal charges. It was "a proposal which a Ministry with enlarged views and a liberal spirit would have grasped at with the utmost avidity," and "an opportunity of facilitating the circulation of knowledge, the interchange of ideas, and the increase of friendly feeling between the two leading nations of Europe." And he went on to stress the importance of the opportunity and to lament its having been missed. But what really incensed Mill was that the British government had thus condoned the perpetuation of "*the peculiar and odious mischief of a monopoly in favour of national prejudices and antipathies*, and against the most valuable of all intercourse, that of human thoughts and feelings" (emphasis added: *CW*, XXIII: 643–6. Cf. *CW*, XXII: 182–3).

But it was especially during the serious crisis of 1840 over the Near East and the activities of the Pasha of Egypt, Mehemet Ali, that Mill's perception of his role as a bridge-maker between British and French view-points fully manifested itself.[25] And yet, Mill's stance on this occasion, and more generally in Franco-British disputes, has been judged as somewhat ethnocentric. John C. Cairns has observed in his Introduction to the volume containing Mill's *Essays on French History and Historians*, when writing on the British thinker's disagreement with Tocqueville on this occasion, that:

> Clearly Mill never understood Tocqueville's concept of national prestige, or his fears for the health of the French national spirit; across more than a century thereafter, few Englishmen did: it remained an impenetrable mystery for most of them, and Mill, for all his francophilism, appeared scarcely better equipped to penetrate it.
>
> (*CW*, XX: xx)[26]

Professor Cairns has also commented that his reaction to "[t]he intense diplomatic crisis of 1839–41 ... showed a very real limitation to Mill's capacity for evaluating the rights and wrongs of the old Anglo-French antagonism" (Cairns 1985: xviii). Raymond Aron has also paid considerable attention to the exchanges between Mill and Tocqueville on this crisis, regarding them as characteristic of broader and recurring attitudes in the two countries with regard to their relationship with each other (Aron 1965: 17–20). While Cairns seems rather critical of Mill's attitude, Aron appears to side, though tacitly, with Mill against Tocqueville.[27]

It will be shown in the following pages that Cairns's statements about Mill's inability to understand the French point of view (Cairns 1985: xviii–xx) need to be qualified, because Mill did show both considerable understanding and receptiveness to French arguments. That this did not prevent him from criticizing the excesses of French reactions to the crisis of 1840 may not mean that he "never understood" Tocqueville's point. It would be fairer to say that Mill understood but did not agree with it, not least for the reasons we have already seen (Chapter 2). What is more, an examination of Mill's correspondence at the time in question shows a steady pattern. He was conspicuously more critical of the French when writing to Tocqueville or d'Eichthal, than he was when writing to British correspondents.

In letters to British correspondents in the autumn of 1840, Mill expressed his "great trepidation," and his indignation at "the two most lightheaded men in Europe, Palmerston and Thiers," who threatened to "embroil the whole world and do mischief which no one now living would have seen repaired." He was angry at the "anti-Gallican tone" in various British periodicals. He informed his British friends that the universal war fervor in France was not due to love of war, but rather to the fact that the French felt themselves "*blessé* and humiliated as a nation." Unlike Nassau Senior – who did not think this was a sufficient explanation for what he saw as French paranoid fears and touchiness (Senior 1842) – Mill's comment was that "[t]his is foolish, but who can wonder at it in a people whose country has within this generation been twice occupied by foreign armies? If that were our case we should have plenty of the same feeling" (*CW*, XIII: 445–6 – letter to John Sterling, 1 October 1840). As weeks went by, he was relaxing in the belief that the immediate danger of war was over, but this did not make him very optimistic. The evil already done was "incalculable": "the confidence which all Europe felt in the preservation of peace" would not for many years be re-established and "the bestial antipathies between nations and especially between France and England have been rekindled to a deplorable extent" (*CW*, XIII: 448 – letter to R.B. Fox, 25 November 1840).

By far the most interesting exchanges on the crisis over the Eastern Question were those between Mill and Tocqueville. In his capacity as a French Deputy, Tocqueville had delivered a speech in the Chamber of Deputies on 30 November 1840, which had caused surprise and consternation to his friends and admirers in Britain. The speech in question represented "the most belligerent moment of his parliamentary career" (Drescher 1964: 155–6). As we have seen (Chapter 2), Tocqueville wrote to Mill (18 December 1840) expressing his grief at the rupture of the intimate alliance between their two countries, but also laying the blame for the situation exclusively on the British side as well as stressing the need for a people such as the French to have their *orgueil national* kept alive and encouraged at any price (Tocqueville 1951– (*Œuvres Complètes*), VI, 1: 330–1). Mill wrote back on 30 December 1840 (*CW*, XIII: 457–60). Besides his British friends and Tocqueville, Mill discussed extensively the developments in Franco-British relations with one more Frenchman, Gustave d'Eichthal. A collation of Mill's letters to d'Eichthal with those he wrote to Tocqueville allows us to have a clear picture as to the message which Mill wanted to bring home to his French correspondents. One can discern three main themes. First, the fact that a Liberal government was in power had prevented reactions against its policy, which would have certainly taken place had the Tories been in power, the Tories being considered anti-Gallican, while the Liberals were not suspected of anything of the kind.[28] Second, Palmerston was able to get away with his policy towards France because of the excessive French reactions that followed, which alienated those who would otherwise have stood up for the French alliance against the Foreign Secretary and made them think that he must have had good reasons for his policy in the first place. Third, the English public were not interested in the Eastern Question or foreign affairs in general, and this was one more reason why they failed to react (a view shared by Nassau Senior, who also tried to make it clear to Tocqueville in his correspondence with him). As for Palmerston, Mill declared that, for his part, he "would walk twenty miles to see him hanged, especially if Thiers were to be strung up along with him" (*CW*, XIII: 459–60).[29]

But it is misleading to judge Mill's stance on the crisis of 1840 only through what he wrote to Frenchmen, especially Tocqueville (as Cairns did). His strictures to the French was only one side of the story. One has to look also at what Mill was writing to his British friends.[30] Thus, meanwhile, on 19 December 1840, Mill had written to John Sterling: "I think and feel very much as you do on the subject of the bad spirit manifested in France by so many politicians and writers and unhappily by some from whom better things were to be expected."[31] But "this does not appear to me to strengthen Palmerston's justification," he stressed.[32] He did not believe that Thiers would have acted, in power, in the manner he did afterwards, "when he knew that he had only the turbulent part of the population to throw himself upon, and no watchword to use but the old ones about making the Mediterranean a French lake, getting rid of the treaties of 1815, etc." Mill had no doubt that Thiers would have attempted "to make such an arrangement as should leave a powerful state at that end of the Mediterranean under French influence,"[33] but he found nothing wrong with this:

I think he had a good right to attempt this, and we no right at all to hinder it if the arrangement was not objectionable on any other account. It appears to me very provoking treatment of France that England and Russia should be extending their influence every year till it embraces all Asia and that we should be so indignant at the bare supposition that France wishes to do a little of what we do on so much larger a scale.[34] It is true we do it almost in spite of ourselves, and rather wish to keep others out than to get ourselves in; but we cannot expect France to think so, or to regard our professing it as anything but attempting to humbug them and not doing it well.

Mill believed that "no harm whatever to Europe would have resulted from French influence with Mehemet Ali," and that it would have been easy "to *bind* France against any future occupation of the country for herself." Had the British acted more wisely, they would have avoided "raising this mischievous spirit in France." No one seemed to him to have raised himself by this but Guizot, who had "done what perhaps no other man could have done and almost certainly none so well" (*CW*, XIII: 451–2).[35]

Mill wrote to Sterling again, on 5 January 1841, and to his correspondent's remarks challenging his earlier assertions about England's provocative treatment of France,[36] Mill replied that the aggressions he meant were "the proceedings by which we are gradually conquering all Asia, from Pekin to Herat." It was, he maintained,

> provoking that France should see England and Russia adding every year on a large scale to their territory and dependent alliances in the East and then crying out at the suspicion of her wishing to do something of the same kind as if it were an enormity never before heard of among the nations of Europe.

However, he felt obliged to warn Sterling against misunderstanding his position. He was not defending France or excusing her conduct "except so far as attacked by people themselves liable to the same accusations in all respects, except (so far as Thiers is concerned) that of duplicity."

Mill then informed his correspondent that he had received a letter from Tocqueville,[37] which he enclosed along with his own letter to Sterling, as the latter might like to see what the French thinker had to say "for the part he has taken in this matter *and how he connects it with his philosophic ideas*" (emphasis added). He went on to say that he had written a long letter to Tocqueville[38] in reply to which he expected "a long and controversial answer." Mill wrote that he had thought it right to try to do some good with Tocqueville "by speaking out with entire frankness, which his personally kind feelings towards me *and his knowledge of my sentiments about France both in itself and in relation to England*, gave me the power of doing without offence" (emphasis added: *CW*, XIII: 462–3).

Concerning the same letter (of 18 December) he had received from Tocqueville, Mill wrote to R.B. Fox, on 23 December 1840:

> He [Tocqueville] touches on politics, mourning over the rupture of the Anglo-French alliance and as the part he took in debate has

excited much surprise and disapproval here it is right to make known
what he professes as his creed on the matter, viz. that if you wish to
keep any people, especially so mobile a people as the French, in the
disposition of mind which enables them to do great things you must
by no means teach them to be reconciled to other people's making no
account of them. They were treated, he thinks, with so great a degree
of slight (to say the least) by our government that for their public
men not to shew a feeling of *blessure* would have been to lower the
standard of national pride which in the present state of the world he
thinks almost the only elevated sentiment that remains in considerable strength.

Mill's comment was that "*[t]here is really a great deal in this*"
(emphasis added) although it did not justify the revival of the old
national animosity or the warlike demonstrations and preparations. A
nation could show itself offended, Mill observed, "without threatening
a vengeance out of proportion to the affront and which would involve
millions that never offended them with units that did, besides ruining
themselves in the end, or rather in the beginning." However, he then
came to the British position, to say that he thought it "quite con-
temptible in England to treat the bare suspicion of France seeking for
influence in the East as something too horrible to be thought of" while
England was "meanwhile progressively embracing the whole of Asia
in her own grasp."[39] Mill wrote that he could not find words to express
his contempt of the whole conduct of the British government and his
admiration for "the man who has conjured away as much as was possible of the evil done and has attained the noblest end, in a degree no
one else could, by the noblest means," namely Guizot, "who now
stands before the world as immeasurably the greatest public man
living."[40]

Thus, Mill's strong opinions on Franco-British relations influenced
decisively his estimation of personalities and parties. Guizot's role in
averting war and helping to forge a Franco-British *entente cordiale*[41] led
Mill to an impressive reversal in his attitude towards Guizot as a politician and to his going out of his way to praise the French minister. On the
other hand, Tocqueville's very different attitude towards the English
alliance led to a cooling of Mill's relations with a man whose overall
political views he found very congenial, certainly more so than those of
Guizot. This example reveals the importance Mill accorded the Franco-
British *entente* and what he hoped could be its concomitants, peace in

Europe, friendly feelings and co-operation between the two peoples, and consequently, the progress of civilization in Europe and the world.

Thus, Mill's correspondence during the crisis of 1840 and its aftermath suggests that he did understand the resentment felt by the French and that he was vehemently opposed to Palmerston's handling of the affair. But at the same time he disapproved strongly of the direction French reactions took, and was infuriated by the prospect that France and Britain could go to war. What he objected to most strongly was the notion that French "honour" was worth starting a Franco-British war that would take European society back to the situation of 1815.

Mill recognized the need for the French to aspire to more than Guizot's notorious (and usually misunderstood) injunction "enrichissez vous"; he himself castigated the July Monarchy's "culte des intérêts matériels."[42] Thus far he went along with Tocqueville. Mill was far from content with a society whose members cared about nothing but their economic and social advancement and the satisfaction of their material needs.[43] But his reaction to the crisis of 1840 revealed the limit to how far he was prepared to go in this direction. He wanted the French – and, of course, the British – to aspire to unselfish goals, to something higher than their own material well-being. But his advocacy of selfless aspiration fell short of endorsing pandering to chauvinistic nationalist feelings and instincts as means to this end.[44]

It might need to be stressed that J.S. Mill was not a "pacifist." The American Civil War induced him, in later years, to declare that he could not "join with those who cry Peace, peace," since "war, in a good cause, is not the greatest evil which a nation can suffer. War is an ugly thing, but not the ugliest of things: the decayed and degraded state of moral and patriotic feeling which thinks nothing *worth* a war, is worse." But what counted was the "good cause": the American Civil War was, to a great extent, for the North, a "war to protect other human beings against tyrannical injustice" ("The Contest in America" (1862): *CW*, XXI: 141–2). In the case of the 1840 Franco-British crisis, it was the irrationality of the cause that infuriated Mill.

Mill adopted a middle position between what he saw as French extremism and irrationality on the one hand and English failure to understand the French on the other. He saw himself in a dual role. When addressing the French (Tocqueville and d'Eichthal) he emphasized the irresponsibility, puerility, and irrationality of their compatriots. In the case of Tocqueville, Mill tactfully indicated to his French correspondent what he regarded as his own failings and misunderstandings. On the other hand, when writing to his British friends (R.B. Fox and Sterling), he stressed the untenable-ness of the British position, Palmerston's provocative treatment of France, etc. and did his best to minimize the negative impression Tocqueville's speeches in the Chamber had made on them, by passing on to them the Frenchman's explanations for his position. It is characteristic in this respect, that he wrote to Tocqueville, on 30 December 1840, presenting to him the view of the recent events taken by Sterling – who had asserted that his was the viewpoint of "the average [man] of the upper classes" in England (see Sterling's letter of 9 December, in Tuell 1941: 131–2). And at the same time, one finds Mill sending Sterling Tocqueville's letter itself, that he might understand Tocqueville's rationale behind his stance. In both cases, Mill did not agree with either completely, but tried to make them do justice to each other's point of view. In each case Mill tried to assist that half of truth which was most in need of assistance – to make each side see "the other side of the shield."

Finally, it needs to be stressed that the fact that a great part of Mill's enthusiasm for France waned over the years (and that the things he was prepared to point to as being done better in France were certainly less numerous in the early 1870s than they were in the early 1830s) should not mislead one into underestimating the significance of his whole experience with regard to France and to studying foreign cultures more generally. It should be remembered that, already in 1836, he had identi-fied as one of the benefits to be derived from the study of foreign coun-tries, besides the fact that a people can in that manner be "admonished of what they want, by what others have," that they would at the same time be "made to feel the value of what they have by what others want" (*CW*, XVIII: 94). This benefit appeared to him to be equally important and it would not be claiming too much to say that his conversance with France was decisive both with regard to his own realization of the positive side of certain aspects of the British experience and to his efforts to bring home to his compatriots the concrete value of these specific areas on which some British (or "English," as he called them) traits were worth cherishing and enhancing.

Notwithstanding his considerable disillusionment with French politics, particularly after Louis Napoleon Bonaparte's coup in December 1851,[45] Mill's efforts to mediate between the two peoples in order to promote a better understanding between them, combat prejudices and misconceptions and encourage the exchange of ideas did not cease. Though he was less optimistic about what such efforts could accomplish (see, for example, *CW*, XXXII: 229), he continued to pursue the same aims as best as he could.[46]

7   Reconciling patriotism and cosmopolitanism

[W]e are so constituted that our affections are more drawn to some among mankind than to others, in proportion to their degrees of nearness to us, and our power of being useful to them. . . . Our regards . . . begin with ourselves, and every man is charged primarily with the care of himself. Next come our families, and benefactors, and friends, and after them our country. We can do little for the interest of mankind at large. To this interest, however, all other interests are subordinate. The noblest principle in our nature is the regard to general justice and that good-will which embraces all the world. . . . this . . . cannot be too often repeated. Though our immediate attention must be employed in promoting our own interest and that of our nearest connexions, yet we must remember that a narrower interest ought always to give way to a more extensive interest. *In pursuing particularly the interest of our country we ought to carry our views beyond it.* We should love it ardently but not exclusively. We ought to seek its good, by all the means that our different circumstances and abilities will allow, but at the same time we ought to consider ourselves as citizens of the world, and take care to maintain a just regard to the rights of other countries.

(Emphasis added: Richard Price: Price 1991: 180–1)

Nationalism will not be easily tamed and categorised to fit the prescriptions of moral and political philosophers.

(Anthony D. Smith: Smith (Anthony D.) 1998: 213)

To count people as moral equals is to treat nationality, ethnicity, religion, class, race, and gender as "morally irrelevant" – as irrelevant to that equal standing. Of course, these factors properly enter into our deliberations in many contexts. But the accident of being born a Sri Lankan, or a Jew, or a female . . . is just that – an accident of birth. It is not and should not be taken to be a determinant of moral worth.

(Martha Nussbaum: Nussbaum *et al.* 1996: 133)

We have seen in Chapter 2 that the distinction between "nationalism" and "patriotism" is far from unproblematic and cannot be as neat as scholars such as Viroli suggest.[1] In the same context we saw that, while both Mill and Tocqueville praised "patriotism," they did have fundamental disagreements as to what forms a commendable feeling of patriotism should take. It is therefore time now to address the question of the exact content of the "patriotism" Mill thought worth cherishing and promoting.

As we have seen already, some of Mill's most direct pronouncements on "patriotism" were made by way of commenting on – and commending – Tocqueville's description of the merits of the patriotism of the Americans, a patriotism conceived as enlightened self-interest. As Mill put it in his review of the first volume of the Frenchman's work (1835), following Tocqueville, there were two kinds of patriotism: one "childlike, unreflecting, and almost instinctive love of country, which distinguishes a rude age," or, in other words, "a love of country which takes its rise principally in the unreflecting, disinterested, and undefinable sentiment which attaches the heart of man to the place of his birth." But, once mankind has outgrown the "rude age" and its modes of thinking which gave legitimacy to this unreflecting kind of patriotism: "There is another kind of patriotism, more reasoning than the former; less generous, less ardent, perhaps, but more fruitful and more durable." This feeling was the result of instruction, it grew with the exercise of political rights, "and ends by becoming, in a manner, identified with personal interest":

> The individual comprehends the influence which the good of the country has over his own good; he knows that the law permits him to bear his part in producing that good; and he takes interest in the prosperity of his country, first, as a thing useful to himself, and, next, as in part the result of his own efforts.
> (Mill, "De Tocqueville on Democracy in America [I]," *CW*, XVIII: 86–8)

In modern times, the feelings of a citizen seemed to Tocqueville to be "inseparable from the exercise of political rights."

In the review of the second volume of Tocqueville's *Democracy in America*, Mill took up the same topic again: "M. de Tocqueville is of opinion, that one of the tendencies of a democratic state of society is to make every one, in a manner, retire within himself, and concentrate his interests, wishes, and pursuits within his own business and household." The members of a democratic community were "like the sands of the seashore, each very minute, and no one adhering to any other." In such a state of society, there were "scarcely any ties to connect any two men together, except the common one of country." "*Now, the love of country is not, in large communities, a passion of spontaneous growth.*"[2] It was difficult for the citizen of a democracy, who could not hope to exercise more than the minutest influence over the running of public affairs, to have "the sentiment of patriotism as a living and earnest feeling": "There being no intermediate objects for his attachments to fix upon, they fasten themselves on his own private affairs." Inevitably:

As, therefore, the state of society becomes more democratic, it is more and more necessary to nourish patriotism by artificial means; and of these none are so efficacious as free institutions – a large and frequent intervention of the citizens in the management of public business.

(Emphasis added: *CW*, XVIII: 182)

Commenting on Tocqueville's discussion of "interest" as the main spring of action in a democratic state of society (as opposed to "pride" in an aristocratic state of society) Mill opined: "Neither the one nor the other of these modes of feeling, our author is well aware, constitutes moral excellence." However, "as an auxiliary" to higher principles, or as a substitute for them when they were absent, it was interest, in the French author's opinion, that "will stand the most wear." And Mill quotes Tocqueville again:

The principle of enlightened self-interest is not a lofty one, but it is clear and sure. . . . By its adaptation to human weaknesses, it easily obtains great dominion; nor is its dominion precarious, since it employs self-interest itself to correct self-interest, and uses, to direct the passions, the very instrument that excites them.

(*CW*, XVIII: 184–5)[3]

According to Tocqueville, "the principle of enlightened self-interest" was "the best suited of all philosophical theories to the wants of the men of our time"; and he regarded it as "the chief remaining security against themselves. Towards it, therefore, the minds of the moralists of our age should turn; even should they judge it incomplete, it must nevertheless be adopted as necessary."

Given the above one could argue that one of the things Mill found objectionable about Tocqueville's stance during the diplomatic crisis of

1840 (see above, Chapters 2 and 6) was that he seemed then to promote a kind of patriotism that did not appeal to enlightened self-interest but rather to "pride." This may be so, but it is more likely that what Mill found most frustrating was the kind of things Tocqueville's stance would encourage the French to take pride in (readiness to avenge a – perceived – slight, military prowess, etc.).

Now, in any discussion about patriotism and cosmopolitanism one needs to establish the group to which ultimate allegiance is paid. Mill, like Bentham before him, adopted a cosmopolitan viewpoint when it came to the group that should command people's supreme and ultimate allegiance.[4] It is simply not true that, in the 1820s, "J.S. Mill ... was but one of several progressive intellectuals – Hazlitt, Moore, and Carlyle were others – who ... found themselves drawn over from what their opponents condemned as the ('French') philosophy of cosmopolitanism, universalism, infidelity, protest, scorn, 'negativity,' and the rest, towards the system of mystical and nationalist enthusiasm enunciated by Wordsworth" (Newman 1987: 243–4).[5] Mill adopted and promoted publicly a cosmopolitan viewpoint throughout his life, and his conception of patriotism was meant to serve that cosmopolitan ultimate allegiance.

To say nothing of his almost melodramatic declarations of solidarity with like-minded French political activists and thinkers in the 1830s and 1840s (see Chapter 6), and his frequent invocations of the interests of "Europe" or mankind throughout his works and correspondence, it may be worth quoting what he had to say on the issue of the proper focus of one's allegiance during his mature years, in the 1850s. In "Utility of Religion," Mill declared that it would be wrong to assume that "only the more eminent of our species, in mind and heart," were "capable of identifying their feelings with the entire life of the human race." There was no gainsaying that "[t]his noble capability implies indeed a certain cultivation," but this cultivation was "not superior to that which might be, and certainly will be if human improvement continues, the lot of all" (*CW*, X: 420–1). Mill adduced the degree of selfless dedication and allegiance inspired by patriotism, love of one's country, as a proof of the capacity of human beings, once properly cultivated and educated, to attain to disinterested devotion to the good of the whole humanity:

> Objects far smaller than this ... have been found sufficient to inspire large masses and long successions of mankind with an enthusiasm capable of ruling the conduct, and colouring the whole of life. Rome was to the entire Roman people, for many generations as much a

religion as Jehovah was to the Jews;... When we consider how ardent a sentiment, in favourable circumstances of education, *the love of country* has become, we cannot judge it impossible that *the love of that larger country, the world*, may be nursed into similar strength, both as a source of elevated emotion and as a principle of duty.

(Emphasis added: *CW*, X: 421)[6]

If, then, people could be trained, "not only to believe in theory that the good of their country was an object to which all others ought to yield, but to feel this practically as the grand duty of life, so also may they be made to feel the same absolute obligation towards the universal good." Thus, a morality

> grounded on large and wise views of the good of the whole, neither sacrificing the individual to the aggregate nor the aggregate to the individual, but giving to duty on the one hand and to freedom and spontaneity on the other their proper province, would derive its power in the superior natures from sympathy and benevolence and the passion for ideal excellence: in the inferior, from the same feelings cultivated up to the measure of their capacity, with the superadded force of shame.

This "exalted morality" would not

> depend for its ascendancy on any hope of reward; but the reward which might be looked for, and the thought of which would be a consolation in suffering, and a support in moments of weakness, would not be a problematical future existence, but the approbation, in this, of those whom we respect, and ideally of all those, dead or living, whom we admire or venerate.

(*CW*, X: 420)

Now, "to call these sentiments by the name of morality ... is claiming too little for them." They were "a real religion." For the essence of religion was "the strong and earnest direction of the emotions and desires towards an ideal object, recognized as of the highest excellence, and as rightfully paramount over all selfish objects of desire." This condition was fulfilled by what Mill was proposing, "the Religion of Humanity." He was convinced "that *the sense of unity with mankind, and a deep feeling for the general good*, may be cultivated into a sentiment and a principle capable of fulfilling every important function of religion and itself justly entitled to the name" (emphasis added: *CW*, X: 420–3).[7]

Now, the idea that the possibility of strong attachment to one's country, patriotism, can be used as a proof of the possibility of cosmopolitan "ideal devotion to a greater country, the world," does not come naturally to all minds. Most people tend to see patriotism and cosmopolitanism as antagonistic to each other. For them, there is a direct correlation between loving one's country and giving preference to one's compatriots at the expense of foreigners. This is not how Mill, or some of his contemporaries, saw things. As H.S. Jones has remarked:

> Most nineteenth-century liberals, at least until the last decade or two of the century, were nationalists[8] because they saw the nation as a step away from the particular and towards the universal, and not because they wished to emphasize their own nation's particularity in relation to other nations. The nation was particular in relation to other nations, but was the most general and universal of actual communities.
>
> (Jones 2000: 49)

It is clearly "as a step away from the particular and towards the universal" that Mill approved of attachment to the nation in the sense of the "enlightened patriotism" he had in mind. This is why Mill could say that what he proposed as one of the three conditions of stability in political society, "a strong and active principle of cohesion among the members of the same community or state," was by no means "nationality in the vulgar sense of the term; a senseless antipathy to foreigners; an indifference to the general welfare of the human race, or an unjust preference of the supposed interests of our own country; . . . ," but, rather: "*We mean a principle of sympathy, not of hostility; of union, not of separation*" (emphasis added: *CW*, VIII: 923).[9] Thus Mill, like Jeremy Bentham or Richard Price before him, saw patriotism as commendable only to the extent that it conduced to the interests of the whole of humanity. This is why he distinguished between different kinds of "patriotism" and tried to promote a certain version of "enlightened patriotism."[10]

At the heart of Mill's philosophy was the desire, through education and the cultivation of intellect and feelings, to overcome selfishness. Ultimately he wanted human beings to develop fellow-feelings with the whole of humanity, those living, those dead and those yet to be born. No less than Burke, he wished people to overcome their self-regarding attitudes and identify with a community. However, the community in question was not the little platoon, or the nation, but the whole of humanity. At the same time, accepting that not all humans were as lofty, generous and high-minded natures as he himself, he conceded that, as a step towards the desired expansion of the circle of fellow-feelings toward the whole of humanity, extending them to include a whole nation was a step of progress in the right direction – as long as the way in which they were expanded was not through "nationality in the vulgar sense." Thus, this is a first sense in which his brand of patriotism can be called "cosmopolitan"; he had a clear answer to what Samuel Scheffler has recently called "Nussbaum's dilemma," arising from the extended debate-symposium on the relationship between patriotism and cosmopolitanism that took place in the mid-1990s in the pages of the *Boston Review* (cf. Nussbaum *et al.* 1996; Scheffler 1996; Scheffler 2001: 118–19). As Scheffler put it, Martha Nussbaum

> appears to think that, in trying to justify our particular attachments and loyalties, we are faced with a choice. . . . Either we must argue that devoting special attention to the people we are attached to is an effective way of doing good for humanity at large, or else we must suppose that those people are simply worth more than others.
>
> (Scheffler 2001: 118)[11]

As Scheffler remarked elsewhere on the same issue, Nussbaum asserts that "a recognition of the equal worth of persons is compatible with the idea that 'we can and should give special attention to our own families and to our own ties of religious and national belonging.'" Thus, "Cosmopolitans, she says, believe that 'it is right to give the local an additional measure of concern.' However, she adds, 'the primary reason a cosmopolitan should have for this is not that the local is better *per se*, but rather that it is the only sensible way to do good.'"[12] As Scheffler observes, the implication for the way in which political action should be constrained by the recognition of the equal moral worth of all persons is

> that, in order to do justice to the idea of equal worth we should aim, both in our own conduct and through our political institutions, to do the greatest possible good for humanity as a whole, counting the interests of all human beings equally. We should give special attention to our families or compatriots just in so far as doing that will

best serve the interests of humanity at large. This formulation moves cosmopolitanism in the direction of utilitarianism, a view that Nussbaum does not discuss and to which there are well-known objections.

(Scheffler 1996: 8)[13]

The mention of utilitarianism as underlying Nussbaum's argumentation is useful here, for it is time to return to our British utilitarian philosopher and his position vis-à-vis love of country and universal benevolence.[14] I would argue that Mill's conception of the relationship between obligations to country and obligations to mankind was close to that of Nussbaum, although his emphases were different, as they were bound to be, given the different contexts.[15] Wherever he had to justify his position on any issue related to international relations or the foreign affairs of Britain, Mill consistently used arguments that assumed the good of mankind as a whole as the ultimate criterion of right and wrong. Moreover, he wrote what proved his most enduring piece on international relations theory in order to convince British politicians to adopt the same kind of language and argumentation, and to stop justifying actions or failures to act in terms of British "interests" alone.[16] And even in the cases where he had to defend a position in terms of the stern realities of power and national survival, he never forgot the ultimate justification. Thus – to give just one of innumerable examples – when, in Chapter XVIII of *Representative Government* he argued in favor of the preservation of the bond between Britain and its overseas dominions for as long as it was not too onerous for the inhabitants of the latter, he adduced arguments like the conduciveness of the existence of entities like the British Empire to the preservation of peace between their members, or that the existence of the British Empire "has the advantage, specially valuable at the present time, of adding to the moral influence, and weight in the councils of the world, of the Power which, of all in existence, best understands liberty" (*CW*, XIX: 565). Such argumentation in terms of the long-term interests of humanity abounds also in Mill's writings on the issues of intervention and nonintervention, those of the observance of treaty obligations, and his writings on international issues more generally.

In all this Mill saw no contradiction between obligations to humanity and love of country. Rather, he tried assiduously to promote a certain conception of love of country which was in his eyes not just compatible, but moreover conducive to the welfare of mankind at large. For him this was the only country worth loving, the country which pursued its interests in ways that promoted the interests of mankind as a whole, and this is the England/Britain he consistently tried to inspire in the consciences of his compatriots (in this respect, idealized Britain as he described it – while prescribing it – in the first part of "A Few Words on Non-Intervention" (1859) was the quintessential cosmopolitan nation).

Some distinctions are necessary here. In a number of extremely interesting and important recent works Julia Stapleton has drawn attention to the national-patriotic dimension of the writings of self-appointed defenders and definers of real "liberalism" and "Englishness" such as J.F. Stephen, R.H. Hutton, and other later thinkers. Stapleton has rightly asserted that authors like J.F. Stephen and Hutton saw their own patriotic discourse in direct and explicit opposition to the utterances of people like Mill (and Matthew Arnold, one could add). I have argued elsewhere that it does not follow, however, that this was the only strand of "patriotic" liberal thought at the time in question, or, to put the same thing in another way, it does not follow that Stephen and Hutton were right in attributing lack of patriotism to Mill and Arnold (Varouxakis 2002: Chapter 1).

A clear distinction should be made between at least two concepts of patriotism during Mill's time. Stapleton has recently argued: "Above all, the growth of English national consciousness after 1850 took place in reaction to the perceived *absence* of *patriotism of any description*[17] among the forces of British radicalism." She went on to comment that: "This perception was not entirely groundless. The English/British *patria* appeared in much radical discourse on citizenship only as an object of abuse." Along with Richard Cobden and John Bright, she included Mill among the radicals who were justly seen as unpatriotic. Although one could find several striking texts written by Mill, published during his time, and read by his critics, in which he tried to shame his compatriots into improving themselves, this does not prove lack of patriotism on his behalf; unless one means by "patriotism" the "my country right or wrong" attitude. Now, apparently this is what J.F. Stephen had in mind when he was identifying "the chief shortcoming of his master turned adversary [Mill] as a lamentable want of patriotism" (Stapleton 2000: 249).[18] Similarly, James Fitzjames's brother, Leslie Stephen, in his volume on J.S. Mill (and obviously including Bentham and James Mill in the observation), opined: "Patriotism, indeed, was scarcely held to be a virtue by the Utilitarians. It meant for them the state of mind of the country squire or his hanger-on the parson; and is generally mentioned as giving a sufficient explanation of unreasoning prejudice."[19] However, Mill spoke, throughout his life and on all sorts of occasions, in favour of "patriotism," of "*patriotisme éclairé*,"[20] or "a strong and active principle of cohesion among the members of the same community or state," as he put it in the later editions of "Coleridge" and *A System of Logic* (*CW*, X: 134–5; *CW*, VIII: 923). It is far from true that Mill was one of the radicals who purportedly ignored or were hostile to "patriotism." It is rather the case that Mill would have no truck with a certain conception of patriotism, very widespread in his time, which saw patriotism as consisting of "a cherishing of bad peculiarities because they are national or a refusal to adopt what has been found good by other countries." This is what he called "nationality in the vulgar sense of the term" (*CW*, VIII: 923; *CW*, X: 135). This is the conception of "patriotism" which the Utilitarians "scarcely held to be a virtue," this is what "meant for them the state of mind of the country squire or his hanger-on the parson." When contemporaries accused Mill (or Arnold) of anti-patriotism or un-English sentiments, it was because Mill (like Arnold) was militantly hostile to all manifestations of feelings and attitudes reflecting such a conception of "patriotism."

It was this, the flag-waving conception of patriotism, that Mill (as well as Bentham and Matthew Arnold) held in profound contempt. To give but a couple of examples, J.F. Stephen wrote in *Liberty, Equality, Fraternity*: "I do not envy the Englishman whose heart does not beat high as he looks at the scarred and shattered walls of Delhi or at the union jack flying from the fort at Lahore."[21] And it was this, their shared conception of "patriotism," that led J.F. Stephen, despite his dislike of popular literature, to make an exception and praise Macaulay, because, as his brother Leslie has put it, "he strongly sympathised with the patriotism represented by Macaulay."[22] Now, it was exactly this that Mill (as well as Matthew Arnold and John Morley) loathed in Macaulay, that his *History of England* "ministers to English conceit."[23] Ministering to English conceit, or giving encouragement to "the already ample self-conceit of John Bull" (*CW*, XXV: 1096) was *not* what a patriot, a man or woman who loved their country, should be doing, according to Mill. Those who loved their country should aim to make it *deserve* to be highly thought of, because of its contributions to the well-being and civilization of mankind. To make their country deserve to be considered great, patriots should strive always to improve it and make it better, for its own sake and for that of mankind. As part of performing this task, patriots should offer their countrymen what they most needed. In smug, ethnocentric, self-congratulating post-1815 Britain, this did not mean reinforcing their self-conceit. It was from a very young age that Mill had decided what loving one's country meant and what it did not mean. Here is what he had to say on these issues in the review article "Modern French Historical Works" at the age of twenty, in 1826,[24] (talking of the reactions in France of those who were attacking historian J.P. Dulaure for his exposure of French vices):

> We own that we are in general predisposed in favour of a man whom we hear accused by a certain class of politicians of being an *enemy to his country*. We at once conclude, that he has either actually rendered, or shown himself disposed to render, some signal service to his country. We conclude, either that he has had discernment to see, and courage to point out, something in his own that stands in need of amendment, or something in another country which it would be for the advantage of his own to imitate; *or that he loved his country well enough to wish it free from that greatest of misfortunes, the misfortune of being successful in an unjust cause;*[25] or . . . that he has given his countrymen to know, that they once had vices or follies which they have since corrected, or (what is worse still), which they have yet to correct. Whoever is guilty of any of these crimes in this country, is a fortunate man if he escapes being accused of *un-English* feelings. This is the epithet which we observe to be appropriated to those, whose wish is that their country should *deserve* to be thought well of. The man of *English* feelings is the man whose wish is, that his country should *be* thought well of; and, above all, should think well of itself, peculiarly in those points wherein it deserves the least. The modern English version of the maxim *Spartam nactus es, hanc exorna*, may be given thus – England is your country, be sure to praise it lustily. *This sort of patriotism*[26] is, it would appear, no less in request with certain persons in France. . . . Accordingly, M. Dulaure's bold exposure of the vices and follies of his countrymen in the olden time, has been thought by many persons extremely *un-French*.[27]

One could see this as a pre-emptive reply, as it were, to J.F. Stephen and to all others who were to criticize Mill subsequently on this count, and it illustrates his clear understanding and articulation of two distinct conceptions, two sorts of "patriotism".

In his own eyes, Mill was consciously and deliberately engaged in a profoundly patriotic exercise, which he believed would benefit the "English nation" far more than the John Bull versions of patriotism associated with his critics or targets such as J.F. Stephen – while, at the same time, it would make the English nation more useful to the general welfare of humanity.

Now, besides its cosmopolitan ultimate aim, what distinguishes Mill's (and Arnold's) version of patriotism is its cosmopolitan language and orientation. Instead of ignoring what the rest of Europe and the world thought of Britain, as most other Victorian thinkers did, to say nothing of the British public a large,[28] Mill believed that it was part of being a good patriot to strive to improve one's country's image abroad, to make its voice heard and respected, and, moreover, to have one's country highly regarded abroad for commendable achievements, for contributions to the common fund of civilization, which other nations could be reasonably expected to recognize as well. Mill seems to have thought that a good way of inculcating in the British people the right kind of patriotism, the patriotism that feeds on the right feelings and aspires to the right sort of collective distinction and greatness, was to make them aware of, and sensitive to, the judgments of (to use two of Bentham's coinages at once) an international "tribunal of public opinion." This is what emerges, for example, from Mill's reaction to Tocqueville's stance during the Franco-British crisis, discussed in Chapter 2. What comes out of the Mill-Tocqueville debate[29] is that Mill's recipe is more compatible with a cosmopolitan outlook which, at the same time, does not underestimate the importance of patriotic attachments but rather tries to direct them to commendable directions. What Mill proposed – not only in this debate, by implication, but also in a great variety of writings – was a patriotism that promoted national solidarity and cohesion without ever indulging in the kind of jingoism to which he thought Tocqueville and his fellow-Frenchmen were succumbing in 1840. This sounds lofty, but how can one achieve it?

A crucial factor that differentiates Mill's version of patriotism from other theories purporting to combine attachment to both cosmopolitanism and patriotism is that Mill, though he was the rationalist heir of the Enlightenment *par excellence* in so many respects, did recognize the importance of a feeling of pride in one's nation and its achievements. Instead of dismissing national pride of any sort as irrational and taking the moral high ground as so many liberal cosmopolitan theorists do, Mill proposed that one should direct one's attention to cultivating the right kind of pride, pride in the right qualities and achievements. Mill consistently promoted a version of patriotism that was feeding on trying to make sure that one can be proud of what one's nation has done and is doing for the welfare of the whole of humanity. It is in this sense that patriotism can be "cosmopolitan." This cosmopolitanism does not consist in shunning nations and fatherlands, but rather in working towards shaping the behavior of one's nation in such a way that it contributes as much as possible to the welfare, "civilization," peace, etc. of the whole of humanity, and one can then be accordingly proud of such contributions. Cosmopolitanism can mean all sorts of things,[30] and it should be obvious by now why this is a peculiar version of cosmopolitanism. Mill's attitude was not compatible with, for example the following use of the term:

> Understood as a fundamental devotion to the interests of humanity as a whole, cosmopolitanism has often seemed to claim universality by virtue of its independence, its detachment from the bonds, commitments, and affiliations that constrain ordinary nation-bound lives. It has seemed to be a luxuriously free-floating view from above.
>
> (Robbins 1998a: 1)

Mill's was a different conception of cosmopolitanism, for it tried to orientate the "national mind" itself to a cosmopolitan outlook, rather than to detach individuals from their nation-bound lives. Mill wanted to use the nation and the ties it generated in the interests of "the improvement of mankind."[31] If individuals could not be induced to pursue the good of the whole of mankind directly, then one way to convince them to act in the interests of mankind is to give them incentives they might be more amenable to. Now, national pride being, in Mill's time (and, it seems, ours) incomparably more likely to serve as an incentive for a much greater number of individuals than love of that greater country, the world (which it was Mill's ultimate aim should become the feeling inculcated in everybody eventually), Mill proposed – and, especially, practised – strategies of using that more limited selfless incentive to promote the good of humanity.

For these reasons, Mill would have agreed with Matthew Arnold that national greatness consists in being admired and loved by the rest of the world (see Arnold 1960–77, V: 96–7).[32] While J.F. Stephen was boasting that foreigners were in no position to judge the achievements of England and very few Englishman cared or should care what foreigners thought of them (Stephen 1866a: 162), Mill (like Arnold) was asking his compatriots to work hard towards deserving the distinct position they claimed for themselves and towards achieving proofs of their greatness in a commonly held (pan-European or pan-Western) system of values and criteria. It is obvious that there is a great difference here between people like J.F. Stephen, on the one hand, and Mill (as well as Arnold, or Bentham) on the other. Whereas the latter went out of their way to elevate the opinion of foreigners (or, at any rate, "civilized," continental European foreigners) as one of the major concerns of the English nation and its governments, Stephen dismissed this criterion and argument as squarely and as explicitly as one could.[33]

Besides the indirect exposition of his opinion on how a nation should entertain and cultivate the "desire to shine in the eyes of foreigners and to be highly esteemed by them" in his debate with Tocqueville (see Chapter 2), it is worth reminding ourselves in this connection that Mill had offered another striking account of his views on these matters in "A Few Words on Non-Intervention" (*CW*, XXI: 109–24). In some sense, this article alone (published in *Fraser's Magazine* in December 1859) should have acquitted Mill from any charges of lack of patriotism, for its first half was, among other things, a panegyric of the even-handedness and morality of England's foreign policy (the opening sentences are striking in this respect). But it was more than that. In this article (which, characteristically, Mill sent to French periodicals in order to have it reviewed in France),[34] one of his intentions was to refute the all but universal belief, on the part of Continental thinkers and public, that British foreign policy was quintessentially selfish and hypocritical,[35] and to convince foreigners that this was far from being the case. But, much more importantly, Mill was using the universally negative image of Britain abroad in order to caution and shame his fellow-countrymen. His main aim was to caution British statesmen against using a discourse (justification of acts or failures to act purely on grounds of national interest) which gave rise to foreign misperceptions about English selfishness. It was "foolish attempting to despise all this": "Nations, like individuals, ought to suspect some fault in themselves when they find they are generally worse thought of than they think they deserve; and they may well know that they are somehow in fault when almost everybody but themselves thinks them crafty and hypocritical" (*CW*, XXI: 112).[36]

An analogy that can be useful in conceptualizing what I mean here by cosmopolitan language, orientation, discourse, and criteria of excellence is provided by Mill's rationale for his rejection of the secret ballot. He wanted people to vote openly in order for them to feel constrained to make electoral choices which they would be able to justify publicly in front of their fellow-constituents, choices therefore for which they could invoke reasons based on common interests and shared principles. If one applies this idea to the international arena, nations would have to "prove" their greatness by invoking what they were contributing to the common fund of humanity, to civilization, and what they were excelling in according to commonly accepted criteria. Thus, the hope was that, like voters, so nations, would shy away from behaviors they would not be able to justify in terms of criteria and principles referring to the common interests of mankind.

There is one more manifestation of this cosmopolitan orientation of the patriotism Mill wanted to inculcate which is worth noting here. In his *Inaugural Address Delivered to the University of St. Andrews* (1867) he included in the ideal curriculum he was proposing the study of International Law, which he "decidedly" thought "should be taught in all universities, and should form part of all liberal education":

> The need of it is far from being limited to diplomatists and lawyers; it extends to every citizen.... Since every country stands in numerous and various relations with the other countries of the world, and many, our own among the number, exercise actual authority over some of these, a knowledge of the established rules of international morality is essential to the duty of every nation, and therefore of every person in it who helps to make up the nation, and whose voice and feeling form a part of what is called public opinion. Let not any one pacify his conscience by the delusion that he can do no harm if he takes no part, and forms no opinion. Bad men need nothing more to compass their ends, than that good men should look on and do nothing. He is not a good man who, without a protest, allows wrong to be committed in his name, and with the means which he helps to supply, because he will not trouble himself to use his mind on the subject. It depends on the habit of attending to and looking into public transactions, and on the degree of information and solid judgment respecting them that exists in the community, whether the conduct of the nation as a nation, both within itself and towards others, shall be selfish, corrupt, and tyrannical, or rational and enlightened, just and noble.
>
> (*CW*, XXI: 246–7)

This is impressive indeed: the thinker who is associated (wrongly)[37] with so-called elitism, asserts that as complex an area of policy as foreign and international policy should be under the close scrutiny of the citizens and that it is a gross dereliction of duty if citizens fail to scrutinize their country's foreign policy and international comportment using as an excuse that international law is too complicated to understand. This is a very demanding conception of citizenship and a very lofty and high-minded perception of what constitutes a good citizen and a good patriot. Note also that this is not the – supposedly – youthful starry-eyed Mill, but the mature Mill.[38]

A final question that may need to be addressed in relation to Mill's conception of patriotism is that raised by the debates among contemporary political theorists disagreeing whether the best way to deal with the threat and challenge of nationalism is to abandon nationhood and adopt instead a form of "new patriotism" (either "republican patriotism" or cosmopolitan "constitutional patriotism") or, alternatively, to stick with nationhood but try to redefine and re-imagine national identities in such ways as for them to be commendable and compatible with liberal democratic values (Canovan 2000). I would argue that if we wish to place Mill in this debate then we have to accept that he tried to do both at the same time. When, in works like "A Few Words on Non-intervention" he tried to convince his compatriots that the enlightened, moral and even-handed foreign policy he was describing (while rather prescribing) was quintessentially English, Mill was trying to cajole them into adopting what he was telling them was already the "English" thing to do. In such works, therefore, Mill was defining or redefining English (or British)[39] national identity to suit his high-minded and enlightened conception of how a nation should comport itself in the international arena. At the same time, however, in various instances Mill seems to have gone a long way towards proposing a conception of universalist cosmopolitan patriotism. It may be fitting to conclude with a text that has been more often quoted than analysed.

In the passage that occurs both in his "Coleridge" (1840: *CW*, X: 134–5) and in his 1843 *System of Logic* (Book VI, Chapter 10: *CW*, VIII: 923) – quoted by, among others, Maurizio Viroli and John Gray as purportedly proving their respective points[40] – Mill effected some changes from the earlier to the later editions that deserve more attention than they have received. While in the earliest version (1840) Mill specified as one of the three conditions of stability in political society "a strong and active *principle of nationality*," in later editions of the text he changed this into: "a strong and active *principle of cohesion among the members of the same community or state*" (emphases added: *CW*, X: 134–5). As if this was not sufficient, in the lines immediately following the above, Mill also changed the original text from: "We need scarcely say that we do not mean a senseless antipathy to foreigners..." into: "We need scarcely say that we do not mean *nationality in the vulgar sense of the term*;[41] a senseless antipathy to foreigners...." Moreover, in the later editions he also added, immediately following this, that he did not mean: "an indifference to the general welfare of the human race, or an unjust preference of the supposed interest of our own country;" (*CW*, X: 135). Although it has escaped attention, the implication is clear: while in the early 1840s Mill was proposing "a strong and active *principle of nationality*" as one of the *sine qua non* of stability in political society, in later editions (1859 and 1867) he did not name what he said was needed "nationality," but rather "a strong and active *principle of cohesion among the members of the same community or state*." And at the same time, he described all the deplorable manifestations of nationalist feeling that he went on to enumerate, as "nationality in the vulgar sense of the term."

Given the topic of this chapter, and the significance of this text as somehow a definition by Mill of what he meant by patriotism (or, as he put it on this occasion, trying to be more precise, "a strong and active principle of cohesion among the members of the same community or state") and what he did not, it may be worth quoting again and using by way of conclusion. The text goes as follows, in the later version:

> We need scarcely say that we do not mean nationality in the vulgar sense of the term; a senseless antipathy to foreigners; an indifference to the general welfare of the human race, or an unjust preference of the supposed interests of our own country; a cherishing of bad peculiarities because they are national or a refusal to adopt what has been found good by other countries.... We mean a principle of sympathy, not of hostility; of union, not of separation. We mean a feeling of common interest among those who live under the same government, and are contained within the same natural or historical boundaries. We mean, that one part of the community shall not consider themselves as foreigners with regard to another part; that they shall cherish the tie which holds them together; shall feel that they are one people, that their lot is cast together ... and that they cannot selfishly free themselves from their share of any common inconvenience by severing the connexion.
>
> (*Logic, CW*, VIII: 923; "Coleridge," *CW*, X: 135–6)

Notes

1 Introduction

1 Mill did not use the word "nationalism" itself; instead, like his contemporaries, he talked of "nationality" and of "patriotism"; and he had a compulsive interest in the concept of "national character" and, more concretely, in the "English national character." For a discussion of the various meanings of "nationality" and of "patriotism" in the nineteenth and twentieth centuries, see Varouxakis 2001a and Varouxakis 2001b.

2 According to Hobhouse, "in his single person he [Mill] spans the interval between the old and the new Liberalism" (Hobhouse 1994: 51). Cf. Freeden 1996: 141–77, 276; Parekh 1994.

3 Collini 1991: 311–41. Cf. Williams 1995; Rees 1956. As one of the pioneers of the study of nationalism put it: "His work and the progress of time combined in changing the creed of a fighting sect into a representative manifestation of the national mind. After John Stuart Mill and through him liberalism in the broad sense of the word became the common basis of all English parties" (Kohn 1946: 19). For two recent works asserting the importance of Mill not only for the historical development of liberalism – which almost nobody disputes – but also as a guide and contributor to contemporary political and moral theorizing, see Eisenach 1998; Stafford 1998.

4 "The discussion of this crucial problem has just commenced."

5 Besides an impressive number of articles in periodicals and collective volumes, book-length contributions around the time in question were: Tamir 1993; Miller 1995; Viroli 1995. Cf. the collective volume by Martha Nussbaum with a great number of respondents in: Nussbaum *et al.* 1996. For a brief but cogent discussion of the background of this academic outpouring, see Benner 1997: 190–2, 203–4. The interest in such issues seems to be increasing since the mid-1990s; to mention but a few examples: Gilbert 1998; Beiner 1999; Poole 1999; Miller 2000; Parekh 2000; Barry 2001; Scheffler 2001. One can add as relevant to this climate the expanded, book-length edition of John Rawls' earlier lecture on "The Law of Peoples": Rawls 1999.

6 In the case of France see the recent collective volumes and special issues in periodicals of political philosophy: *La Pensée politique*, special issue: "La Nation," 1996; *Philosophie politique: Revue internationale de Philosophie politique*, No. 8, special issue: "La Nation," 1997; Wieviorka 1997; Kymlicka and Mesure 2000.

7 Cf. Burrow 1981.

8 Kohn 1944; Plamenatz 1976. For a French version of a binary distinction, see Winock 1982.

9 I will argue further on that Acton's disagreement with Mill has been overplayed by

subsequent commentators, and that Acton and Mill were closer to each other than existing scholarship would have one believe.

10 See, for the most recent examples: Hall 2001: 173, 175–6; Moore 2001: 3, 7, 17. Cf. Kymlicka's claims for Mill's influence on subsequent liberal but also socialist thought, from Ernest Barker in the inter-war period through late-twentieth-century American liberals to David Miller's social-democratic argument for nationality as a prerequisite for egalitarian justice (the claim that "egalitarian justice is only possible if citizens are bound to each other by 'common ties,' by a strong sense of 'common membership' and 'common identity' which 'must exist at a national level' " – which, Kymlicka claims, "is yet another version of Mill's position"); see Kymlicka 1995a: 53, 72–3, 209 n.14. Mill is still being blamed, among other things, for the results of Woodrow Wilson's peace settlement in 1919, and the subsequent World War II, to the more recent events in Yugoslavia. A recent such attribution of blame has come from Lord Acton's latest biographer (Hill 2000: 413).

11 Cf. Fred Rosen's criticisms of Kedourie's notion of a "Whig theory of nationality" in Rosen 1997.

12 Hereafter: *Representative Government*.

13 Cf. Ronald Beiner's recent claim that "the Mill–Acton debate" constitutes one of the very few existing "significant texts in the history of modern political thought that one must read in order to think normatively about nationalism," one of the scarce "intellectual landmarks in the history of modern thought"; the others he mentions are "the writings of Herder," "Fichte's *Addresses to the German Nation*," "Renan's famous lecture" and "Julien Benda's *The Treason of the Intellectuals*" (Beiner 1999: 3). Cf. Jones 2000: 62–3; Miller (David) 2000: 34.

14 For specimens of Bagehot's views (strikingly echoing those of Mill in *Representative Government*), see "The Meaning and the Value of the Limits of the Principle of Nationalities" (1864): Bagehot 1965–86, VIII: 149–53; "The Gains of the World by the Two Last Wars in Europe" (1866): Bagehot 1965–86, VIII: 154–60; cf. Bagehot 1965–86, VIII: 190. As far as Acton's later views are concerned, Fasnacht has observed that "The best clue to Acton's mature views on nationality is his support of Home Rule for Ireland" (Fasnacht 1952: 182, n.3).

15 This was very far from true in the case of Mill: he never saw Russia as "civilized," and as one of "the carriers of historical development," but rather as barbarian to such an extent that he believed the rest of Europe should prevent even by arms the absorption of any smaller, more "civilized" nationalities by the Russian Empire. This is one of the many instances where Kymlicka misunderstands Mill's position: for Mill it was *not* a matter of size.

16 According to Kymlicka, "This debate [between Mill and Acton] was revisited by British liberals during and after World War I. For example, Alfred Zimmern defended Acton's claim that a multination state checks the abuse of state power (Zimmern 1918), while Ernest Barker defended Mill's belief that a nation-state can best sustain free institutions (Barker 1948)" (Kymlicka 1995a: 53).

17 Kymlicka also noted: "Mill also opposed the attempts of the Québécois to maintain a distinct francophone society in Canada, and encouraged their assimilation into the more 'civilized' English culture." Kymlicka gives reference to Parekh 1994 for evidence (Kymlicka 1995b: 22–3, n.8). We will see further on that Parekh's views misrepresent Mill's attitude to a significant extent. For another instance where Kymlicka is misled into misrepresenting Mill's thought by following Parekh, see Kymlicka 1995a: 207, n.4.

18 We will see (particularly in Chapters 6 and 7) that Mill may be blamed for many things, but ethnocentrism should be very low in the list.

19 See, for one example among many, in Chapter XVI of *Representative Government* itself: *CW*, XIX: 549–50. For Matthew Arnold's similar attitude see Pecora 1997–8; for Bagehot's emphatic assertion of the advantages of the *"mixture of races"* (emphasis in original) see Bagehot 1965–86, VII: 57; Bagehot 1965–86, VIII: 187–91. For more on this issue see Varouxakis 2002: Chapter 4.

20 Even this concession is an understatement, given the extent of Mill's deliberate and sustained efforts to discredit and denounce his contemporaries' facile racial explanations (see below, Chapter 3).

21 Parekh offers a footnote at this point: "Among the Europeans, Mill did not think much of the 'bureaucracy-ridden nations of the continent. . . .' In his view the English were the only people likely to 'do most to make the world better.' On them lies 'the best hope' for human progress." This comment clearly implies a degree of ethnocentrism and Anglocentrism in Mill's thought which is very unfair to his strenuous efforts to avoid ethnocentrism both for himself and for his compatriots. The quotations Parekh offers are taken out of context, and Mill's relationship with the nations of the Continent, and particularly the one implied here, France, was a very complex and fruitful one (see Varouxakis 2002).

22 Note that here Mill had written "nations," not "states." The quotation from Mill is from *On Liberty* (*CW*, XVIII: 273–4)

23 There is no need to remind anyone how highly Mill thought of the achievements in civilization of the ancient Greeks, for example.

24 Cf. Varouxakis 1999: 296–305.

25 Mill did not say they had a right, he only said it was desirable and in the interests of the more backward group.

26 Both here and in Parekh 2000, Parekh misquotes Mill by quoting "enlightened liberty"; Mill wrote "enlightened liberality": *CW*, XIX: 563.

27 Cf. Coupland 1945; Martin 1972: 42–74.

28 "Report on the Affairs of British North America, from the Earl of Durham," *Parliamentary Papers*, 1839, XVII.

29 See "Radical Party and Canada: Lord Durham and the Canadians" (January 1838), *CW*, VI: 405–35; "Lord Durham and His Assailants" (August 1838), *CW*, VI: 437–43; "Lord Durham's Return" (December 1838), *CW*, VI: 445–64.

30 Emphasis added. Parekh wrote this in reference to Mill's recommendations for the Welsh and the Scottish Highlanders, but he implies the same in the case of the French Canadians. I argue that Mill did not mean forcing the "English" *way of life* either on the French Canadians or on Britain's "Celtic fringes."

31 For more on these disagreements and on the whole issue of Mill's relationship with India, see particularly Zastoupil 1994. Cf. Brady 1977: xlvi–li. Cf. also Rosen 1999.

32 He used the term "nationality" in at least two senses: first, to designate a group of people constituting a nation; and, second, to designate what is called today "nationalism" (nationalist feeling or attachment). For more on the meaning of "nationality" in the nineteenth century, see Varouxakis 2001b.

33 In this wish Mill was at one with other thinkers, most notably Matthew Arnold (Varouxakis 2002).

34 For works stressing the overwhelming significance of Mill's commitment to rationality see Jones 1992; Skorupski 1989.

35 For a recent work asserting that Mill had "consciously situated himself right at the boundaries of what is today the liberal–communitarian divide – at the crossroads where abstract rights claims meet shared identities and common experiences," see Eisenach 1998: 4–5. According to Eisenach.

In a language much older than his own, Mill struggled with reconciling the logic of "contract" with the meaning of "birth-right." This powerful defender of individuality and rights is also a historically sophisticated analyst of the moral, psychological, and national/cultural resources necessary for the recognition and defense of these rights.

(Eisenach 1998: 5)

2 "A liberal descent"?

1 The book that made the term "liberal nationalism" fashionable among English-speaking political theorists and sparked off an animated debate that is still going on, was Yael Tamir's *Liberal Nationalism* (Tamir 1993). In that book there is no mention at all of the classic work in the older literature on nationalism where "liberal nationalism" appears prominently, in Hayes' fivefold classification of nationalism that was received as authoritative for decades after its appearance (see Hayes 1931). There is no mention of this classification in any of the other major works by political theorists in the second part of the 1990s. Hayes had presented British political and legal thinker Jeremy Bentham as the major exponent of what he had identified as "liberal nationalism." Cf. Kayser 1932.

2 On "nationality" – and specifically on the attribution of the notion to J.S. Mill – see Miller 1995: 10. On the distinction between "nationalism" and "patriotism," see Viroli 1995.

3 The most cogent refutation seems to me to be that by Erica Benner in her brilliant review article on Viroli's *For Love of Country* and Miller's *On Nationality*: see Benner 1997. See also O'Leary 1996; Vincent 1997.

4 A number of articles on specific thinkers have shown, in the case of each of these thinkers respectively, the tensions between liberalism and support for nationalism. See, in particular: Rosen 1997: 177–88 (focusing on Jeremy Bentham and several Benthamites, but also with broader implications); Jennings 1991: 497–514; cf. Rosen 1992; Haddock 1999: 313–36. Although a Tocqueville scholar has written on these issues in the case of Tocqueville, she does not address the tensions in question: Mélonio 1991: 17. Thus, the cases of Tocqueville and Mill and what they reveal with regard to these tensions will have to be discussed in this chapter.

5 Cf. Gray 1983: 213–15.

6 I use the phrase "liberal descent" as an allusion to John Burrow's classic study of that title (Burrow 1981).

7 *The Guardian Higher*, 20 January 1998, p. iii. In the same strain, in an essay in the *New Statesman*, Gray outlines what he calls "an altogether different liberal tradition – the tradition of social liberalism that runs from John Stuart Mill through L.T. Hobhouse and T.H. Green to Maynard Keynes, James Meade and Isaiah Berlin" (Gray 1998). On Gray's intellectual-political itinerary until about the time when he decided to place himself in the tradition described above, see Colls 1998. Cf. Gamble 1999.

8 J.S. Mill, *A System of Logic* (first edition: 1843), Book VI, Chapter x. Cf. *CW*, X: 134–5 ("Coleridge" (1840)). For more on this passage, see *infra*, Chapter 7.

9 Emphasis added.

10 Cf. Gray 1995: 100.

11 Recently David Miller turned to this debate once more in order to argue that, when all is said and done, it is Mill's view that was right, rather than Acton's. He did so at a paper entitled "Nationality and Political Liberty," delivered at the Seventh Annual Conference of the Association for the Study of Ethnicity and Nationalism [ASEN], LSE, 18 April 1997. Cf. Miller (David) 2000: 34.

12 See more on the context and the broader issues involved in this disagreement in Chapter 6.

13 For a short but extremely sharp comment on Tocqueville's rationale for his stance on these issues, see Tombs 1997: 325. For criticisms of Tocqueville's "blindness" to national differences by some of his contemporaries, see Mélonio 1993: 106–7.

14 For a succinct analysis of Tocqueville's account of the new, democratic, social state and its repercussions for politics and culture, see Manent 1996.

15 The crisis was over the Near East, where France's *protégé*, the Pasha of Egypt, Mehemet Ali, had made moves which put in danger the integrity or even the very existence of the Ottoman Empire (under whose suzerainty he held his Egyptian dominions). What brought matters to a head, and sparked off a crisis that threatened to cause a war between France and Britain, was the treaty of 15 July 1840 concluded between Britain, Russia, Austria and Prussia, stipulating that the Pasha should evacuate Syria or face concerted action against him by these powers. The exclusion of France from this treaty, which was not known in Paris before 26 July, was received by the French press as a humiliating act against France and there was a general outcry for war. See Lawlor 1959: 43–9.

16 See Tocqueville 1985: 136–8, 142–6, 149–52. See also A. de Tocqueville, *Correspondance Anglaise: Correspondance d'Alexis de Tocqueville avec Henry Reeve et John Stuart Mill*, in Tocqueville 1951– (*Œuvres Complètes*), VI, 1: 330–1.

17 Cf. another Frenchman's famous pronouncement, concluding his well-known passage describing his "certain idea of France": "Bref la France ne peut être la France sans la grandeur": Charles de Gaulle, *Mémoires de guerre*.

18 Cf. Jeremy Bentham's statements: "national honour consists in justice"; and: "the glory of being able to hit the hardest blow ought to be left to schoolboys"; quoted in Conway 1989: 93.

19 See in Chapter 6.

20 Cf. Conor Cruise O'Brien's definition of nationalism: "strong national emotion, combined with a strong tendency to exalt the idea of the nation above all other ideas" (O'Brien 1988: 18). If we were to follow strictly such a definition, it would be misleading to call Tocqueville a nationalist. It is one thing to say that the nation is the supreme and paramount value and another to say: let us cultivate solidarity and social feelings, if need be, by myths, by using irrational or sentimental attachments, or even by condoning or actively seeking war. (Cf. Drescher 1964: 154: "the Eastern crisis was the occasion for, rather than the cause of, Tocqueville's appeal for a bold foreign policy.") The danger is, of course, that if you go down that path, you may end up, unwittingly, elevating the nation and its perceived pride or honour as the supreme value.

21 Cf. Kelly 1992: 6.

22 Mill, "De Tocqueville on Democracy in America I," *CW*, XVIII: 86–9. Tocqueville's text quoted and commented upon by Mill can be found in Tocqueville 1994: 235–7. See also Mill, "De Tocqueville on Democracy in America II," *CW*, XVIII: 182–3.

23 If I understand her correctly, this is the attitude towards nationalism proposed by Benner.

24 Cf. Habermas 1995. Political theorists tend to associate the notion of "constitutional patriotism" (*Verfassungspatriotismus*) with Habermas in particular, but the term was coined by Dolf Sternberger, in his: "Verfassungspatriotismus" (Sternberger 1982). For more on "constitutional patriotism" see Chapter 7.

An earlier version of this chapter has been given as a paper at the 1998 Annual Conference of the Political Studies Association of the UK and printed in the Conference proceedings (*Contemporary Political Studies* 1998, ed. by Andrew Dobson and Jeffrey Stanyer, pp. 1085–96).

3 Nations and nationhood I

1 See Bolt 1971, *passim*; Watson 1973: 198–212; Rich 1994: 779; Varouxakis 2002 (Chapter 4).

2 See, for instance, George W. Stocking's remarks on Leslie Stephen's use of "race" (Stocking 1987: 138–9). For the confusion and imprecision characterizing the use of the type of race not just in common discourse, but also among specialists, see Banton 1987: xii–xv, 29–32.

3 On the question of race in French historiography at this time, see Crossley 1993: 56–7, 90–2.

4 Bentham had mentioned "*race* or *lineage*" as one of the many "circumstances influencing sensibility" (Bentham 1996: 67); another of these circumstances was climate.

5 Steele's statement quoted above was preceded by the remark that "Mill was sometimes critical of the doctrine, common in his day, that certain races or peoples were inferior to others in their aptitude for free and progressive institutions: but only when he thought it was being strained, and used in too deterministic a fashion" (Steele 1970: 435). I will try to show in the following pages that, given the extent to which Mill fought against racial determinism, both with regard to Mill's reaction to racial theories in general and to their application to the case of the Irish in particular, Steele's concession is an understatement.

6 See the passage quoted in the (second) epigraph to this chapter.

7 Cf. Parekh 1994.

8 The passage quoted is to be found in *CW*, XIII: 404.

9 The fact that Mill went on to ascribe to the peoples of the south of Europe (as opposed to those of the north) characteristics similar to those he agreed with d'Eichthal in attributing to the black race (as opposed to the whole of the white race) goes some way towards suggesting that he was not speaking in strictly biological terms.

10 D'Eichthal had adduced the researches of W.-F. Edwards and E. Geoffroy Saint-Hilaire (Eichthal and Urbain 1839: 15). Both were well known scientists. Edwards was one of the major exponents of theories asserting the importance of race in history and society (see Banton 1987: xiii, 31).

11 On 25 December 1840, after having received one more of d'Eichthal's ethnological works, Mill wrote to him: "You are very usefully employed in throwing light on these dark subjects – the whole subject of the races of man, their characteristics and the laws of their fusion is more important than it was ever considered till late and it is now quite *a [sic] l'ordre du jour* and labour bestowed upon it is therefore not lost even for immediate practical ends" (*CW*, XIII: 456). By this time d'Eichthal had become a leading member of the *Société ethnologique* which was presided over by W.-F. Edwards (Ratcliffe 1977: 151).

12 Cf. Crossley 1993: 205–6.

13 Cf. Guizot's explanation of the peculiarities of English history in terms of the circumstances of the Norman conquest, translated and endorsed by Mill in: J.S. Mill, "Guizot's Essays and Lectures on History" (*CW*, XX: 291–2); see also: Barzun 1941: 318–29; Crossley 1993: 91–3.

14 "that of attributing all variations in the character of peoples and individuals to indelible natural differences, without asking oneself whether the influences of education and of the social and political environment do not offer a sufficient explanation."

15 "but as regards their predilection for or against centralization, I would ask you whether the differences in the historical development of France and England, of which you have given such a true and instructive outline, do not alone suffice as an explanation."

16 In a letter to Charles Wentworth Dilke, referring to the latter's book *Greater Britain: a Record of Travel in English-speaking countries during 1866 and 1867* (1868), Mill's only criticism "of a somewhat broader character" was "that (in speaking of the physical and moral characteristics of the populations descended from the English) you sometimes express yourself almost as if there were no sources of national character but race and climate," while Mill himself believed "the good and bad influences of education, legislation, and social circumstances ... to be of prodigiously greater efficacy than either race or climate or the two combined" (*CW*, XVII: 1563) – Dilke's book was "very successful" (Bolt 1971: 38, 103). Also, in a letter to John Boyd Kinnear (referring to Kinnear's *Principles of Reform: Political and Legal*, London 1865), Mill stated as one of the chief points on which he differed from the author that the latter ascribed "too great influence to differences of race and too little to historical differences and to accidents as causes of the diversities of character and usage existing among mankind" (*CW*, XVI: 1093).

17 J.S. Mill, "The Negro Question," *Fraser's Magazine*, xli (January 1850), 25–31; now in *CW*, XXI: 85–95.

18 Cf. *CW*, XVIII: 196–7 ("Tocqueville on Democracy in America"); *CW*, XX: 269–70 ("Guizot's Essays and Lectures on History").

19 This statement could be a direct retort also to Hume's statement (1748): "I am apt to suspect the negroes, and in general all the other species of men ... to be *naturally inferior* to the whites. There scarcely ever was a civilized nation of any other complexion than white, nor even any individual, eminent either in action or speculation. No ingenious manufactures amongst them, no arts, no sciences" (emphasis added: Hume 1994: 86n). Cf. Immerwahr 1992: 481–6.

20 Cf. Hume 1994: 84.

21 "The French, and the Italians, are undoubtedly by nature more nervously excitable than the Teutonic races, and, compared at least with the English, they have a much greater habitual and daily emotional life: but have they been less great in science, in public business, in legal and judicial eminence, or in war? There is abundant evidence that the Greeks were of old, as their descendants and successors still are, one of the most excitable of the races of mankind. It is superfluous to ask, what among the achievements of men they did not excel in. The Romans, probably, as an equally southern people, had the same original temperament: but the stern character of their national discipline, like that of the Spartans, made them an example of the opposite type of national character; *the greater strength of their national feelings being chiefly apparent in the intensity which the same original temperament made it possible to give to the artificial*" (Emphasis added: *CW*, XXI: 309–10).

22 Many instances in Mill's other writings would suggest that he was not always as sanguine as he appears to be here about the prospects of various nations, particularly the French, by the time he wrote *The Subjection*. But one has to distinguish between the short-term prospects of various nations and states and the potentialities that there were theoretically. In addition, of course, the exigencies of the case he wanted to defend in this work may go some way towards accounting for the unequivocal stress on human malleability.

23 Cf. J.S. Mill, *A System of Logic: Ratiocinative and Inductive, CW*, VIII: 856–60 (Book VI, Chapter iv, section 4: "*Relation of mental facts to physical conditions*").

24 See Banton 1987: 54–60, and *passim*; Stocking 1987: 102–9, and *passim*. Cf. Sternhell 1987: 413: "As a political theory and as the basis for a theory of history, racism became a factor in European history in the second half of the nineteenth century."

25 See, in particular, Mill's letter to Comte of 30 October 1843 (*CW*, XIII: 604–11). On Mill's disagreement with Comte, see also Mandelbaum 1971: 168–9; Mueller 1968:

107–15. Mill's attitude towards race and its influence on the formation of national character was, in the main, similar to that of Tocqueville. While conceding that physical factors such as race must have some part in the formation of national character, he rejected any practical conclusion that would be based exclusively or even mainly on the influence of race, and sought to discredit any deterministic inferences that could be drawn from observable racial differences. On Tocqueville's attitude to race see Schleifer 1980: 62–72; Richter 1958; Todorov 1993: 126–9; and Alexis de Tocqueville, *Correspondance d'Alexis de Tocqueville avec Arthur de Gobineau*: Tocqueville 1951– (*Œuvres Complètes*), IX.

26 See also Rainger 1978: 51–70; Bolt 1971: 4, 6–7, 15, 18–19; Banton 1987: 59–60.

27 Hunt began his article by quoting Mill's forceful statement (in the *Principles of Political Economy*) about the vulgarity of "attributing the diversities of conduct and character to inherent natural differences" (Hunt 1866: 113). Mill's statement is in *CW*, II: 319.

28 For other such attacks on Buckle and Mill jointly (coming from people including Lord Acton for instance), see Varouxakis 2002: Chapter 4.

29 Hunt is not mentioned anywhere in Mill's works or extant correspondence, nor is Knox.

30 See above. In fact, Mill's almost tedious invocation of a great number of historical examples that seemed to serve his argument in *The Subjection of Women* may have something to do with the intensification of debates about racial and physical determinism after around 1850.

31 According to Rainger: "In the British scientific community of the 1860s, Huxley was among the best known for his work in government and political affairs, but, unlike Hunt or others who espoused an applied anthropology, his political beliefs were not rooted in, nor apparently related to, his scientific research" (Rainger 1978: 65; cf. 64). Hunt's was what scholars have called "the anthropological approach," while that adopted by scientists like Huxley and the members that remained in the Ethnological Society of London after Hunt's defection (and establishment of the breakaway Anthropological Society) was "the ethnological approach" (Banton 1987: 30–1).

32 Mill was referring to Huxley 1865. Huxley did accept a biological basis for differences of character (which is apparently why Mill found his physiology "heretical"), but did not want to draw the usual conclusions from that acceptance (see Mandelbaum 1971: 207, 455 n.69).

33 On the state of Mill's knowledge about Darwin, see Robson 1968a: 273–5; Mazlish 1975: 423–4.

34 Cf. Mill's "Michelet's History of France," *CW*, XX: 235: "yet the same readiness to submit to the severest discipline...": Was it a Gaelic characteristic, was it a southern characteristic, or was it a result of despotism? Also *CW*, XXIII: 335: "The discussion has been stormy; the natural consequence, among an excitable people, of the arrival of two hundred new deputies unused to the forms of debate, and the violent passions excited by a division of parties so nearly equal as to afford a hope of victory to each and every division." What is the cause? The excitability of the people, or their being new to the procedures of constitutionalism along with the equal division of parties? The same confounding of different kinds of causes appears here. Cf. J.S. Mill, *Inaugural Address Delivered to the University of St. Andrews*, *CW*, XXI: 254–5.

35 See, for instance, Matthew Arnold, *On the Study of Celtic Literature* (1867) (Arnold 1960–77, III: 291–395) – "which was more an essay in the comparative analysis of national character than about Celtic literature as such" (Collini 1993: 264). See also: Faverty 1951: *passim*; Houghton 1957: 212–13; Semmel 1962; Mandelbaum 1971: 199, 451 (n.32); Watson 1973: 198–212; Trilling 1974: 232–43; Paul 1981; Le

Quesne 1993: 83–4; Francis and Morrow 1994: 211, 213–18, 219, 229, 231 (n.56); Varouxakis 2002 (Chapter 4 and *passim*).
36 For a version of such a view of Mill, see Skorupski 1989: 1–47, and *passim*.
37 Cf. *CW*, XIII: 605; *CW*, XXI: 263.

4 Nations and nationhood II

1 This is not meant to ignore or play down the importance of Mill's interest in, and conversance with, other national or cultural groups, such as the inhabitants of the Indian subcontinent and Ireland. For their significance in this context, see, notably, Robson 1998.
2 Cf. Noiriel 1995: 4–23 (especially pp. 9–10). For an account of uses of national character, political culture, and related categories in the social sciences especially since the 1940s, see Claret 1998.
3 Cf. Ferguson 1995, *passim*.
4 Walter Bagehot, Matthew Arnold, Hippolyte Taine, are among the thinkers who dedicated pride of place to national character. Discussions of national characters went on well into the twentieth century: see, for instance, Barker 1927. Cf. Claret 1998.
5 See, for a discussion of the way in which "national character" has been treated by historians and social scientists, Potter 1954: 3–72 ("The Study of National Character").
6 These two senses are not always sufficiently differentiated. An instance where the two senses in which the term was used by Mill need to be discerned from each other occurs in F.E.L. Priestley's comments on Mill's "Whewell on Moral Philosophy" (Priestley 1969: xxxvi–xxxvii).
7 Reference is given to *CW*, VIII: 861, 864, 862.
8 Reference is given to *CW*, VIII: 867n.
9 Mill went on:

> But even here there is a large margin of doubt and uncertainty. These things are liable to be influenced by many circumstances: they are partly determined by the distinctive qualities of that nation or body of persons, but partly also by external causes which would influence any other body of persons in the same manner. In order, therefore, to make the experiment really complete, we ought to be able to try it without variation upon other nations: to try how Englishmen would act or feel if placed in the same circumstances in which we have supposed Frenchmen to be placed; to apply, in short, the Method of Difference as well as of Agreement. Now these experiments we cannot try, nor even approximate to.
>
> (*CW*, VIII: 867n)

10 In the example given above, of English stereotypes on the French, Mill would invite the ethologist to take them into account and study them as manifestations of *the English* national character.
11 What is said here does not mean to exculpate Mill from the criticism that he indulged in national stereotyping through many of his writings (cf. Varouxakis 2002: Chapter 4). All I am asserting is that he did not sanction such stereotyping here, in the "footnote on groups" Carlisle refers to, in the *Logic*, with the kind and degree of "scientific" status that Carlisle would have one believe he does. For an instance where Mill did take what people thought of a nation as a valid description of its national character, in an early article (1832), more than a decade prior to his enunciation of the principles of ethology in the *Logic*, see *CW*, XXIII: 397 ("our evidence is public

notoriety"). Of course, instead of considering this statement to be an indication of inconsistency, one could suggest that it shows the distance Mill had covered in his speculations on national characters in the course of a decade, his substitution of scientific methods for idle national stereotypes. It remains to be seen of course to what extent he lived up to the methods he stipulated since he wrote the *Logic*. Cf. Robson (John M.) 1968a: 141–2.

12 In "State of Society in America" (1836) Mill asserted that one could never know a foreign country as well as one could hope to know one's own country, but rather could be aided by the study of foreign countries in understanding – and aiming at improving – one's own. And he added: "and the wisdom acquired by the study of ourselves, and of the circumstances which surround us, can alone teach us to interpret the comparatively little which we know of other persons and other modes of existence; to make a faithful picture of them in our own minds, and to assign effects to their right causes" (*CW*, XVIII: 93).

13 See, for example, *CW*, VIII: 867n; *CW*, XIX: 410, 420–1; *CW*, XXI: 309–10. Cf. Mazlish 1975: 406: "England and France, and their respective national characters, lived in perpetual tension and dialectic in Mill's soul. He alone, he felt, understood the two countries."

14 See, for instance, Robson 1968a: 223; Mandelbaum 1971: 165.

15 It has been pointed out by J.W. Burrow that James Mill, for all the criticism his *Essay on Government* has received, did insert a qualification to his generalizations, when, in the *Fragment on Mackintosh*, he wrote that there was a set of circumstances – the most important circumstances in his opinion – "which nations have in common; *at least nations which are on the same level in point of civilization*" (emphasis added: Burrow 1968: 59–60). To the extent that James Mill was not blind to differences between different states of civilization, J.S. Mill's presentation of his own relativism as an improvement on his father's thought must be seen as more emphatically focused on his appreciation of differences of national character and their significance for politics.

16 Emphasis added: *CW*, XII, 43 (letter of 7 November 1829). In the account of his conversation with Mill on centralization that Tocqueville has left, it comes out that, as early as in 1835, Mill distinguished between national character and what Tocqueville meant by "state of society," and accorded the former much more importance than Tocqueville did (Tocqueville 1957: 132–3).

17 "Stage of civilization" was interchangeable in his writings with "state of civilization" or "state of society."

18 See the list of the "social facts and phenomena" that follows: *CW*, VIII: 911–12. Mill then stresses that "there exist Uniformities of Coexistence between the states of the various social phenomena."

19 "Comparison of the Tendencies of French and English Intellect": *CW*, XXIII: 442–3; for the French version of the same text ("Lettre à Ch. Duveyrier") see *CW*, XXV: 1251–5.

20 Thus, as we saw earlier in the first section of this chapter, Janice Carlisle's assertions concerning the function of "ethology" in Mill's writings have to be qualified; see Carlisle 1991: 144–5.

21 On the proportion of his articles on France to his overall output, see Robson and Robson 1982: 76–7 (n.12).

22 See *CW*, XXII: 146, 177, 247. Some of the tendencies, habits, or feelings of the French people, or the French "mind," that seem to correspond to what Mill called national character, discussed in these articles, are worth noting. He wrote that "almost all Frenchmen resemble republicans in their habits and feelings" (*CW*, XXII: 152);

that they were "an eminently place-hunting people" (*CW*, XXII: 159); he noted "the generosity of their national character" (*CW*, XXIII: 560). The tendency to over-government in France was described as a development of recent decades, "from the reign of Napoleon to the present time" (*CW*, XXII: 184–5). Another theme in these early newspaper writings was the frequent reference to the "excitability" and "mobility" of the French character. The French were "a people ... susceptible of strong emotions" (*CW*, XXII: 226) and "an excitable and confiding people" (*CW*, XXII: 283). See also *CW*, XXIII: 335; *CW*, XXII: 246–7; cf. *CW*, XIII: 448. A hereditary peerage was an institution "radically incompatible with the feelings and habits of the French people" (*CW*, XXIII: 342). The French despised hereditary distinctions and valued highly personal ones. Birth and wealth conferred no moral ascendancy in France (*CW*, XXII: 200–1). This was "*one of those broad and all-pervading differences between nations, which render it absurd to transfer institutions ready-made from one country to the other*" (emphasis added: *CW*, XXII: 343). Cf. *CW*, XXIII: 682.

23 Cf. Spitzer 1987: 174.
24 Mill was responding to an article (critical of the French) in *The Times*, 11 May 1831, p. 2.
25 Mill stressed the distance of his own generation from the "eminent thinkers of fifty years ago" in a British context as well, patently overplaying the differences (Collini, Winch, and Burrow 1983: 133). And a lot has been written on Mill's youthful rebellion towards his father and his "Oedipal conflict" (Mazlish 1975: 15–43, 279, and *passim*).
26 Cf. Spitzer 1987: 10, and *passim*; also McLaren 1971: 59–60.
27 See more on this issue below, Chapters 5 and 6.
28 In this insistence he was following Comte; cf. Skorupski 1989: 267–9. Mill went on to assert that: "States of society are like different ages in the physical frame; they are conditions not of one or a few organs or functions, but of the whole organism. Accordingly, the information which we possess respecting past ages, and respecting the various states of society now existing in different regions of the earth, does, when duly analysed, exhibit uniformities. It is found that when one of the features of society is in a particular state, a state of *many* [MS, 1843, 1846: "*all the*"] other features, more or less precisely determinate, always *or usually* [MS, 1843, 1846, 1851: "*spontaneously*"] coexists with it" (emphasis added: *CW*, VIII: 912). From the changes he introduced to his phrasing of this last sentence, it is clear that Mill himself had second thoughts, in the later editions of the *Logic*, about the degree of "uniformity" or "consensus" exhibited by such phenomena.
29 Letter to Sarah Austin of 26 February 1844: *CW*, XIII: 622.
30 For Tocqueville's use of "state of society", see Lamberti 1989: 13–39.
31 Collini speaks of "the portmanteau term 'state of society'": Collini, Winch and Burrow 1983: 151.
32 On 9 February 1834 he had written in the *Examiner*, concerning a bill introduced by the French government aimed at the suppression of cheap political publications: "We shall watch the progress of this Bill. There is no doubt that it will pass; for *public opinion is not yet sufficiently advanced in France*, to maintain any struggle in behalf of freedom of discussion for its own sake, when they take no personal or party interest in those who are the victims of the infringement" (emphasis added: *CW*, XXIII: 683).
33 (Letter to Henry S. Chapman). Mill went on to lament the fact that the man best qualified to direct such a movement, Armand Carrel, was dead, adding that "[w]ithout Carrel, or, I fear, any one comparable to him, the futurity of France and of Europe is

most doubtful." (Mill was not alone in missing Carrel at that time.) Besides lamenting Carrel's absence, Mill did not conceal that he saw serious dangers. The first danger was that of war, and the second was the inordinately high expectations raised by the spread of "Communism."

34 Hereafter: "Vindication," first published in *Westminster Review*, April 1849; now in *CW*, XX: 319–63.

35 Cf. Mill, "Prospects of France, IV" (10 October 1830): "Almost all Frenchmen resemble republicans in their habits and feelings": *CW*, XXII: 152. Cf. Bagehot 1965–86, VIII: 236–7.

36 The remarks Mueller refers to are in *CW*, XX: 200.

37 Cf. "Guizot's Essays and Lectures on History," *CW*, XX: 280.

38 The third – closely related – condition was that "they must be willing and able to do what it requires of them to enable it to fulfil its purposes."

39 The last case seems to allude to French experience in the aftermath of the revolution of 1848. Although "great man" Mill never considered Louis Napoleon Bonaparte to be!

40 The phrase "institutions *alien from*, or *too much in advance of*" (emphasis added) would seem to suggest such an understanding of the distinction. If a set of institutions is said to be "too much in advance of the condition of the popular mind" (*CW*, XIX: 357), it can be expected to be appropriate for the people in question one day, if, and when, the popular mind would advance. If, on the other hand, a set of institutions is said to be "alien from" the particular popular mind, then the difficulty may be assumed to be more insuperable, and to have to do with the deeper traits of the national character of that people, which would be even more difficult to change than their state of society.

41 On the protean character of the republic, see Nicolet 1982 (particularly pp. 16–34).

42 Mill noted that in regard to the "infirmities" he was about to refer to it was "not ... obvious that the government of One or a Few would have any tendency to cure or alleviate the evil" (*CW*, XIX: 418).

43 Cf. the review article "Guizot's Essays and Lectures in History" of 1845 (*CW*, XX: 290–4), where Mill had exhibited the reverse mode of reasoning. Of course, Mill apparently still implied, in *Representative Government*, that national character was formed through history (this is clear in "Centralisation," which he wrote in 1862 (*CW*, XIX: 581–613 – especially pp. 594, 605)); cf. *The Subjection of Women, CW*, XXI: 277. Yet, he now seemed to consider it more durable, less easily changeable.

44 Cf. "Centralisation" (*CW*, XIX: 610–11), where Mill spoke, referring to the French once more, of the "confounding of the love of liberty with the love of power, the desire not to be improperly controlled with the ambition of exercising control." Cf. Montesquieu 1989: 155.

45 Cf. Benjamin Constant, "The Liberty of the Ancients compared with that of the Moderns" (Constant 1988: 316).

46 Cf. *CW*, XXII: 159; and *CW*, XX: 193.

47 Cf. "Centralisation": *CW*, XIX: 583.

48 They were "very jealous of any attempt to exercise power over them, not sanctioned by long usage and by their own opinion of right." But they cared "very little for the exercise of power over others" (*CW*, XIX: 421).

49 This was a commonplace belief at the time; cf. Swart 1964: 123–37.

50 "Qu'il y ait ou non décadence morale en France je n'oserais le dire. Il est certain que le caractère français a des très grands défauts, qui ne sont jamais plus montrés que dans l'année malheureuse qui vient de s'écouler. Mais il n'est rien moins qu'assuré que ces défauts n'ont pas existé au même degré dans ce qu'on appelle les plus beaux

jours de la France" ("I do not have the temerity to say whether or not there is moral decadence in France. It is certain that the French character has great faults, which have never become more apparent than in the unhappy year which has just passed. But it is no less certain that these faults existed to the same degree in what are called the most glorious days of France") (*CW*, XVII, 1864).

51 "On the New Constitution of France, and the Aptitude of the French Character for National Freedom" (January 1852). For more on Bagehot's views on this issue, see Varouxakis 2002 (Chapters 3 and 4).

5 International relations, intervention/non-intervention and national self-determination

1 See, for example, Miller (Kenneth) 1961; Souffrant 2000; Grader 1985; Ellis 1992; Sullivan 1983; Beitz 1979: 82, 84n, 85–7, 112–4; Vincent 1974: 54–6, 61–3, and *passim*; Walzer 1992: 87–97, 101; Holbraad 1970: 162–5, 168, 170, 176; Kohn 1946: 11–42.

2 Vincent concludes his chapter entitled "Theory" as follows: "In the Cold War, Mill's doctrine of counter-intervention to enforce nonintervention has seen service on both sides of the battle, and Cobden's doctrine has survived as a protest against it. The recurrence of these different themes will be apparent in the chapters that follow" (Vincent 1974: 63). And Vincent does make good his promise (Vincent 1974: 112, 173, 225, 230, 245, 314, 314n, 318, 388–9). See also: Beitz 1979: 82, 85–7; and Forbes and Hoffman 1993: 66–7, 69, 70, 82.

3 First published in *Fraser's Magazine* (Vol. 60, December 1859), pp. 766–76; now in *CW*, XXI: 109–24. This article has been the focus of attention for existing accounts of Mill's views on non-intervention; some of these also looked at the "Vindication of the French Revolution of February 1848," written in 1849 (*CW*, XX: 317–63), and at the earlier article "The Spanish Question," written in 1837, to which Mill had contributed the theoretical part (*CW*, XXXI: 359–88). None of the existing accounts has referred to the early newspaper writings of 1830–1.

4 Another "fundamental distinction" that Mill had already made in that article was that between "civilized" and "barbarian" peoples. The principles that are presented here are those he held to apply in the relations between "civilized" countries (*CW*, XXI: 118–20). For a criticism of Mill's attitude towards what he called "barbarian" peoples, see Parekh 1994.

5 So far, Mill agreed with Cobden, who also used this argument – among others – against intervention. But this is as far as their agreement went. See Vincent 1974: 53.

6 The main "despotic" powers Mill was referring to were the Russian, Austrian and Ottoman Empires, as well as Prussia.

7 For a succinct analysis of the philosophical premises underlying Mill's views on non-intervention presented here, see Walzer 1992: 87–91.

8 On Mill's familiarity with France, see Chass 1928; Mueller 1968; Filipiuk 1991; Varouxakis 2002.

9 Wight gives reference to Thomas Raikes, *A Portion of the Journal* (Longmans, 1856), vol. i, p. 106.

10 "It is a metaphysical and political word which means almost the same thing as intervention."

11 Emphasis added: Wight 1966b: 115. Wight went on to explain: "Without adopting the tacit premises of the remark, one may recognize that it is very difficult to give precision to the terms intervention and non-intervention, and very difficult to erect either of them into a theoretical norm of international conduct."

12 "This interpretation of the function of the nonintervention doctrine after 1815 allowed

Mazzini to assert his view of the real meaning of the doctrine in words which were to be echoed by John Stuart Mill eight years later" (Vincent 1974: 59–60). The above statement is followed by a footnote referring the reader to p. 56 of Vincent's book, which is where he had dealt with Mill's advocacy of "the case for counter-intervention," basing his discussion exclusively on "A Few Words on Non-Intervention" (1859). On Mazzini's arguments cf. Wight 1966b: 114.

13 See Collingham 1988: 186–93; Jennings 1991: 507–10; Pilbeam 1991: 60–79 and *passim*; Tombs 1996: 358–63; Tombs 1997: 320. Cf. Betley 1960; Brown 1980.

14 See, especially, Carrel 1857–59, I: 150–1, 220, 230–1, 320–1, 338–41, 379–434; II: pp. 5–12, 52–7 (especially p. 56), 176–83, 184–90. Given Mill's pronounced admiration and affection for Carrel, there is a *prima facie* case for suspecting and investigating some connection. Significantly, Carrel, who played an active role in the July revolution and initially supported the government of the July monarchy, passed gradually to the ranks of the opposition exactly because of frustration at the government's foreign policy, which he saw as pusillanimous and dishonorable for France: see McLaren 1971: 246–78; Jennings 1991: 507–10.

15 Cf. Carrel 1857–9, I: 409–14.

16 For the General's speech, see *Moniteur Universel* (hereafter: *Moniteur*), 1831: 109–10 (15 January 1831). On Lamarque's advocacy of war, with special reference to this particular speech, cf. Tombs 1994: 169–77 (particularly p. 171).

17 Maximilien Lamarque and François Mauguin were members of the opposition. They were the two politicians for whom *Le National* reserved its most unqualified support, due precisely to their intensely nationalistic speeches and pleas for war, of which Mill was critical in this article. See McLaren 1971: 122. For Mauguin's speech, see *Moniteur*, 1831: 111. Mill went on to report: "That able and highly-principled paper, the *Courrier Français*, has answered both speeches in an article, which, we trust, will be read in every corner of France" (*CW*, XXII: 248). The article Mill referred to was: "De la paix et de la guerre," *Courrier Français*, 17 January: 1–2.

18 That Mill was reading *Le National* before he met its chief editor personally in 1833 (and developed an extraordinary admiration for him) can be surmised, for example, from *CW*, XXIII: 466–7, 525–30; and *CW*, XII: 194–5, 220.

19 Some of those who championed intervention did advocate a "mission libératrice" on the Napoleonic model (Lochore 1935: 79). Mill apparently was not referring to them, but, most notably, to Lafayette, who had based his argument on the grounds Mill goes on to present.

20 "War, the Left argued, was inevitable anyway, because the reactionary monarchies of Europe would not dare to let a revolutionary regime survive. France must therefore seize the most favourable moment to fight, which was while the Poles, the Belgians and the Italians were still up in arms" (Tombs 1996: 360).

21 Cf. Lafayette's speech of 28 January in *Moniteur*, 1831: 193–4.

22 The French government had declared that the entry of foreign troops into Belgium would be considered a declaration of war. The result had been, in Mill's words, that "all Europe applauded, and the Cabinets reluctantly acquiesced." Though France had been at that time "almost without an army," and many of its frontier fortresses were "in a state almost incapable of defence," the "imposing unanimity which reigned in the July revolution, struck terror into the Powers, and they feared to stir" (*CW*, XXII: 300–1).

23 He concluded: "This being the melancholy fact, the attempt to enforce non-intervention against Austria in the case of the Papal states would probably lead to war; and the co-operation of such a spiritless people as that of Romagna, in case of future hostilities, is so little worth, that it would be unwise in France to accelerate

such a calamity in order to save them. Her policy now is to throw her shield over Belgium and Switzerland; leave events in other countries to take their course; and, if war is coming, wait till it comes" (*CW*, XXII: 301).

24 In "The Spanish Question" (*CW*, XXXI: 373–4). There Mill had taken issue with Roebuck's complete condemnation of interference.

25 See Lafayette's speech on external affairs of 28 January in *Moniteur*, 1831: 193–4.

26 He alluded to the Crimean War. Compare the above with what Carrel had written in the *National* in 1831 (22 January): Carrel 1857–59, II: 51.

27 In this switch, Mill was not alone of course. Alexis de Tocqueville, by no means favorable to Britain's international ambitions before Louis-Napoleon Bonaparte's coup (in December 1851), became, after the latter event, an ardent supporter of Britain's international greatness as the only guarantee for the survival of liberty: see Drescher 1964: 170–92. See also Mazzini 1852: 272–3, 296.

28 See also Mill's reported reply to the question *"What are your principles of non-intervention?"* during one of the meetings before the Westminster election, on 8 July 1865, in *CW*, XXVIII: 39. Cf. also his reply to the same effect on 3 July, 1865: *CW*, XXVIII: 17.

29 The French intervention in Italy in 1849, of which Mill said he disapproved, was directed, in its crucial phase (from June to October 1849), by the foreign minister of the Second Republic at that time, who happened to be a well-known acquaintance of Mill's, Alexis de Tocqueville. See Mélonio 1984.

30 This latter seems to be the case in the example Mill employed, namely the Russian intervention to aid Austria in keeping down the Hungarians. See also his statement in the same text "that not a gun shall be fired in Europe by the soldiers of one Power against the revolted subjects of another..." (*CW*, XXI: 124).

31 *Westminster Review* (Vol. 51, April 1849): 1–47; now in *CW*, XX: 317–63 (for the part of the article dealing with international relations, see 340–8).

32 Cf., on Lord Brougham's advocacy of strict non-intervention in the 1820s, Little 1975: 25.

33 Alphonse de Lamartine was the foreign minister of the Provisional Government. On the overall issue of British reactions to his stance and role during those crucial months, see Bensimon 1999.

34 For another such vehement denunciation of Lamartine's Manifesto and overall foreign policy, as well as of "[t]his barbarous feeling of nationality" which "has become the curse of Europe," see Senior 1973a: 60–5; cf. Senior 1973b, I: 262.

35 Mill follows John Austin rather than Jeremy Bentham here. Cf. *CW*, XXI: 177, 246.

36 Cf. *CW*, XXI: 121.

37 The cases Mill referred to were the interference by the great powers between Greece and Turkey at Navarino, between Holland and Belgium at Antwerp, and between Turkey and Egypt at St. Jean d'Acre (*CW*, XX: 346).

38 See Vincent 1974: 56. See also Walzer 1992. On p. 90, Walzer discerns three different cases in which non-intervention can be abandoned. The third case is, what he later calls, "humanitarian intervention" (Walzer 1992: 101–8). In view of the description he gives of cases under this heading (pp. 90, 101–8), Walzer is wrong in asserting that Mill did not discuss "humanitarian intervention" (p. 90). Both in the 1849 "Vindication..." and in "A Few Words...," a decade later, Mill vindicated the case for foreign intervention when "the war either continues long undecided, or threatens to be decided in a way involving consequences repugnant to humanity or to the general interest": *CW*, XX: 346. Cf. *CW*, XXI: 121.

39 This is what late twentieth-century commentators (such as Vincent and Walzer) call "humanitarian intervention" (Walzer 1992: 101–8).

40 Mill asserted that the era of the Reformation was such a time – when "sympathy of religion [was] held to be a perfectly sufficient warrant for assisting anybody." The same applied "in the present age," with regard to *political* sympathies: "What religious sympathies were then, political ones are now; and every liberal government or people has a right to assist struggling liberalism...; as every despotic government... never scruples to aid despotic governments" (*CW*, XX: 346).

41 In his *Autobiography* Mill wrote, with reference to his *Principles of Political Economy*, that he promulgated there his views on socialism "less clearly in the first edition, rather more so in the second, and quite unequivocally in the third." His explanation of the differences may be relevant to the promulgation of his views on intervention in 1849:

> The difference arose partly from the change of times, the first edition having been written and sent to the press before the French Revolution of 1848, after which the public mind became more open to the reception of novelties in opinion, and doctrines appeared moderate which would have been thought very startling a short time before.
>
> (*CW*, I: 241)

42 A partial exception is Holbraad's footnote, which implies that a new principle was added in 1859 that was not there in 1849 (Holbraad 1970: 164–5n).

43 Quotations from Brougham's essay cited by Mill: *CW*, XX: 347. Cf. Senior's equally vehement attack on the principle of nationality: Senior 1973a: 64–5; Senior 1973b, I: 262.

44 Cf. his reference to the Italians in the *Manifeste*, in Mill's translation: *CW*, XX: 341.

45 In the 1849 – original – version Mill had written "both" instead of "all."

46 In 1849: "unfit for."

6 Foreign policy and the public moralist

1 "I would wish to see crucified the first man who would dare pour out in the tribune of one people abuse against another people. It takes whole generations to heal the harm that this can cause in one day. This is very despicable in a century which needs so much the help of the energetic and enlightened men of all advanced countries for the difficult task of the reorganization of European society."

2 Cf. *Autobiography*, *CW*, I: 169–71, where Mill spoke of "the battle about the shield, one side of which was white and the other black."

3 I am borrowing the term "public moralist" from Collini's seminal study (Collini 1991). For some extremely sharp comments on Mill's activity and strategies as a public moralist, see Collini 1991: 121–69, and *passim*.

4 On the importance of this early experience, and of the younger Mill's conversance with France more generally, see Mueller 1968; Filipiuk 1991. Cf. Varouxakis 2002. Cf. Mill's own assessment of the importance of his boyhood stay in France in his *Autobiography*:

> The chief fruit which I carried away from the society I saw, was a strong and permanent interest in Continental Liberalism, of which I ever afterwards kept myself *au courant*, as much as of English politics: a thing not at all usual in those days with Englishmen, and which had a very salutary influence on my development, *keeping me free from the error always prevalent in England ... of judging universal questions by a merely English standard.*
>
> (Emphasis added: *CW*, I: 63)

5 For the most succinct and accurate accounts of what is implied here about M. Arnold, see Trilling 1974; Collini 1993. For similarities between Arnold and Mill in this respect cf. Varouxakis 2002: *passim*. Cf. also Robson (John M.) 1968b.

6 On the proportion of Mill's articles dedicated to French politics during the early 1830s, see Robson and Robson 1982: 76–7 n.12.

7 Arnold's first foray into social and political criticism, the pamphlet *England and the Italian Question*, was written in 1859. Mill's attacks on English smugness and ethnocentric myopia started already in the mid-1820s, with his onslaughts on the *Edinburgh Review*'s "offerings both to national antipathies and to national vanity" – on account of its unfavorable comments on the French (*CW*, I: 307–11), as well as on the *Quarterly Review*'s and Walter Scott's complacency with things English as opposed to everything French (*CW*, XX: 17, 60).

8 Cf. *CW*, XXIII: 443. It was not the least of the attractions that the Saint-Simonians held for Mill that, besides their acute interest in questions related to differences of national character, they were particularly keen to bring as close as possible the two nations Mill was most interested in, France and Britain.

9 Bain added: "Mill had a great partiality for France, until the usurpation of Louis Napoleon; and his opinion of England was correspondingly low" (Bain 1882: 161). For Collini's agreement with Bain's assessment of Mill's attitude towards France, see Collini 1999: 139. Even more critical of Mill's depreciation of the English character and his "one-sided and declamatory counter-eulogy of things foreign" with particular reference to his "perilous assumptions" and "half-truths" about the merits of the French had been F.T. Palgrave in his (anonymous) review of Mill's *Autobiography* in the *Quarterly Review* (Palgrave 1874): 166–7; cf. *ibid.*: 155. Many other contemporaries on both sides of the English Channel had noticed Mill's extraordinary interest in France. Mill himself was by no means less explicit about the extent of his involvement with France. He seems to have believed that no Briton knew France better than he did (see, for example, *CW*, XII: 78; *CW*, XIII: 431).

10 He had used this phrase while speaking of Bulwer-Lytton, but there can be little doubt that he regarded himself as one of "the moral teachers of England."

11 "Like all elevated spirits, who want to enhance the civilization of their homeland by comparing it to different civilizations, he despises flattering his country, and does not fear at all to point out to it the qualities of its rivals which he would like to see it acquire. If he has incurred a reproach among his compatriots, it is that he is the rather morose censor of England and the rather indulgent panegyrist of France." The last remark (written before Bain's and Palgrave's criticisms were voiced) indicates that there had been similar criticisms of Mill's partiality in favor of France earlier as well. When Michelet published the fifth volume of his *Histoire de France*, which he spoke of as "ce volume si peu favorable aux Anglais," he hoped he could enlist for its defence "la haute impartialité d'un Anglais, de M. Mill" (quoted – from a letter by Michelet to Gustave d'Eichthal – in Mill, *CW*, XIII: 432–3n). Mill did in fact write a favorable review of the first five volumes of Michelet's work (*Edinburgh Review*, January 1844): see *CW*, XX: 217–55.

12 "the help of the energetic and enlightened men of all advanced countries for the difficult task of the reorganization of European society."

13 Cf. *CW*, I: 169–71.

14 In turn, the preservation of peace was necessary if the repetition of what Mill regarded as Napoleon's attempt "to uncivilize human nature" (*CW*, XXII: 307) was to be averted.

15 In a letter to Tocqueville (20 February 1843); quoted in the epigraph to this chapter.

16 See above, Chapter 5.

17 See "Banquet allemand à Paris," *Le National*, 28 May 1832: 3. Thus, apparently, Mill was not completely blind to Carrel's anti-English tone (cf. McLaren 1971: 265).

18 See, for instance, *CW*, XXIII: 388: "But we solemnly assure our friends in France,..." In fact, the article, in which this phrase appears, published on 8 January 1832 in the *Examiner* (pp. 24–5), was, within all probability, actually sent to French political activists, as Mill wrote to d'Eichthal, on 28 January: "Would it be inconvenient to you to take with you to Paris some numbers of the Examiner for Marchais and for M. de Lasteyrie?": *CW*, XII: 95 (cf., on Marchais, *CW*, XII: 121–2). Some of Mill's articles *were* actually published in France as well as in Britain (*CW*, XXIII: 691–7). Cf. *CW*, XII: 197, 281–2, 343–4; *CW*, XXII: 173; *CW*, XXIII: 442–7, 717–27.

19 Translated by Mill in his article of 2 December 1832 (as was the whole article from the *National*): *CW*, XXIII: 525–7. Then Mill proceeded to comment on Carrel's article: *CW*, XXIII: 527–30.

20 The *juste-milieu*, the *Doctrinaires* in particular. See Jardin and Tudesq 1983: 147–8.

21 Carrel had excepted *The Times* from his complaints (see *CW*, XXIII: 527).

22 It should be noted that throughout this article Mill translated the word "confrères" as "brothers." This text was written before Mill met Carrel personally.

23 According to Weill, Marchais was "le bras droit de Lafayette": Weill 1928: 109.

24 Cf. Mill's letter to John Taylor (1 September 1832): *CW*, XII: 115. Mill had given one more such "public testimony of sympathy and fraternity" the previous April, when he had sent his "Lettre à Ch. Duveyrier" to be published in *Le Globe*: see *CW*, XXIII: 442.

25 For details on the crisis see Chapter 2, note 15.

26 Cairns had also written, earlier on, that the crisis of 1839–41 "revealed clearly that [Mill] had by no means lost his native bearings" (Cairns 1985: xviii).

27 See in particular Aron 1965: 19 (where Aron wrote that "probablement, la réponse de J.S. Mill ... n'a-t-elle pas encore perdu toute signification"). See also Todorov 1993: 191–207 (especially 195–7); Todorov is more overtly critical of Tocqueville's stance.

28 Cf., on the Liberal party's Francophiles or "Foxites," Bullen 1974: 2–4, 20–4.

29 Cf. what Mill wrote to Tocqueville two years later (20 February 1843), referring to the same affair and the same man with the words quoted in the epigraph to this Chapter (*CW*, XIII: 571).

30 On 19 November 1840 Mill wrote to Sir William Molesworth, congratulating him for his speech to his constituents at Leeds, during which Molesworth had attacked Palmerston's policies and deplored the possibility of any rupture of peace with France (see *Examiner*, 15 November 1840, p. 721). It was, according to Mill, "a very proper thing, done in the very best way," and he thought that it had done, and would do, "good both in France and here." In the same letter Mill went on to praise Fonblanque's stance towards the whole affair, in the *Examiner*: he had "been doing admirably on this war question." Mill must have been referring to the leading articles in the *Examiner* of 8 November (p. 705) and of 15 November (p. 721). Cf. Mill's letter to Albany Fonblanque himself, on 17 June 1841, where he took the opportunity "to express the great admiration I have felt for the writing and conduct of the Examiner during the last year and especially on the Eastern question on which it alone resisted an almost universal madness, and did so with an ability and in a spirit which seemed to me quite perfect" (*CW*, XIII: 478–9). According to Mill, *The Times* also had "been rendering good service of late" (*CW*, XVII: 1995–6) – on the stance of *The Times*, cf. Taylor (A.J.P.) 1993: 48.

31 For part of Sterling's letter of 9 December to which this is an answer, see Tuell 1941: 131–2. Sterling had written: "I had no conception that there could be a number of able

men in an important public position in a great civilized country showing themselves such knaves and fools as the war Party at Paris" (p. 131).

32 Sterling's remarks deploring French reactions to the events of 1840 had been followed by the comment: "Lord Palmerston went on much stronger grounds than I supposed in his bellicose policy." Sterling proceeded to denounce what he supposed Thiers's plans to have been (Tuell 1941: 131–2).

33 Sterling had argued to this effect in his letter of 9 December (Tuell 1941: 131–2).

34 Cobden had denounced English hypocrisy in the same vein with regard to attitudes towards Russia's aggrandizement (Cobden 1903, I: 153).

35 Mill did not exaggerate the difficulties of the task Guizot had set himself in trying to avert war and revitalize the Anglo-French alliance. See Johnson (Douglas) 1963: 268–73; Bullen 1974: 23, 26–8 and *passim*; Bullen 1991: 187–201.

36 In Sterling's letter of 4 January 1841; partly in Tuell 1941: 132.

37 Tocqueville's letter of 18 December 1840: in *Œuvres Complètes*, VI, 1: 329–31.

38 Mill was referring to his letter of 30 December 1840: *CW*, XIII: 457–60.

39 And Mill continued in the same strain as in the two letters to Sterling of 19 December and of 5 January (*CW*, XIII: 451, 462).

40 Mill went on to admit that he could not think without "humiliation" of some things he had written in the past "of such a man as this," when he had thought him a dishonest politician (*CW*, XIII: 454–5). Cf. what Mill had said, parenthetically, concerning Guizot's political career in two instances where Guizot's historical work was the main subject: *CW*, XX: 185–6; *CW*, XX: 259. For the oscillations of Mill's estimation of Guizot as a politician, cf.: *CW*, XII: 61; *CW*, XIII: 654, 714. Significantly, it was again a question of foreign policy and Franco-British relations, the Spanish Marriages, that modified, to an extent, Mill's favorable view of Guizot (letter to J. Austin, *CW*, XIII: 714).

41 Guizot was called from the London Embassy back to Paris in order to become Foreign Minister as well as virtual head of the new French government, after Thiers' fall, in October 1840.

42 In his analysis of the causes of the fall of the July monarchy, in "Vindication" (1849), Mill wrote that the second great characteristic of the government of Louis Philippe, "discreditable" and "fatal to the government," had been that:

> It wrought almost exclusively through the meaner and more selfish impulses of mankind. Its sole instrument of government consisted in a direct appeal to men's immediate personal interests or interested fears. It never appealed to, or endeavoured to put on its side, any noble, elevated, or generous principle of action. It repressed and discouraged all such, as being dangerous to it.

Louis Philippe had striven "to immerse all France in the *culte des intérêts matériels*, in the worship of the cash-box and of the ledger. It is not, or [1849: 'at least'] it has not hitherto been, in the character of Frenchmen to be content with being thus governed. Some idea of grandeur, at least some feeling of national self-importance, must be associated with that which they will voluntarily follow and obey" (*CW*, XX: 325).

43 Cf. Varouxakis 2002: Chapter 2.

44 See above, Chapter 2. Cf., on Bentham's denunciation of "honour" and "glory" as causes for war, Conway 1989: 92, 93–4. On Bentham's views in this respect see also Kohn 1946: 17–19. Cf. Yasukawa 1991: 179–97.

45 Alexander Bain has written of Mill that "up to the fatality of December, 1851, he had a sanguine belief in the political future of France" (Bain 1882: 93). Mill loathed Napoleon III and dreaded his foreign policy ambitions.

46 Mill sent his article "A Few Words on Non-Intervention" to French periodicals in order to have it reviewed in France (see his letter to J.W. Parker: *CW*, XV: 652). One of his intentions in that article was to dissipate the very widespread belief, on the part of Continental thinkers and public, that British foreign policy was quintessentially selfish and hypocritical. In the same years Mill tried assiduously to promote Hare's plan of representation in France. And, in a manner true to his attitude in earlier decades, he complained in a letter to his step-daughter, Helen Taylor (2 February 1860), about the writers in the *Saturday Review*: "The best service they have rendered is by being always strenuous for arming, and against Louis Napoleon, but in doing so they have become anti-French to a degree I do not like" (*CW*, XV: 667).

7 Reconciling patriotism and cosmopolitanism

1 Cf. Stephen Nathanson's argument that there are liberal and illiberal versions of both nationalism and patriotism and that therefore a neat distinction between nationalism and patriotism does not suffice (Nathanson 1993). Cf. Canovan 2000; Benner 1997.
2 Emphasis added.
3 The texts quoted from Tocqueville can be found in: Tocqueville 1994: 526–32.
4 On Bentham's cosmopolitanism, see Ellis 1992: 164:

> The utilitarians were fundamentally cosmopolitan; the citizen of a nation is also a citizen of the world ... whose basic duty is to the good of mankind in general. Of course, we have duties to particular sections of mankind that we do not have to other sections – our families, friends, countrymen, and so on – but this is so only because and insofar as utility is maximized by recognizing such duties. Similarly, utility is maximized by accepting the natural disposition that a government has to foster the interests of its own citizens ... but a government's fundamental duty is again to mankind in general. So Bentham can write that it should be a crime for a nation "to do more evil to foreign nations taken together ... than it should do good to itself," or even "to refuse to render positive services to a foreign nation, when the rendering of them would produce more good to the last mentioned nation, than it would produce evil to itself."

Cf. Hayes 1931: 128: "Bentham was an English patriot, but he was also, in the best eighteenth-century manner, a good deal of a cosmopolite, and he felt no inner conflict between the two loyalties." Cf. also: Conway 1990: 231: "Bentham declared himself 'an Englishman by birth' but 'a citizen of the world by naturalization.'" On J.S. Mill's comment on the "cosmopolitan character" of Bentham's writings, see: *CW*, XVII: 1812.
5 Newman also argued that: "the unhappy young Mill ... [l]ike Coleridge in the late nineties ... was painfully finding his way home; he was making his way from the great broad idea of 'universal benevolence' to the narrower but surer one of 'national improvement.'" (Newman 1987: 243–4).
6 Mill continues here:

> He who needs any other lesson on this subject than the whole course of ancient history affords, let him read Cicero *de Officiis*. ... [in *de Officiis*] on the subject of duty to our country there is no compromise. That any man, with the smallest pretensions to virtue, could hesitate to sacrifice life, reputation, family, everything valuable to him, to the love of country is a supposition which this eminent interpreter of Greek and Roman morality cannot entertain for a moment.
>
> (*CW*, X: 421)

7 As Mill had asserted earlier on in the same text: "The power of education is almost boundless: there is not one natural inclination which it is not strong enough to coerce, and, if needful, to destroy by disuse." To prove this assertion, Mill adduced the example of what he called "the greatest recorded victory which education has ever achieved over a whole host of natural inclinations in an entire people – the maintenance through centuries of the institutions of Lycurgus": "the root of the system was devotion to Sparta, to the ideal of the country or State: which *transformed into ideal devotion to a greater country, the world*, would be equal to that and far nobler achievements" (emphasis added: "Utility of Religion," *CW*, X: 409).

8 Here some comment is necessary. There is a confusion in the use of the term "nationalist" in English, as it may mean at least two very different things. First, one can be nationalist in the sense of elevating one's own nation to the supreme value, putting one's own nation first, etc. Second, now, "nationalist" was used, especially in the nineteenth and in the early twentieth century, to describe British liberal thinkers who sympathized with and supported the national liberation movements of other nations (usually smaller or less powerful than their own). Jones seems to be using the term in this latter sense here.

9 This is why Viroli, try as he might, cannot really convince that this statement by Mill is fully compatible with the kind of "republican patriotism" he talks about (Viroli 1995; Viroli 2000).

10 For an instance of Mill's using the term 'enlightened patriotism' in French ("patriotisme éclairé"), see CW, XVII: 1769. Cf. Bagehot 1965–86, IV: 122–3.

11 "What we cannot do," Scheffler continues, "is to affirm that all people are of equal worth, while simultaneously insisting that our special relationships to particular people obligate us to devote special attention to those people, whether or not doing so will promote the good of humanity at large" (Scheffler 2001: 118).

12 As Scheffler explains:

> Rather than trying to divide one's attention among all the children of the world, for example, one should give special attention to one's own children, but only because that is the most effective way of allocating one's benevolence. One must not suppose that one's own children are worth more than other children.
>
> (Scheffler 1996: 8)

13 Thus, Scheffler concludes that, "[i]f there is a genuinely controversial ethical position underlying Nussbaum's cosmopolitanism it is this: that, at some fundamental level, our responsibilities to all people are the same, and that special responsibilities arising out of our participation in particular groups and relationships can be justified only derivatively." As Scheffler notes, "[n]on-cosmopolitans reject this position" (Scheffler 1996: 8).

14 Obviously, the broader controversies surrounding the extent and the sense in which Mill was consistently utilitarian cannot be discussed here. For them see, notably, Crisp 1997. Also, Riley 1998: 151–66.

15 Mill kept a much closer eye on concrete issues of national security and the realities of power in international relations than most academic political philosophers feel called upon or inclined to do in relatively secure English-speaking countries today. Cf. the cogent remarks by Margaret Canovan on the differences in the discourses of patriotism between earlier periods and today: "It is highly characteristic of the new discourse of patriotism (bearing witness to changed political conditions in the West) that the military concerns that loomed so large in the past have almost dropped out of view" (Canovan 2000: 290). More generally on contemporary liberal political theorists' neglect of the underlying realities of power, see Canovan 1996.

16 I am alluding to Mill's "A Few Words on Non-Intervention," on which more will be said further on.

17 The former emphasis (*"absence"*) is in the original, the latter is mine.

18 Cf. the remark of his brother, Leslie Stephen, that what J.F. Stephen desiderated in Mill's theory of liberty was "the great patriotic passions which are the mainsprings of history": see Stapleton 1998: 247.

19 Stephen (Leslie) 1900: 12–13. For an impressive collection of strictures on Mill's "un-Englishness" at the time of his death and shortly afterwards, see Collini 1991: 311–41.

20 *CW*, XVIII: 86–9, 182–3; *CW*, XVII: 1769.

21 See Stapleton 1998: 251.

22 Stapleton 1998: 244. Among the things J.F. Stephen found worthy of praise in his article on Macaulay was that "[h]e was ... full of patriotic feelings ... He was an enthusiastic Englishman" (Stephen 1866(b): 208).

23 *CW*, XIV: 6. Mill's disciple, Morley, complained scathingly of Macaulay's complacent pandering to "the commonplaces of patriotism" ("Macaulay," in Morley 1970: 73–97).

24 During the 1820s Mill spent a lot of ink attacking the *Edinburgh Review*'s "offerings both to national antipathies and to national vanity" (on account of its unfavorable comments on the French), as well as the *Quarterly Review*'s and Walter Scott's complacency with things English as opposed to everything French (*CW*, I: 307–11; *CW*, XX: 17, 60).

25 Emphasis added.

26 Emphasis added.

27 *CW*, XX: 17, 21–2. Cf. what Mill wrote to Macvey Napier on 20 October 1845: *CW*, XIII: 683.

28 Cf. Senior 1842: 18–20; Stephen 1866a: 162; Mill, *CW*, XXI: 112.

29 See Chapter 2.

30 Cf. Samuel Scheffler, "Conceptions of Cosmopolitanism," in Scheffler 2001: 111–30. Cf. also Robbins 1998b.

31 I am alluding here to the title of John M. Robson's classic study of Mill's social and political thought (Robson 1968a).

32 Compare also what Arnold had to say in a letter to his mother (10 March 1866), commenting on one of the many attacks he had received on account of his essay "My Countrymen": "I should be sorry to be a Frenchman, a German, or American, or anything but an Englishman; but I know *that this native instinct which other nations, too, have, does not prove one's superiority, but that one has to achieve this by undeniable, excellent performance*" (emphasis added: Arnold 1996–2000, III: 17–18). The word "prove" is significant here. Like Mill, Arnold has in mind some sort of international tribunal of public opinion, in front of which it would not be enough for Englishmen, Frenchmen, Americans and so on to boast they were great and superior following their "native instinct," but rather would have to "prove" their superiority and greatness "by undeniable, excellent performance," presumably in identifiable, commonly accepted domains of excellence.

33 It is not unrelated here to remind ourselves of the crucial importance Bentham had accorded to international public opinion for the purposes of supervising the observance of international law.

34 See his letter to J.W. Parker (*CW*, XV: 652). It was – very favorably – reviewed in the *Revue des Deux Mondes* (Forcade 1859).

35 Cf. Cornick 1995; Cornick 2000.

36 Nassau Senior believed that England did not care at all about what foreigners thought

of her, and contributed an interesting analysis of the reasons for English disregard for the opinion of foreigners (Senior 1842: 18–20, 31, 32–3, 42, and *passim*).

37 For a recent succinct refutation of the imputation of elitism to Mill's thought, see Miller (Dale) 2000.

38 The reminder that Mill had a demanding concept of citizenship brings us to the question of so-called "republican citizenship." It is difficult for anyone to deny completely the existence of republican elements and themes in Mill's thought. In an article examining liberal attitudes to the obligation to military service, April Carter has argued that the major liberal thinkers had no adequate conception of the requirements of citizenship. However, Mill comes out as an exception to the rule argued by Carter, of liberal thinkers not having addressed the issue adequately. Carter to all intends and purposes concedes that Mill did, but claims that this does not diminish the validity of the argument because the works in which he addressed the issue were not published or widely circulated at the time for them to have influenced the liberal tradition decisively. In this context Carter addresses briefly the question of the presence of republican elements in Mill's thought (Carter 1998). This broader topic is the focus of recent work by Dale Miller. Moreover, Miller not only identifies a number of republican elements in Mill's thought, but also argues cogently against the more or less accepted view that Mill's republican themes were not compatible with his liberalism, and claims that there was unity in what he calls Mill's "civic liberalism" (Miller (Dale) 2000). In the context of such debates it is worth examining the extent to which Mill's attitude towards patriotism can be taken as an instance of "republican patriotism" as the latter is defined by Viroli (Viroli 1995; Canovan 2000; Viroli 2000). Although Mill did wish to promote "public spirit" through civic education in the way republican patriots did; although pride in, and active vigilance in order to defend the liberty of the fatherland were elements shared by Mill and republican patriots; and although he clearly came closer to sharing republican notions of the obligation to military service and service in the militia than most liberal thinkers, his version of patriotism cannot be taken to be an example of republican patriotism as defined by Viroli. Mill was too keen to dissociate his conception of patriotism from exclusive particularism for it to be purely republican patriotism. While it does contain and even emphasize some themes associated mainly with republicanism, Mill's version of patriotism was too universalist and cosmopolitan for it to be a simple instance of republican patriotism. (For a succinct delineation of the two main versions of "new patriotism" referred to as "republican patriotism" and "cosmopolitan constitutional patriotism" respectively, see Canovan 2000).

39 In "A Few Words" Mill kept using "British" and "English" interchangeably within the same breath.

40 See above, Chapters 1 and 2.

41 Emphasis added.

Bibliography

Acton, [First Baron], John Emerich Edward Dalberg-Acton (1985–88) *Selected Writings of Lord Acton*, ed. by J. Rufus Fears, 3 vols, Indianapolis: Liberty Classics (Vol. I: *Essays in the History of Liberty* (1985); Vol. II: *Essays in the Study and Writing of History* (1986); Vol. III: *Essays in Religion, Politics, and Morality* (1988)).

Alter, Peter (1994) *Nationalism*, second edition, London: Edward Arnold.

Arnold, Matthew (1960–77) *The Complete Prose Works of Matthew Arnold*, ed. by R.H. Super, 11 vols, Ann Arbor: University of Michigan Press. (Vol. I: *On the Classical Tradition* (1960); II: *Democratic Education* (1962); III: *Lectures and Essays in Criticism* (1962); IV: *Schools and Universities on the Continent* (1964); V: *Culture and Anarchy with Friendship's Garland and Some Literary Essays* (1965); VI: *Dissent and Dogma* (1968); VII: *God and the Bible* (1970); VIII: *Essays Religious and Mixed* (1972); IX: *English Literature and Irish Politics* (1973); X: *Philistinism in England and America* (1974); XI: *The Last Word* (1977)).

—— (1996–2000) *The Letters of Matthew Arnold*, ed. by Cecil Y. Lang, 4 vols, Charlottesville and London: University Press of Virginia. (Vol. I: 1829–59 (1996); II: 1860–65 (1997); III: 1866–70 (1998); IV: 1871–78 (2000)).

Aron, Raymond (1965) *Auguste Comte et Alexis de Tocqueville Juges de l'Angleterre* (*The Zaharoff Lecture for 1965*), Oxford: Clarendon Press.

Bagehot, Walter (1965–86) *The Collected Works of Walter Bagehot*, ed. by Norman St John-Stevas, 15 vols, London: The Economist. (Vol. I, II: *The Literary Essays* (1965); III, IV: *The Historical Essays* (1968); V, VI, VII, VIII: *The Political Essays* (1974); XII, XIII: *The Letters* (1986); XIV, XV: *Miscellany* (1986)).

Bain, Alexander (1882) *John Stuart Mill: a criticism with personal recollections*, London: Longmans.

Banton, Michael (1987) *Racial Theories*, Cambridge: Cambridge University Press.

Barker, Ernest (1927) *National Character and the Factors in its Formation*, London: Methuen and Co.

Barry, Brian (2001) *Culture and Equality: an egalitarian critique of multiculturalism*, Cambridge: Polity.

Barzun, Jacques (1932) *The French Race: theories of its origins and their social and political implications*, New York: Columbia University Press.

—— (1941) "Romantic historiography as a political force in France," *Journal of the History of Ideas*, 2: 318–29.

—— (1965) *Race: a study in superstition*, New York: Harper and Row.

Beiner, Ronald (ed.) (1999) *Theorizing Nationalism*, Albany: State University of New York Press.

Beitz, Charles R. (1979) *Political Theory and International Relations*, Princeton, NJ: Princeton University Press.

Benner, Erica (1997) "Nationality without nationalism" (review article), *Journal of Political Ideologies*, 2, 2: 189–206.

Bensimon, Fabrice (1999) "Lamartine pendant la révolution de 1848, vu de Grande-Bretagne," *Franco-British Studies*, 27: 1–17.

Bentham, Jeremy (1843) "Principles of International Law," *The Works of Jeremy Bentham*, ed. by John Bowring, 11 vols, Edinburgh, William Tait II: 535–60.

—— (1990) *Securities Against Misrule and Other Constitutional Writings for Tripoli and Greece* (*The Collected Work of Jeremy Bentham*, UCL Bentham Project edition), ed. by Philip Schofield, Oxford: Oxford University Press.

—— (1996) *An Introduction to the Principles of Morals and Legislation*, ed. by J.H. Burns and H.L.A. Hart, with a new introduction by F. Rosen, Oxford: Oxford University Press.

Betley, Jan Andrej (1960) *Belgium and Poland in International Relations, 1830–1831*, The Hague: Mouton and Company.

Bolt, Christine (1971) *Victorian Attitudes to Race*, London: Routledge and Kegan Paul.

Brady, Alexander (1977) "Introduction," in John Stuart Mill (1963–1991) *Essays on Politics and Society*, *CW*, XVIII: vii–lxx.

Brougham, Henry Peter, Lord (1848) *Letter to the Marquess of Lansdowne, K.G., Lord President of the Council, on the late Revolution in France*, London: Ridgway.

Brown, Mark (1980) "The Polish question and public opinion in France, 1830–46," *Ante-murale*, 24.

Bullen, Roger (1974) *Palmerston, Guizot and the Collapse of the Entente Cordiale*, London: Athlone Press.

—— (1991) "La politique étrangère de Guizot," in Marina Valensise (ed.), *François Guizot et la Culture Politique de son Temps* (Colloque de la Fondation Guizot-Val Richer), Paris: Gallimard-Le Seuil: 187–201.

Burrow, John W. (1968) *Evolution and Society: a study in Victorian social theory*, Cambridge: Cambridge University Press.

—— (1981) *A Liberal Descent: Victorian historians and the English past*, Cambridge: Cambridge University Press.

Cairns, John C. (1985) "Introduction," in John Stuart Mill (1963–91) *Essays on French History and Historians*, *CW*, XX: vii–xcii.

Canovan, Margaret (1996) *Nationhood and Political Theory*, Cheltenham: Edward Elgar.

—— (2000) "Patriotism is not enough," in Catriona McKinnon and Iain Hampsher-Monk (eds) (2000) *The Demands of Citizenship*, London and New York: Continuum: 276–97.

Carlisle, Janice (1991) *John Stuart Mill and the Writing of Character*, Athens, Georgia: University of Georgia Press.

Carrel, Armand (1857–59) *Œuvres Politiques et Littéraires d'Armand Carrel*, ed. by E. Littré and A. Paulin, 5 vols, Paris: Librairie de F. Chamerot.

Carter, April (1998) "Liberalism and the obligation to military service," *Political Studies*, XLVI: 68–81.

Chass, Charles (1928) "Stuart Mill et la France," *Bulletin de l'Association France-Grande Bretagne*, 76: 2–13.

Claret, Philippe (1998) *La Personnalité collective des Nations: Théories anglo-saxonnes et conceptions françaises du caractère national*, Brussels: Bruyant.

Cobban, Alfred (1969) *The Nation State and National Self-Determination*, London: Collins (The Fontana Library).

Cobden, Richard (1903) *The Political Writings of Richard Cobden*, 4th edition, 2 vols. London: T. Fisher Unwin.

Collingham, H.A.C. (1988) *The July Monarchy: a political history of France 1830–1848*, London and New York: Longman.

Collini, Stefan (1991) *Public Moralists: political thought and intellectual life in Britain, 1850–1930*, Oxford: Clarendon Press.

—— (1993) [1988] "Arnold," in Keith Thomas (series editor, *Past Masters* series), *Victorian Thinkers*, Oxford: Oxford University Press: 195–326 [first published as an independent volume, 1988].

—— (1999) *English Pasts: Essays in History and Culture*, Oxford: Oxford University Press.

Collini, Stefan, Donald Winch, and John W. Burrow (1983) *That Noble Science of Politics: a study in nineteenth-century intellectual history*, Cambridge: Cambridge University Press.

Colls, Robert (1998) "Ethics Man: John Gray's new moral world," *Political Quarterly*, 69, 1: 59–71.

Constant, Benjamin (1988) *Political Writings*, trans. and ed. by Biancamaria Fontana, Cambridge: Cambridge University Press.

Conway, Stephen (1989) "Bentham on peace and war," *Utilitas*, 1: 82–101.

—— (1990) "Bentham, the Benthamites, and the nineteenth-century British peace movement," *Utilitas*, 2: 221–43.

Cornick, Martyn (1995) "The myth of 'perfidious Albion' and French national identity," in David Dutton (ed.), *Statecraft and Diplomacy in the Twentieth Century: Essays presented to P.M.H. Bell*, Liverpool: Liverpool University Press.

—— (2000) "Distorting mirrors: problems of Franco-British perception in the *fin de siècle*," in Martyn Cornick and Ceri Crossley (eds), *Problems in French History*, Basingstoke: Macmillan: 125–48.

Coupland, Reginald (1945) "Introduction" to *The Durham Report* (an Abridged Version with an Introduction and Notes by Sir Reginald Coupland), Oxford: Clarendon Press: vii–lxviii.

Crisp, Roger (1997) *Mill on Utilitarianism*, London and New York: Routledge.

Crossley, Ceri (1993) *French Historians and Romanticism: Thierry, Guizot, the Saint-Simonians, Quinet, Michelet*, London and New York: Routledge.

Drescher, Seymour (1964) *Tocqueville and England*, Cambridge, Massachusetts: Harvard University Press.

—— (1968) *Dilemmas of Democracy: Tocqueville and modernization*, Pittsburgh: University of Pittsburgh Press.

Eichthal, Gustave d' and Ismayl Urbain (1839) *Lettres sur la Race Noire et la Race Blanche*, Paris.

Eisenach, Eldon J. (ed.) (1998) *Mill and the Moral Character of Liberalism*, University Park, Pennsylvania: The Pennsylvania State University Press.

Ellis, Anthony (1992) "Utilitarianism and international ethics," in Terry Nardin and David R. Mapel (eds), *Traditions of International Ethics*, Cambridge: Cambridge University Press: 158–79.

Fasnacht, G.E. (1952) *Acton's Political Philosophy: an analysis*, London: Hollis and Carter.

Faverty, Frederic E. (1951) *Matthew Arnold the Ethnologist*, Evanston, Illinois: Northwestern University Press.

Ferguson, Adam (1995) *An Essay on the History of Civil Society*, ed. by Fania Oz-Salzberger, Cambridge: Cambridge University Press.

Filipiuk, Marion (1991) "John Stuart Mill and France," in Michael Laine (ed.), *A Cultivated Mind: essays on J.S. Mill presented to John Robson*, Toronto: University of Toronto Press: 80–120.

Forbes, Ian and Mark Hoffman (eds) (1993) *Political Theory, International Relations, and the Ethics of Intervention*, London: Macmillan.

Forcade, E. (1859) "Chronique de la quinzaine," *Revue des Deux Mondes*, 24 (seconde période): 984–97.

Francis, Mark and John Morrow (1994) *A History of English Political Thought in the Nineteenth Century*, London: Duckworth.

Freeden, Michael (1996) *Ideologies and Political Theory: a conceptual approach*, Oxford: Clarendon Press.

Gamble, Andrew (1999) "The last utopia" (review article), *New Left Review*, 236: 117–27.

Gilbert, Paul (1998) *The Philosophy of Nationalism*, Boulder, Colorado and Oxford: Westview Press.

Grader, Sheila (1985) "John Stuart Mill's theory of nationality: a liberal dilemma in the field of international relations," *Millennium: Journal of International Studies*, 14: 207–16.

Gray, John (1983) *Mill on Liberty: a defence*, London: Routledge & Kegan Paul.

—— (1995) *Berlin*, London: Fontana Press.

—— (1998) "A strained rebirth of Liberal Britain," *New Statesman*, 21 August 1998: 28–9.

Habermas, Jürgen (1995) "Citizenship and national identity: some reflections on the future of Europe," in Omar Dahbour and M.R. Ishay (eds), *The Nationalism Reader*, New Jersey: Humanities Press: 333–43.

Haddock, Bruce (1999) "State and nation in Mazzini's political thought," *History of Political Thought*, 20: 313–36.

Hall, John A. (2001) "Liberalism and nationalism," in Athena S. Leoussi (ed.) *Encyclopaedia of Nationalism*, New Brunswick and London: Transaction Publishers: 173–6.

Harvie, Christopher (1976) *The Lights of Liberalism: university liberals and the challenge of democracy 1860–86*, London: Allen Lane.

Hayes, Carlton J.H. (1931) *The Historical Evolution of Modern Nationalism*, New York: R.R. Smith.

Hill, Roland (2000) *Lord Acton*, New Haven and London: Yale University Press.

Hobhouse, L.T. (1994) *Liberalism and Other Writings*, ed. by James Meadowcroft, New York and Cambridge: Cambridge University Press.

Hoffmann, Stanley (1996) "Mondes idéaux," commentary in John Rawls, *Le Droit des Gents*, Paris: Éditions Esprit: 113–54.

Holbraad, Carsten (1970) *The Concert of Europe: a study in German and British international theory 1815–1914*, London: Longman.

Horowitz, Donald (1994) "Democracy in Divided Societies", in Larry Diamont and Mark F. Plattner (eds), *Nationalism, Ethnic Conflict and Democracy*, Baltimore: The Johns Hopkins University Press, pp. 35–55.

Houghton, Walter E. (1957) *The Victorian Frame of Mind 1830–1870*, New Haven and London: Yale University Press.

Hume, David (1994) "Of national characters," in D. Hume, *Political Essays*, ed. by Knud Haakonssen, Cambridge: Cambridge University Press: 78–92.

Hunt, James [anon.] (1866) "Race in legislation and political economy," *The Anthropological Review*, 4: 113–35.

Huxley, T.H. (1865) "Emancipation – Black and White", *Reader*, 5: 561–2.

Immerwahr, John (1992) "Hume's revised racism," *Journal of the History of Ideas*, 53: 481–6.

Jardin, André and Tudesq, André-Jean (1983) *Restoration and Reaction, 1815–1848*, Cambridge: Cambridge University Press.

Jennings, Jeremy (1991) "Nationalist ideas in the early years of the July Monarchy: Armand Carrel and *Le National*," *History of Political Thought*, Vol. 12: 497–514.

Johnson, Douglas (1963) *Guizot: aspects of French history 1787–1874*, London: Routledge and Kegan Paul.

Johnson, Peter (1993) "Intervention and moral dilemmas," in Ian Forbes and Mark Hoffman (eds), *Political Theory, International Relations and the Ethics of Intervention*, London: Macmillan.

Jones, H.S. (1992) "John Stuart Mill as moralist," *Journal of the History of Ideas*, 53: 287–308.

—— (2000) *Victorian Political Thought*, Basingstoke and London: Macmillan.

Judt, Tony (1994) "The new old nationalism," *The New York Review of Books*, Vol. XLI, No. 10 (26 May 1994): 44–51.

Kayser, Elmer Louis (1932) *The Grand Social Enterprise: a study of Jeremy Bentham in relation to liberal nationalism*, New York: Columbia University Press.

Kedourie, Elie (1985) *Nationalism*, London: Hutchinson.

Kelly, George Armstrong (1992) *The Humane Comedy: Constant, Tocqueville and French liberalism*, Cambridge: Cambridge University Press.

Kohn, Hans (1944) *The Idea of Nationalism*, New York: Macmillan.

—— (1946) *Prophets and Peoples: studies in nineteenth-century nationalism*, New York: Macmillan.

Kymlicka, Will (1991) [1989] *Liberalism, Community and Culture*, Oxford: Clarendon Press.

—— (1995a) *Multicultural Citizenship: a liberal theory of minority rights*, Oxford: Clarendon Press.

—— (ed.) (1995b) *The Rights of Minority Cultures*, Oxford: Oxford University Press.

—— (2000) "Les droits des minorités et le multiculturalisme: l'évolution du débat anglo-américain," in Kymlicka, Will and Mesure, Sylvie (eds) (2000) *Les Identités culturelles* (2000 issue of *Comprendre: Revue annuelle de Philosophie et de Sciences Sociales*, No. 1): 141–71.

Kymlicka, Will and Mesure, Sylvie (eds) (2000) *Les Identités culturelles* (2000 issue of *Comprendre: Revue annuelle de Philosophie et de Sciences Sociales*, No. 1).

Laborde, Cécile (2000) *Pluralist Thought and the State in Britain and France, 1900–25*, Basingstoke: Macmillan.

Lamberti, Jean-Claude (1989) *Tocqueville and the Two Democracies*, Cambridge, Massachusetts and London: Harvard University Press.

Lawlor, Mary (1959) *Alexis de Tocqueville in the Chamber of Deputies: his views on foreign and colonial policy*, Washington, D.C.: The Catholic University of America Press.

Leary, David E. (1982) "The fate and influence of John Stuart Mill's proposed science of ethology," *Journal of the History of Ideas*, XLIII: 153–62.

Le Quesne, A.L. (1993) "Carlyle," in Keith Thomas (series editor), *Victorian Thinkers*, Oxford: Oxford University Press: 1–101.

Lichtenberg, Judith (1999) "How liberal can nationalism be?," in Ronald Beiner (ed.), *Theorizing Nationalism*, Albany: State University of New York Press: 167–88.

Little, Richard (1975) *Intervention: External Involvement in Civil Wars*, London: Martin Robertson.

—— (1993) "Recent literature on intervention and non-intervention," in Ian Forbes and Mark Hoffman (eds), *Political Theory, International Relations and the Ethics of Intervention*, London: Macmillan: 13–31.

Lochore, R.A. (1935) *History of the Idea of Civilization in France (1830–1870)*, Bonn: Ludwig Roehrscheid Verlag.

Mandelbaum, Maurice (1971) *History, Man, and Reason: a study in nineteenth-century thought*, Baltimore: The Johns Hopkins University Press.

Mandler, Peter (2000) " 'Race' and 'nation' in mid-Victorian thought," in Stefan Collini, Richard Whatmore, and Brian Young (eds), *History, Religion, and Culture: British intellectual history 1750–1950*, Cambridge: Cambridge University Press: 224–44.

Manent, Pierre (1996) *Tocqueville and the Nature of Democracy*, Lanham, Maryland: Rowman & Littlefield.

Martin, Ged (1972) *The Durham Report and British Policy*, Cambridge: Cambridge University Press.

Mayall, James (1991) "Non-intervention, self-determination and the 'New World Order,' " *International Affairs*, 67, 3: 421–9.

Mazlish, Bruce (1975) *James and John Stuart Mill: father and son in the nineteenth century*, London: Hutchinson.

Mazzini, Giuseppe (1852) "Europe: its condition and prospects," in *Essays: Selected from the Writings, Literary, Political, and Religious, of Joseph Mazzini*, ed. by William Clarke, no date, London: The Walter Scott Publishing Co.: 261–98 (first published in the *Westminster Review*, 2 April 1852).

McCarthy, Leon (1993) "International anarchy, realism and non-intervention," in Ian Forbes and Mark Hoffman (eds), *Political Theory, International Relations and the Ethics of Intervention*, London: Macmillan.

McLaren, Angus G. (1971) "The *National* under the editorship of Armand Carrel" (unpublished Ph.D. thesis), Harvard University.

Mehta, Uday Singh (1999) *Liberalism and Empire: a study in nineteenth-century British liberal thought*, Chicago: University of Chicago Press.

Mélonio, Françoise (1984) "Tocqueville et la restauration du pouvoir temporel du Pape (Juin–Octobre 1849)," *Revue Historique*, 271, 1: 109–23.

—— (1991) "L'Idée nationale et l'idée de démocratie chez Tocqueville," *Littérature et Nation*, 7 (second series): 5–24.

—— (1993) *Tocqueville et les Français*, Paris: Aubier.

Michelet, Jules (1974) [1846] *Le Peuple*, ed. by Paul Viallaneix, Paris.

Mill, James (1975) *The History of British India*, ed. by William Thomas, Chicago.

Mill, John Stuart (1963–1991) [referred to as: *CW*] *The Collected Works of John Stuart Mill*, general editor F.E.L. Priestley and subsequently John M. Robson, University of Toronto Press: Toronto and London, 33 vols. (Vol. I: *Autobiography and Literary Essays* (1981); II, III: *Principles of Political Economy* (1965); VI: *Essays on England, Ireland and the Empire* (1982); VII, VIII: *A System of Logic: Ratiocinative and Inductive* (1973); X: *Essays on Ethics, Religion and Society* (1969); XII, XIII: *Earlier Letters, 1812–1848* (1962); XIV, XV, XVI, XVII: *Later Letters, 1848–1873* (1972); XVIII, XIX: *Essays on Politics and Society* (1977); XX: *Essays on French History and Historians* (1985); XXI: *Essays on Equality, Law and Education* (1984); XXII, XXIII, XXIV, XXV: *Newspaper Writings* (1986); XXVIII, XXIX: *Public and Parliamentary Speeches* (1988); XXX: *Writings on India* (1990); XXXI: *Miscellaneous Writings* (1989); XXXII: *Additional Letters* (1991); XXXIII: *Indexes to the Collected Works of John Stuart Mill* (1991)).

Miller, Dale E. (2000) "John Stuart Mill's civic liberalism," *History of Political Thought*, 21, 1: 88–107.

Miller, David (1995) *On Nationality*, Oxford: Clarendon Press.

—— (2000) *Citizenship and National Identity*, Cambridge: Polity.

Miller, Kenneth E. (1961) "John Stuart Mill's theory of international relations," *Journal of the History of Ideas*, 22, 4: 493–514.

Montesquieu, Charles-Louis de Secondat (1989) [1748] *The Spirit of the Laws*, ed. by Anne Cohler, Basia Miller and Harold Stone, Cambridge: Cambridge University Press.

Moore, Margaret (2001) "Normative justifications for liberal nationalism: justice, democracy and national identity," *Nations and Nationalism*, 7, 1: 1–20.

Morgenthau, Hans J. (1957) "The paradoxes of nationalism," *The Yale Review*, XLVI, 4: 481–96.

Morley, John (1970) *Nineteenth-Century Essays*, selected and with an introduction by Peter Stansky, Chicago: University of Chicago Press.

Mueller, Iris Wessel (1968) *John Stuart Mill and French Thought*, Freeport, NY: Books for Libraries Press.

Nathanson, Stephen (1993) *Patriotism, Morality and Peace*, Lanham, MD: Rowman & Littlefield.

Newman, Gerald (1987) *The Rise of English Nationalism: a cultural history 1740–1830*, London: Weidenfeld and Nicolson.

Nicolet, Claude (1982) *L' Idée Républicaine en France (1789–1924): essai d'histoire critique*, Paris: Gallimard.

Noiriel, Gérard (1995) "Socio-histoire d'un concept. Les usages du mot 'nationalité' au XIXe siècle," *Genèses: Sciences Sociales et Histoire*, 20: 4–23.

Norman, Wayne (1999) "Theorizing nationalism (normatively): the first steps," in Ronald Beiner (ed.), *Theorizing Nationalism*, Albany: State University of New York Press: 51–65.

Nussbaum, Martha C. *et al.* (1996) *For Love of Country: debating the limits of patriotism*, ed. by Joshua Cohen, Boston: Beacon Press.

O'Brien, Conor Cruise (1988) "Nationalism and the French Revolution," in Geoffrey

Best (ed.), *The Permanent Revolution: The French Revolution and its legacy, 1789–1989*, Fontana Press.

O'Grady, Jean (1991) Introduction to *Indexes of the Collected Works of John Stuart Mill*, *CW*, XXXIII: vii–xxx.

O'Leary, Brendan (ed.) (1996) "Symposium on David Miller's *On Nationality*," *Nations and Nationalism*, 2, 3: 407–52.

Palgrave, Francis Turner [anon.] (1874) "*Autobiography*. By John Stuart Mill," *Quarterly Review*, 136: 150–79.

Parekh, Bhikhu (1994) "Decolonizing liberalism," in Aleksandras Shtromas (ed.), *The End of 'Isms'? Reflections on the fate of ideological politics after Communism's collapse*, Oxford: Blackwell: 85–103.

—— (2000) *Rethinking Multiculturalism: cultural diversity and political theory*, Basingstoke and London: Macmillan.

Paul, Diane (1981) "'In the interests of civilization': Marxist views of race and culture in the nineteenth century," *Journal of the History of Ideas*, 42: 115–38.

Pecora, Vincent P. (1997–8) "Arnoldian ethnology," *Victorian Studies*, 41: 355–79.

Perkins, John A. (1987) "The right of counter-intervention," *Georgia Journal of International and Comparative Law*, 17.

Pilbeam, Pamela M. (1991) *The 1830 Revolution in France*, London: Macmillan.

—— (1995) *Republicanism in Nineteenth-Century France, 1814–1871*, Basingstoke: Macmillan.

Plamenatz, John (1976) "Two types of nationalism," in Eugene Kamenka (ed.), *Nationalism: the nature and evolution of an idea*, London: Edward Arnold.

Poole, Ross (1999) *Nation and Identity*, London and New York: Routledge.

Potter, David M. (1954) *People of Plenty: economic abundance and the American character*, Chicago: University of Chicago Press.

Price, Richard (1991) [1789] "A discourse on the love of our country," in Richard Price, *Political Writings*, ed. by D.O. Thomas, Cambridge: Cambridge University Press: 176–96.

Priestley, F.E.L. (1969) "Introduction," in J.S. Mill, *Essays on Ethics, Religion and Society*, *CW*, X: xxxvi–xxxvii.

Rainger, Ronald (1978) "Race, politics, and science: the Anthropological Society of London in the 1860s," *Victorian Studies*, 22: 51–70.

Ratcliffe, Barrie M. (1977) "Gustave d'Eichthal (1802–1886): an intellectual portrait," in Barrie M. Ratcliffe and W.H. Chaloner (eds), *A French Sociologist looks at Britain: Gustave d'Eichthal and British society in 1828*, Manchester: Manchester University Press: 109–61.

Rawls, John (1999) *The Law of Peoples* (with "The Idea of Public Reason Revisited"), Cambridge, Massachusetts: Harvard University Press.

Rees, J.C. (1956) *Mill and his Early Critics*, Leicester: University College Leicester.

Rich, Paul B. (1994) "Social Darwinism, anthropology and English perspectives of the Irish, 1867–1900," *History of European Ideas*, 19: 777–85.

Richter, Melvin (1958) "Debate on race: Tocqueville-Gobineau correspondence," *Commentary*, 25: 151–60.

Riley, Jonathan (1998) *Mill on Liberty*, London: Routledge.

Robbins, Bruce (1998a) "Actually existing cosmopolitanism," in Pheng Cheah and Bruce Robbins (eds), *Cosmopolitics: thinking and feeling beyond the nation*, Minneapolis and London: University of Minnesota Press: 1–19.

—— (1998b) "Comparative cosmopolitanisms," in Pheng Cheah and Bruce Robbins (eds), *Cosmopolitics: thinking and feeling beyond the nation*, Minneapolis and London: University of Minnesota Press: 246–64.

Robson, Ann P. and John M. Robson (1982) "'Impetuous eagerness': the young Mill's radical journalism," in Joanne Shattock and Michael Wolff (eds), *The Victorian Periodical Press: samplings and soundings*, Leicester: Leicester University Press: 59–77.

Robson, John M. (1968a) *The Improvement of Mankind: the social and political thought of John Stuart Mill*, Toronto: University of Toronto Press.

—— (1968b) "Mill and Arnold: liberty and culture – friends or enemies?," in G.S. McCaughey (ed.), *Of Several Branches: Studies from the Humanities Association Bulletin 1954–65*, Toronto: 125–42.

—— (1998) "Civilization and culture as moral concepts," in John Skorupski (ed.), *The Cambridge Companion to Mill*, Cambridge: Cambridge University Press: 338–71.

Rosen, Fred (1992) *Bentham, Byron, and Greece: Constitutionalism, Nationalism, and Early Liberal Political Thought*, Oxford: Clarendon Press.

—— (1997) "Nationalism and early British liberal thought," *Journal of Political Ideologies*, 2, 2: 177–88.

—— (1999) "Eric Stokes, British Utilitarianism and India", in Martin I. Moir, Douglas M. Peers and Lynn Zastoupil (eds), *J.S. Mill's Encounter with India*, Toronto: University of Toronto Press: 18–33.

Scheffler, Samuel (1996) "Family and friends first?," *Times Literary Supplement*, 27 December: 8–9.

—— (2001) *Boundaries and Allegiances: problems of justice and responsibility in liberal thought*, Oxford: Oxford University Press.

Schleifer, James (1980) *The Making of Tocqueville's "Democracy in America,"* Chapel Hill: North Carolina University Press.

Seliger, M. (1958) "Race-thinking during the Restoration," *Journal of the History of Ideas*, 19: 273–83.

Semmel, Bernard (1962) *The Governor Eyre Controversy*, London: MacGibbon and Kee.

—— (1984) *John Stuart Mill and the Pursuit of Virtue*, New Haven: Yale University Press.

Senior, Nassau W. (1842) "France, America, and Britain," *Edinburgh Review*, 75: 1–48.

—— (1973a) [1850] "Sketch of the Revolution of 1848," in N.W. Senior, *Journals Kept in France and Italy from 1848 to 1852, with a Sketch of the Revolution of 1848*, ed. by M.C.M. Simpson, 2 vols, New York: Da Capo Press, I: 1–89 [first published in *Edinburgh Review*, January 1850].

—— (1973b) [1871] *Journals Kept in France and Italy from 1848 to 1852, with a Sketch of the Revolution of 1848*, ed. by M.C.M. Simpson, 2 vols, New York: Da Capo Press.

Silberner, Edmund (1946) *The Problem of War in Nineteenth Century Economic Thought*, trans. by Alexander H. Krappe, Princeton, NJ: Princeton University Press.

Skorupski, John (1989) *John Stuart Mill*, London: Routledge.

—— (ed.) (1998) *The Cambridge Companion to Mill*, Cambridge: Cambridge University Press.

Smith, Anthony D. (1998) *Nationalism and Modernism*, London: Routledge.

Smith, Michael Joseph (1992) "Liberalism and international reform," in Terry Nardin and David R. Mapel (eds), *Traditions of International Ethics*, Cambridge: Cambridge University Press.

Souffrant, Eddy M. (2000) *Formal Transgression: John Stuart Mill's philosophy of international affairs*, Lanham, Maryland: Rowman & Littlefield.

Spitzer, Alan B. (1987) *The French Generation of 1820*, Princeton: Princeton University Press.

Stafford, William (1998) *John Stuart Mill*, Basingstoke: Macmillan.

Stapleton, Julia (1998) "James Fitzjames Stephen: liberalism, patriotism, and English liberty," *Victorian Studies*, 41: 243–63.

—— (2000) "Political thought and national identity in Britain, 1850–1950," in Stefan Collini, Richard Whatmore, and Brian Young (eds), *History, Religion, and Culture: British intellectual history 1750–1950*, Cambridge: Cambridge University Press: 245–69.

Steele, E.D. (1970) "IV. J.S. Mill and the Irish Question: reform, and the integrity of the Empire, 1865–1870," *The Historical Journal*, 13: 419–50.

Stephen, James Fitzjames (1866a) "Mr. Arnold on the Middle Classes," *Saturday Review*, 21 (10 February 1866): 161–3.

—— (1866b) "Lord Macaulay's Works," *Saturday Review*, 22 (18 August 1866): 207–9.

Stephen, Leslie (1900) *The English Utilitarians*, 3 vols, London: Duckworth and Co. (Vol. III: *John Stuart Mill*).

Sternberger, Dolf (1982) "Verfassungspatriotismus," in *25 Jahre Akademie für Politische Bildung*, Tutzing: 76–87.

Sternhell, Zeev (1987) "Racism," in David Miller *et al.* (eds), *The Blackwell Encyclopaedia of Political Thought*, Oxford: Blackwell: 413–16.

Stocking, George W., Jr. (1987) *Victorian Anthropology*, New York: Free Press.

Sullivan, Eileen P. (1983) "Liberalism and imperialism: J.S. Mill's defence of the British Empire," *Journal of the History of Ideas*, 44, 4: 599–617.

Swart, Koenraad W. (1964) *The Sense of Decadence in Nineteenth-century France*, The Hague: Martinus Nijhoff.

Tamir, Yael (1993) *Liberal Nationalism*, Princeton, NJ: Princeton University Press.

Taylor, A.J.P. (1993) *The Trouble Makers: Dissent over Foreign Policy 1792–1939*, London: Pimlico.

Tocqueville, Alexis de (1951–) [referred to as: *Œuvres Complètes*]: *Œuvres, Papiers et Correspondances d'Alexis de Tocqueville*, édition definitive sous la direction de J.-P. Mayer, Paris: Gallimard. (Vol. VI, 1: *Correspondance Anglaise: Correspondance d'Alexis de Tocqueville avec Henry Reeve et John Stuart Mill*; Vol. VI, 2: *Correspondance Anglaise: Correspondance et Conversations d'Alexis de Tocqueville et Nassau William Senior*; Vol. IX: *Correspondance d'Alexis de Tocqueville et d'Arthur de Gobineau*; Vol. III, 2: *Écrits et Discours Politiques*; Vol. XVI: *Mélanges*).

—— (1957) *Voyages en Angleterre et en Irlande*, ed. by J.P. Mayer, Paris: Gallimard.

—— (1985) *Selected Letters on Politics and Society*, ed. by Roger Boesche, Berkeley: University of California Press.

—— (1994) [1835, 1840] *Democracy in America*, trans. by George Lawrence, ed. by J.P. Mayer, Hammersmith, London: Fontana Press.

Todorov, Tzvetan (1993) [1989] *On Human Diversity: nationalism, racism and exoticism in French thought* (trans. from the French), Cambridge, Mass., and London: Harvard University Press.

Tombs, Robert (1994) "Was there a French *Sonderweg*?," *European Review of History*, 1, 2: 169–77.

—— (1996) *France 1814–1914*, Harlow, Essex: Longman.

—— (1997) "A la recherche d'une famille politique nationaliste: les cas britannique, français et allemand de 1800 à 1870," in *Les Familles politiques en Europe occidentale au XIXe Siècle*, École Française de Rome: 315–33.

Trilling, Lionel (1974) [1939] *Matthew Arnold*, London: G. Allen and Unwin.

Tuell, Anne Kimball (1941) *John Sterling: a representative Victorian*, New York: Macmillan.

Varouxakis, Georgios (1999) "Guizot's historical works and J.S. Mill's reception of Tocqueville," *History of Political Thought*, 20, 2: 292–312.

—— (2001a) "Patriotism," in Athena S. Leoussi (ed.), *Encyclopaedia of Nationalism*, New Brunswick and London: Transaction Publishers: 239–42.

—— (2001b) "Nationality," in Athena S. Leoussi (ed.), *Encyclopaedia of Nationalism*, New Brunswick and London: Transaction Publishers: 233–4.

—— (2002) *Victorian Political Thought on France and the French*, Basingstoke: Palgrave (forthcoming).

Vincent, Andrew (1997) "Liberal nationalism: an irresponsible compound?," *Political Studies*, 45, 2: 275–95.

Vincent, R.J. (1974) *Nonintervention and International Order*, Princeton, NJ: Princeton University Press.

Viroli, Maurizio (1995) *For Love of Country: an essay on patriotism and nationalism*, Oxford: Clarendon Press.

—— (2000) "Republican patriotism," in Catriona McKinnon and Iain Hampsher-Monk (eds), *The Demands of Citizenship*, London and New York: Continuum: 267–75.

Walzer, Michael (1992) [1977] *Just and Unjust Wars: a moral argument with historical illustrations*, New York: Basic Books.

Watson, George (1973) *The English Ideology: studies in the language of Victorian politics*, London: Allen Lane.

Weill, Georges (1928) *Histoire du Parti républicain en France (1814–1870)*, Paris.

Wieviorka, Michel (ed.) (1997) *Une Société fragmentée? le multiculturalisme en débat*, Paris: La Découverte.

Wight, Martin (1966a) "Why is there no International Theory?," in Herbert Butterfield and Martin Wight (eds), *Diplomatic Investigations: Essays in the Theory of International Politics*, London: George Allen & Unwin: 17–34.

—— (1966b) "Western values in international relations," in Herbert Butterfield and Martin Wight (eds), *Diplomatic Investigations: essays in the theory of international politics*, London: George Allen & Unwin.

Williams, Geraint (1995) "Changing reputations and interpretations in the history of political thought: J.S. Mill," *Politics*, 13, 3: 183–9.

Winock, Michel (1982) "Nationalisme ouvert et nationalisme fermé," in Michel Winock, *Nationalisme, antisémitisme et fascisme en France*, Paris: Seuil.

Yasukawa, Ryuji (1991) "James Mill on peace and war," *Utilitas*, 3, 2: 179–97.

Zastoupil, Lynn (1994) *John Stuart Mill and India*, Stanford, California: Stanford University Press.

Index